THE QUEEN
HERSELF

Helen Cathcart

W.H. ALLEN · LONDON
A Howard & Wyndham Company
1982

Typeset by Phoenix Photosetting, Chatham
Printed and bound in Great Britain by
Mackays of Chatham Ltd, Kent
for the Publishers, W.H. Allen & Co. Ltd,
44 Hill Street, London W1X 8LB

ISBN 0 491 02755 9

THE QUEEN HERSELF

CONTENTS

LIST OF ILLUSTRATIONS

(Between Pages 128 & 129)

Princess Elizabeth, aged five	*Edmund Brock*
The Duchess of Edinburgh, 1947	*Stella Marks*
Pastel study, 1950	*Alfred Lawrence*
The State Portrait	*Sir James Gunn*
Colonel-in-Chief, Irish Guards	*Timothy Whidborne*
The Queen, aged thirty-seven	*Douglas Anderson*
An American portrait, 1972	*Wallace King*
With favourite dogs, 1975	*Terence Cuneo*
As if approaching guests	*William Narraway*
Looking into the future	*Pietro Annigoni*

The State Portrait of The Queen
in her Coronation Robes, by Sir
James Gunn, is reproduced by
gracious permission of Her Majesty
The Queen

Author's Note

This book is published to commemorate the thirty years' reign of Queen Elizabeth II: one should say the first thirty years, under Providence. Middle life is lined by milestones and anniversary garlands, and there could be no happier meridian than the marriage year of the Prince of Wales as an opportunity to assess the warmer, more private side of the Queen's personality, the Queen *herself*.

It is twenty years since the writing of my earlier study, *Her Majesty*, inaugurated my perhaps over-numerous books which the Queen is pleased to term 'the series', and I should like to express my deep appreciation of all the help and useful advice I have been given, from the days of the late Commander Colville to the present Mr Michael Shea and Mrs Michael Wall, among others.

Authors seldom thank their readers or reviewers, but I am grateful for the generous response of my previous book *The Queen Mother Herself* which has naturally evoked this sequel. At the outset, I am also indebted to my honorary nieces, Jacqueline and Catherine Matters, who encouraged me to write in some depth of the upbringing and education of the Queen, already little known within their own quarter-century. My quotations from the Queen's early letters are from the Curtis Publishing Co. records within the catalogued maze of the Library of Congress, and hitherto restricted material has been drawn from the uncut original text of *The Little Princesses* by Marion Crawford. I have similarly referred to the annotated private typescripts of the 'family portrait' of Prince Philip by Queen Alexandra of Yugoslavia, supplemented by family reminiscences.

In writing of Princess Frederica of Hanover I have felt it

proper to describe apparent coincidences and circumstance without intruding too freely into privacy and I am grateful to Her Royal Highness for her patient correction on relevant detail. In British Columbia, Miss Margaret Ford, head of the Sociology Division, Vancouver Library, prepared the groundwork for my personal research with friendly efficiency; and I am similarly indebted for information to Herr K. D. Galler of the German Consulate, and Mrs Hawkes of the Vital Statistics Division in Victoria. Among the officials who hospitably welcomed me to Simon Fraser University, Mr Dennis Roberts notably dealt with my many questions with exemplary discretion wedded to helpfulness.

I further gratefully acknowledge brief incidental quotations from *King George VI* by Sir John Wheeler-Bennett and *Queen Mary* by the late James Pope-Hennessy. As indicated to his family, I have also drawn on my correspondence with the late Lord Louis Mountbatten, in which – as with Royal Archives material – copyright is reserved.

Helen Cathcart

Part One

Elizabeth of York

1

The baby of Bruton Street

In the early hours of Wednesday 21 April 1926, the child who was to become Queen Elizabeth II was ushered into the world by Caesarean section. A daughter was thus born to the Duke and Duchess of York, an infant third in line to the British throne 'for the time being', as *The Times* said next day.

In preparation for her first baby the little Duchess of York had 'gone home to Mother', as family humour averred, and was installed towards the end of February at her parents' London home, No. 17 Bruton Street, in those days five doors east of Berkeley Square. There were hopes of the baby being born perhaps at Easter, a first grandchild in the male line for King George V. But Easter Day on 4 April was passed in unmarred serenity, and in mid-April the editors of the illustrated magazines hastily revised their headlines and regaled their readers with unexplained photospreads of the young Duke and Duchess. Waiting in calm contentment, the Duchess is credited with preparing a mock bulletin that at least mother and child were comfortable.

On Monday 19 April it was of pertinent news interest that the Duke and Duchess of York lunched at Buckingham Palace with the King and Queen. The following day increased family anxiety until, late that evening at Windsor Castle, the King learned that the three doctors – Sir Henry Simson, surgeon to the Hospital for Women; Sir George Blacker, obstetric physician to University College Hospital, and Mr Walter Jagger, of the Samaritan Hospital for Women – had been summoned to Bruton Street, and the King told his duty equerry to awaken him at any hour, in the middle of the night if need be, if any news came.

The birth of the little Princess Elizabeth has been described by poetic souls as 'occurring in spring at its brightest' but Arnold Bennett, equally concerned just then with the advent of a daughter, noted in his journal that the weather had been 'evil for a week' and late that night he found it 'pouring with cold rain' on leaving his nearby club in Pall Mall.

At Windsor Castle it fell to Captain Reginald Seymour to awaken the King and Queen at 4 a.m. to tell them that they had a granddaughter and to approach the royal bedside with the first official bulletin, 'Her Royal Highness the Duchess of York was safely delivered of a Princess at 2.40 this morning. Both mother and daughter are doing well.' The emotional stress in the word *safely* remained evident in Queen Mary's delighted entry in her diary later that morning: 'We were awakened at 4 a.m. by Reggie Seymour who informed us that darling Elizabeth had got a daughter. Such a relief and joy!'

At 10 a.m. a second reassurance was forthcoming in the signed bulletin, 'The Duchess of York has had some rest since the arrival of her daughter. Her Royal Highness and the infant Princess are making very satisfactory progress. Henry Simson. Walter Jagger.' At the Tower of London and in Hyde Park a twenty-one-gun salute was fired, and the guns still sounded when the King's daughter, Princess Mary, arrived at Bruton Street as the baby's first recorded visitor, to be prettily followed by a girl of eighteen, the daughter of the Lord Mayor of London, bringing the first tribute of flowers.

That same morning, like Shakespeare's 'harbingers preceding still the fates', three Mountbatten ladies conveniently called at Windsor Castle and the *Court Circular* testifies that 'The Crown Princess of Sweden, Princess Andrew of Greece and the Dowager Marchioness of Milford Haven visited Their Majesties and remained to luncheon.' In due order of precedence we are watching the late Earl Mountbatten of Burma's two sisters and his mother.

Queen Mary must have talked happily of the new baby and of her thankfulness after the difficult time Elizabeth had gone through. Lord Mountbatten's younger sister, Princess Louise, who had married the widowed Crown Prince Gustaf Adolf of Sweden, was full of news of the five youngsters to whom she was stepmother. The elder Mountbatten sister, Princess Andrew, had a family of four girls, aged eleven to twenty-one, the four bridesmaids at her brother's wedding four years earlier. Yet, above all, she revelled in the pranks of her lively four-year-old son, Prince Philip, safe with his nanny that morning at his grandmother's home in Kensington Palace. Whatever the topics, the fates had cause for eavesdropping on that lunch-table conversation at Windsor Castle on the day Queen Elizabeth II was born.

That afternoon the King and Queen motored up to Bruton Street where a small crowd had gathered outside No. 17 for their arrival and greeted them with cheers. 'At 2.30 we went to London to congratulate Bertie and we found Celia Strathmore there, saw the baby, a little darling with a lovely complexion and pretty fair hair,' Queen Mary confided to her diary.

In 1926 Bruton Street remained stalwartly residential. The dignified doorways along its quarter-mile length were those of Tennants and Pakenhams, Herberts, Stonors and others discreetly listed in Boyle's *Court Guide*, and a light traffic of horsed carriages with ducal crests mingled with the Daimlers. It would be nine years before, with trade creeping in, Norman Hartnell established his salon in Lord Hereford's house, and twelve years before the demolition picks destroyed No. 17 and its neighbours, which were replaced early in 1939 by the modern brickwork and monolithic heights of Berkeley Square House.

Today only a plaque of Welsh slate at the entrance of an American bank records that Queen Elizabeth II was born there, yet undeniably the spirit of history defied expulsion. During the war, the bombproofed ground floor of the new building served for the storage of Hansard, the official records of Parliamentary free speech. In the naval chart-rooms in the basement were planned the merchant navy convoys supporting the D-day landings on the Normandy beaches; while among the upper floors, occupied by the Ministry of Economic Warfare, David Bowes Lyon realised one day that below his desk in times past there had stood his niece Lilibet's first cradle.

In the unchanged calm of 1926, however, 17 Bruton Street seemed good for centuries, a noble mansion of Palladian splendour, its façade graced with six Corinthian columns reputed to have been retrieved from the first ruins of Whitehall Palace. It would indeed seem fitting if materials from Charles II's building store had survived to strengthen the birthplace of the fifteenth successor to his throne. Yet in firmer fact Lord and Lady Strathmore had resided at No. 17 for less than five years and, with ample room for their two unmarried sons, and sufficient occasional guest-rooms for her large family, Lady Strathmore regarded it as a godsend.

The richness of family life when her sons and daughters were growing up had belonged to their former London home, the lovely Adam house at 20 St James's Square, in memory filled always with music and the voices of young people. In particular, with the tranquil country weeks at St Paul's Walden Bury and the high summers spent at Glamis. No. 20 had provided the carefree London scene of her youngest daughter Elizabeth's girlhood. With its theatres and exhibitions and fun, all London had been the background of Lady Elizabeth Bowes Lyon's youthful explorations with her younger brother David; and even as far back as King George V's Coronation summer in 1911, the presence of the King's shy fifteen-year-old second son, Prince Albert, can be noted – though he attracted little attention – at a Strathmore junior dance.

With the tragic passage of the 1914 war, it was to be eight or nine years before young Elizabeth Lyon, as she called herself, and Prince Albert met again, recollecting one another and their earlier meetings. By this time Elizabeth was more firmly one of Princess Mary's community of younger friends, and Bertie occasionally dropped into his sister's sitting-room at the Palace for the fun of an impromptu gramophone dance session. When they were seen dancing together at a ball at the Farquhars' mansion in Grosvenor Square, he and Elizabeth were obviously accustomed partners. The King had noticed the attraction of Elizabeth Lyon, 'a pretty and charming girl'.

On 5 June 1920, the King created Bertie Duke of York, Earl of Inverness and Baron Killarney . . . 'the same titles that I had', he noted, as if giving his son a sharp reminder of the life of royal duties ahead. And on the Strathmores that summer a thunderbolt fell, in the form of legal notice that their fourteen-year lease of 20 St James's Square had expired. Casually taking its renewal for granted, Lord Strathmore grimly learned that the house had been irrevocably sold over his head.

At this juncture, in utter dismay at the prospect of seeing less of Elizabeth if her family left London, Bertie dutifully consulted his father for permission to ask her to marry him. 'Ask by all means,' the King grunted. 'You'll be lucky if she accepts you.' Such was the badinage with which he cloaked his respect for his son's good qualities, but events sadly confirmed his opinion, for Bertie plucked up his courage to propose one weekend at St Paul's Walden Bury, and was gently refused.

Elizabeth's decision seemed resolute and definite as thought and emotion could make it, and the preserved correspondence suggests the disappointment of the parents on both sides. The Duke looked 'so disconsolate' as Lady Strathmore wrote to her Scottish neighbour, Lady Airlie. 'I do hope he will find a nice wife who will make him happy. I like him so much and he is a man who will be made or marred by his wife.' Queen Mary, too, now felt convinced that Lady Elizabeth was 'the one girl to make Bertie happy'. But, she added, 'it seemed best to say nothing to either of them. Mothers should never meddle in their children's love affairs.'

We shall probably never know who saved the situation. For one factor, Princess Mary became engaged to Viscount Lascelles and drew Elizabeth further into the family fabric by asking her to become one of her eight bridesmaids in Westminster Abbey, the only bridesmaid indeed without cousinly or official Court connections. But, best of all, Lady Strathmore's house-hunting ended with a fourteen-year Berkeley estate lease of 17 Bruton Street, more domestic in scale than her St James's home but amply renewing the pleasures of town and country for Elizabeth and the family.

After needful refurbishment, it was nearly the eve of Princess Mary's wedding before the family moved in, and early on the wedding day – 28 February – the polite gazers from every nearby window had the pleasure of seeing the daughter of the house, a headdress of silver rose-leaves above her gleaming furs, stepping into the State landau sent for her from Buckingham Palace.

'Mary looked lovely in her wedding dress,' the Duke of York wrote to his brother, the Prince of Wales, who was away in India, but he forebore to mention the bridesmaids, Elizabeth the most touchingly beautiful in her shimmering silver dress. Nor was it long before the Duke was seen at No. 17. He was persistent but no longer patient, and the King and Queen were delighted when he succeeded at last in his courtship and conveyed the joyful news in a three-word telegram to Sandringham, 'ALL RIGHT BERTIE'. This was on 13 January 1923 and Queen Mary's first jotting in her diary two days later was of her son's happiness. 'He looks beaming.' A few days later, in one of the few private letters to her brother, Lord Cambridge, that have leaked into the Royal Archives she scribbled, 'Elizabeth is with us now, perfectly charming, so well brought up, a great addition to the family.'

This mirrored the King's view. He had dreaded the idea of future daughters-in-law but in a paternal way, without plumbing psychological depths, he had fallen more than a little in love with Elizabeth himself. 'You have endeared yourself to the people,' he wrote to Bertie. 'I am quite certain that Elizabeth will be a splendid partner in your work and share with you and help you in all you have to do.'

King George V was then a man of sixty, a bearded father figure who had reigned for fifteen years with his wife, Queen Mary, his dear May. He had first grown the beard as a young naval lieutenant. 'You will think that it has altered me rather,' he broke the news to his mother, and thereupon tended it for the rest of his life, an asset to dignity and formality, a shield against self-revelation and a defence against change. An addict of routine and discipline, the well-trimmed beard amplified his principles of good order and absolute precision in every detail of everyday living, though he was not without jovial humour.

Drowned partridge would be served for lunch, he chaffed Princess Mary during the rainy February of her wedding. But Queen Mary records that poor Papa quite 'broke down' at the parting from his daughter. She left 'a terrible blank . . . the corridors of Windsor so empty and silent'. However, three weeks after Bertie – the Duke of York's – engagement, Mary presented the King with his first grandson (the present seventh Earl of Harewood), which being in the female line was an event of no more than tender sentiment. Mary's absence, too, was less disturbing, and the King's letters to his friends increasingly show the transfer of his interest and affection to 'Bertie and E'.

Their wedding day on 26 April 1923 was showery, and now Lady Elizabeth Bowes Lyon attracted all the world's interest as she drove for the last time from Bruton Street in a State landau. The King noted with approval that 'the sun actually came out as the bride entered the Abbey' and mentions in his journal that he found the Archbishop of York's address both moving and beautiful, words he used only seldom. 'You cannot resolve that your new life shall be happy,' the Archbishop had oddly enjoined the bridal couple. 'You can and will resolve that it shall be noble.'

From his wartime naval service, from Cranwell air training and his Cambridge studies, the Duke of York had gained a popular post-war reputation as the Industrial Prince. 'Industrial affairs?' the King said to Mr Clynes. 'That's my second son's department.' One of the first tasks facing the Duke and Duchess on their return from honeymoon was an industrial tour in Liverpool and they were not long installed in White Lodge, their grace-and-favour home in Richmond Park, than they faced a visit to Ulster. The Duchess of York's range of special interests was felt to comprise art, music and child welfare, but her father-in-law soon saw that her good sense and strength of character would be effective in any field. With intuitive sympathy, she appeared to analyse small personal worries almost before he had begun to consider them and had a delightful way of proving them no problem at all.

'Unlike his own children, I was never afraid of him,' she once wrote in recollection. 'In all his twelve years of having me as a daughter-in-law he never spoke one unkind or abrupt word to me and was always ready to listen and give advice on one's own silly little affairs. He was so kind and so *dependable*. And when in the mood he could be deliciously funny. . . .'

In 1924 Princess Mary gave birth to a second son and, with the King's persuasion, the baby was named Gerald David, not only in compliment to the family name of the Prince of Wales but also for Elizabeth's favourite name, that of *her* brother David. From August 1925 the Duke and Duchess kept to themselves the secret anticipation of possibly another David of their own, and the King was not, in fact, told of their hopes until the autumn. White Lodge had been given them because Queen Mary wished 'to keep it in the family': she had lived there in childhood and her eldest son had been born there as a June baby; which was very different, the Yorks found, to the hazards of being lost in the fogs apt to cloak the scene from November to February. The Duchess's decision to await her baby in London with her mother followed naturally on a risk that the doctors might never find their way to the Lodge in bad weather. Besides, on the topic of motherhood Lady Strathmore was both knowledgeable and reassuring. The new baby would be her eighteenth grandchild.

After a bronchial attack the previous year, King George had undertaken a health cruise in the Mediterranean, but in March 1926 his private anxiety for Elizabeth and her baby deterred him from going so far from home. Besides there were industrial worries to demand his attention; the risk of a coal strike had been narrowly averted and the King's anxieties were heightened by the risk of a General Strike, an attempt 'to coerce the government' which he viewed as the danger-line of revolution. On the previous 20 November, Queen Alexandra had died at Sandringham, and the sad interest of sorting his mother's possessions provided the King with lighter preoccupations. But time moved forward beyond any possibility of miscalculation and the family were on tenterhooks until, in the small hours of 21 April, the gynaecologists foregathered and 'a certain line of treatment was adopted', the only phrase to satisfy propriety at the time.

The possibility that the April night had seen the advent of a future Queen Regnant occurred to few. Lady Strathmore rejoiced in her first royal grandchild, her thirteenth granddaughter, while the news columns merely reminded readers that 'the little Princess of Great Britain and Ireland' affected the position of her younger uncles in the succession. The Duke of York felt unsure of his parents' welcome for a girl, but lost no time in attempting to put things right, clearly at Elizabeth's behest.

'You don't know what a tremendous joy it is to Elizabeth and me to have our little girl,' he wrote on 22 April. 'We always wanted a child to make our happiness complete, and now that it has at last happened, it seems so wonderful and strange. I am so proud of Elizabeth at this moment after all that she has gone through during the last few days, and I am so thankful that everything has happened as it should and so successfully. I do hope that you and Papa are as delighted as we are to have a granddaughter. I know Elizabeth wanted a daughter. May I say I hope you won't spoil her?'

The Queen's response was to hurry to pay her daughter-in-law – and the baby – a second visit. Though usually fast asleep, the baby held court every afternoon to friends and relatives: Elphinstones, Plunkets, Pagets, Ogilvys, Viners. After two further reports of satisfactory progress the medical bulletins were discontinued, and a week later the newspapers disappeared or shrank to single sheets in the bitter but brief confrontation of the General Strike.

It seemed debatable whether a policeman should be spared for the doorway of No. 17, and a Palace equerry then stood sentinel there from time to time wearing the armband of a special constable. Residents of Bruton Street were to be seen at their basement windows peeling potatoes for transport volunteers, and the baby's milk came down from St Paul's Walden without recourse to the guarded milk-churns in Hyde Park. On 24 April the Duke warily sought his father's consent on 'the names of our little girl. We should like to call her Elizabeth Alexandra Mary. I hope you will approve. I am sure there will be no muddle over two Elizabeths. We are so anxious for her first name to be Elizabeth as it is such a nice name. Elizabeth of York sounds so nice, too.'

In a desk memo, the King commented to Queen Mary, 'he says nothing about Victoria. I hardly think that necessary', and the family noticed with glee that the Duchess had contrived the same initials as her own, E. A. M. for Elizabeth Angela Marguerite.

The General Strike collapsed on 13 May and, calling at 17 Bruton Street next day with a promised flask of Jordan christening water, Lady Airlie was startled at the number of people waiting outside to see the baby taken for an airing. 'There have never been so many as today,' the Duke told her. 'I can't imagine why.' But Lady Airlie looked at the crowd, 'people of all ages and all classes' as she wrote, and thought she knew the reason. 'Here, in this country, in the throes of strife and bitterness, was something of continuity and of hope in the future.'

On Saturday 29 May the little Princess was christened by the Archbishop of York in the private chapel at Buckingham Palace and baptised with the promised names, Elizabeth Alexandra Mary. The day was propitiously fine, the gold lily font of 1840 was brought from Windsor, and the baby maintained the tradition of wearing the robe of cream Brussels lace used for all Queen Victoria's children and many of her lineal descendants. The six sponsors were the King and Queen and Lord Strathmore as grandparents, Princess Mary and Lady Elphinstone as aunts and, a notable link with the past, there was the distinguished figure of Queen Victoria's last surviving son, the Duke of Connaught.

At his own christening seventy-six years earlier he had been named Arthur after his senior godfather, the great Duke of Wellington. 'You will see her grow up. I shan't,' he said sadly, taking the baby's hand. Yet, with his memories of the Prince Consort and the panorama of Victorian splendour and prosperity, he was to live into his ninety-second year and died only three months before Princess Elizabeth registered for National Service in 1942. White-moustached, grey-waistcoated, upright, he dominates the christening photographs.

'Of course poor baby cried,' Queen Mary noted. 'In fact, she cried so much all through the ceremony', Lady Airlie adds, 'that immediately after it her old-fashioned nurse dosed her well from a bottle of dill water, to the intense amusement of the Prince of Wales.' A few newspapers published pictures of the single-tier christening cake, with its cherubs and white sugar roses of York, but it was not long before the baby could be taken out in her pram in the June sunshine without attracting undue attention. From royal babies and industrial strife public interest was wandering to other themes. Mr Alan Cobham had completed his first air flight from London to the Cape in three months and was laying plans for a seaplane flight to Australia. A year before anyone had heard of Lindbergh, Spain cheered the fourth successful 'crew of aviators' to fly the Atlantic. In London the aluminium figure of Eros had been banished from Piccadilly Circus and a chaos of cranes and hutments covered the site of the future 'subterranean piazza' of the Underground. The flying age, an era of flight and international rivalries and reconstruction, was in the making.

After the weekends of early summer at St Paul's Walden Bury, Princess Elizabeth of York was first taken to Scotland, in early August, travelling by a day train in the arms of Nanny Clara Knight. 'Big blue eyes, tiny ears and the whitest skin in the world', a family friend described the young traveller. Sheltered within the clipped yews of the Dutch garden at Glamis Castle, she beamed upon Scottish cousins, friends and uncles and aunts innumerable. Back in London, in October, a friend found the Duchess kneeling on the floor beside a couch, playing with her six-month-old treasure. 'No doubt about it, a Princess, sitting up by herself in the middle of a huge chesterfield. Her hair, very fair, is beginning to curl charmingly, owing much to the untiring attention of her nurse. The baby is always good . . . she has the sweetest air of complete serenity.'

Within three months, however, mother and child were to

be separated, the 'little Duchess' restraining as best she could the sad knowledge that six enjoyable months of a babyhood were to be denied to her. The Australian Premier, Mr Bruce, had asked that one of the King's elder sons might open the first Parliament in the new Federal capital of Canberra in May 1927 and, since the Prince of Wales had already toured Australia, the choice clearly fell on the Duke and Duchess of York. With visits to Jamaica, Fiji and New Zealand, the outward voyage aboard the battleship *Renown* would take two months. The Duchess gave her daughter a necklace of coral beads as a parting Christmas gift and it appears in photographs like a signal. 'I felt very much leaving,' the Duchess confessed to her mother-in-law, writing from the ship. 'The baby was so sweet playing with the buttons on Bertie's uniform that it quite broke me up.'

The plan was that little Elizabeth should stay with her grandparents alternately, in January to Alah's – Clara Knight's – familiar old family nursery at St Paul's Walden Bury, where she had brought up the Duchess and so many Bowes Lyon children, and then to the King and Queen in early February. 'Our sweet little grandchild Elizabeth arrived here yesterday and came to see us after tea,' the King mentions in his journal. And so, curiously, Elizabeth went to lodge at the Palace twenty-five years to the month before she first went there as Queen.

From that moment the King's references to 'little Elizabeth' grow increasingly frequent in his diaries and letters. Queen Mary would greet the baby after tea, 'Here comes the bambino!' But, once displayed, when Nanny had given an account of the day, the Queen quickly detached herself. It was the King who usually responded to outstretched arms, who took the baby on his lap and suffered tugging fingers at his beard. 'I am glad to be able to give you the most excellent accounts of your sweet little daughter, who is growing daily,' he reported in a special advance birthday letter to the parents. 'She has four teeth now, which is quite good at eleven months old, she is very happy and drives in a carriage every afternoon, which amuses her.' The Duke sensibly replied, 'I am so glad little Elizabeth is behaving herself so well. I do hope you will not spoil her too much, as I have always been told grandfathers are apt to.'

Queen Mary dwelt less on the topic. Her interest was to deepen with her granddaughter's schooling. But as her biographer has pointed out, she was not unmaternal but lacked any spontaneous understanding of a child's ways. 'Baby was sweet at teatime,' she once said of a two-year-old son. 'I really believe he begins to like me at last.'

The threat of spoiling little Elizabeth came from afar. 'It is extraordinary how popular our baby is out here,' Bertie wrote to his mother from New Zealand. 'Wherever we go cheers are given for her as well, and children write to us about her.' Few civic ceremonies were without a presentation of toys for 'Princess Betty'. From New Zealand alone more than a ton were crated home aboard the *Renown*, including dolls taller than the Princess herself and a battalion of teddy-bears. The unforeseen generosity and every new tribute to the baby helped to soften the separation, and the parents eagerly welcomed an account of the first birthday party, at which the two Lascelles boys eagerly wolfed the sponge cake. In May, the Strathmores could write of Elizabeth's powers of getting about, more like swimming than crawling, sitting on her left leg and paddling vigorously with the right.

Nanny Knight had described her earlier charge of long ago, the baby's mother, as 'an exceptionally happy easy baby, crawling early and speaking very young'. With little Elizabeth, it was difficult to teach the word 'Mama' with no mother in sight. But, at fourteen months, the baby references to 'sweet little Lilibet' appear in the King's journal: the baby had improvised a name for herself. The Duke and Duchess returned home on 27 June and the King was cautious of their welcome. 'We will not embrace at the station before so many people,' he instructed his son. 'When you kiss Mama, take your hat off.' Lilibet, too, would not be brought to the station. She awaited her mother at the Palace in Clara Knight's arms, a moment of unfathomable emotion and surprise, and the cry, 'Oh, you little darling!'

Outside the Palace the people were calling and cheering and the young Duchess presently appeared with her husband on the balcony, her child in her arms. In perspective the delight of the crowd ranks as Elizabeth II's first public ovation and, within the hour, many hundreds had massed at Hyde Park Corner, intent on a more personal welcome. Under Queen Mary's approving eye No. 145 Piccadilly had been made ready as the Yorks' future London home. Alah and the baby and domestic staff had already been there for a week and, with a Persian rug hastily draped over the balcony, the happy Duchess carried out her fourteen-month-old daughter again and again to meet the affectionate demonstration.

2

One Four Five

In those days 145 Piccadilly was one of an opulent terrace of late nineteenth-century mansions adjoining Apsley House where the traffic flows south from Hyde Park. A dignified four-storey town house, behind the railings of a cobbled forecourt shared with the Allendale family next door, it was to be the home of the Yorks for the next ten years, the London scene of Princess Elizabeth's childhood.

Successively the home of Baron Albert Rothschild and then of the brewer, Sir William Bass, No. 145 had remained un-tenanted for three or four years when the Duchess of York discovered that her husband might gain a grace-and-favour lease in the gift of the King. The Crown Estate Commissioners had advertised it as an 'Important mansion, with electric passenger lift, drawing-room, dining-room, ballroom, study, library, about twenty-five bedrooms. . .' omitting to mention the first consideration to the Duchess, that a gate at the back opened on the small enclosure of Hamilton Gardens, with sooty shrubs and paths affording a degree of sheltered play space for the children. The house also had the advantage, remarkable at the time, of double glazing which created an oasis of quiet at Hyde Park Corner; and near the garden door there soon stood an aviary with the canaries given for 'Princess Betty' in New Zealand, their song deepening the serenity of the pleasant home atmosphere.

In the entrance hall, the chimes of a notable eighteenth-century Scottish clock welcomed visitors. The time was to come when the pipe of young voices echoed from the circular landing of the nursery quarters at the top of the house, but for weeks after her homecoming in 1927 the Duchess could hardly bear to be separated from her baby daughter. 'Elizabeth is learning to walk. Very dangerous!' she wrote to a friend within the month, and visitors would often find the child playing at her feet in the sitting-room.

The early Marcus Adams photographs were taken at this time, stylish with the charm of Hoppner's princesses. 'She stood so sweetly, without the slightest shyness, waiting to be kissed,' wrote the author Lady Cynthia Asquith, after being offered 'quite fantastic payment' for a royal serial. The little girl delved into the visitor's handbag, 'spectacles promptly perched on nose, pennies pocketed, the mirror ogled, face-powder applied', and we glimpse her descending a staircase, resolutely announcing 'Lilibet walk self'. Talking was presently improved, Cynthia Asquith noted, with 'long conversations through an imaginary telephone, in a quaint blend of all the grown-up voices familiar to her, her pantomime technique perfect'.

When her grandfather, the King, fell seriously ill with a lung infection in the winter of 1928–9, a token of his recovery was that he asked to have 'sweet little Lilibet' with him, and the little Princess and her capable Alah went to stay with him at Craigweil, near Bognor, during his convalescence. 'G delighted to see her,' wrote Queen Mary, and next day noted in her diary, 'I played with Lilibet making sand pies! The Archbishop of Canterbury came . . . so kind and sympathetic.' One finger on the little girl's shoulder, King George began to walk again, and on Easter Monday he made a brief appearance with the Queen and Lilibet on the sea wall and 'there was great cheering', says Queen Mary. The Princess's photographs, her pictures on chocolate boxes, the magic of the camera and the printed word were endearing their grandchild to the public far faster than the essentially homely royal couple had thought possible.

Celebrating her third birthday by 'picking cherries off a cake', just as her mother had done, the Duke of York similarly experienced the ground-swell of popularity in taking up a round of duties as Lord High Commissioner in Edinburgh. 'The one thing I regret is that we have not got Lilibet here,' the Duchess wrote to the Queen from Holyroodhouse. 'I fear that has been a very great disappointment to the people. Not that they would have seen her, but they would have liked to feel that she was here. This morning, in the solemn old Assembly, the Moderator mentioned "our dear Princess Elizabeth" which is, I believe, almost unique. It almost frightens me that the people should love her so much. I suppose that it is a good thing. . . . I hope that she will be worthy of it, poor little darling.' Meanwhile, when the Archbishop called on the King, he found him on hands and knees searching the carpet. 'We are looking for Lilibet's hair-slide,' the King explained. Before so trusted a friend, the King joined Lilibet unabashed in the games of childhood, and in his notebooks the Archbishop mentions the pleasant sight of 'the King-Emperor shuffling on hands and knees along the floor, while the little Princess led him by the beard'.

Of Bognor itself, the child retained only a misty impression that she did not like the sea. But the sight of horses trotting past 145 became etched on her mind, in Alah's view, at two or three years old. Her own brown legs became a pair of pretended horses with special names. A fall would be followed by the cry, 'Oh dear, I've bruised poor Flycatcher!' or 'I've cut poor Harmony!'

At Sandringham she made a round of the stables with her grandfather, conversing with each of the six horses in turn, offering sugar from the palm of her hand. In 1929 she had her first riding lessons and went to her first meet of the hounds that winter as the smallest of spectators. Her father, then an ardent huntsman, rented Naseby Hall and, as Master of the Hunt, the seventh Earl Spencer told of riding over one day to be greeted by the small Princess in the doorway, 'How nice to see you! Do please come in, but you'd better leave your horse outside.'

For her fourth birthday, the King gave her a Shetland pony named Peggy, a timely mind-occupying gift in view of grown-up intimations of a baby brother 'perhaps, in summer'. Her anniversary occurred on Easter Monday, and the strolling crowds at Windsor had the amusement of seeing the diminutive figure in pink responding to the salute of the Scots Guards, as if clearly aware of the distinction of the occasion.

By now the nursery landing at 145 stabled a troop of toy horses and grown-up visitors were methodically harnessed; Cynthia Asquith finding herself reined in by her own string of pearls. But real horses were as individual as people, and from her nursery windows the little Princess could watch the largest traffic space of central London, the sinewy horses of the brewer's drays, the lone pullers with their delivery vans, the jingling troop of the Horse Guards, an ever-changing spectacle replaced in high summer by the friendly village horses and fell ponies at Glamis.

Princess Margaret was born at Glamis Castle late in the evening of 21 August 1930 and on the following day any expectations of a baby brother were strategically dispensed for Lilibet by news of 'a baby sister for you'.

The young Duke and Duchess of York had indeed expected a son, the surprise element of the birth indeed evident in their indecision in choosing names for another daughter. It was not until 27 August that the Duchess of York wrote to Queen Mary, 'I think that Ann of York sounds pretty, and Elizabeth and Ann go well together. I wonder what you think? Lots of people have suggested Margaret but it has no links really on either side.' Her father-in-law was, however, averse to Ann and the question was still unresolved when the King and Queen first saw their new granddaughter at Glamis on 30 August. 'The baby a darling', wrote Queen Mary, but another week passed before the Duchess decided to write to the Queen at Balmoral with explicit firmness, 'Bertie and I have decided now to call our little daughter "Margaret Rose", instead of M. Ann, as Papa does not like Ann. I hope that you like it. I think that it is very pretty together.' And ten weeks later Princess Margaret was christened in the private chapel at Buckingham Palace, as her sister had been, and *The Times* noted that four-year-old Princess Elizabeth was among those present.

The transition from only child to the happy possessor of a sister was smoothly accomplished. They drilled Lilibet in considering which of her toys 'would be best for Baby'. While Mrs Knight took charge of the baby, an assistant nurse from Lady Linlithgow's Scottish household, Margaret Macdonald, had become Lilibet's special nanny, perhaps a shade more amenable to tantrums. She was an auburn-haired girl in her mid-twenties, whom Lilibet occasionally ambushed with a 'Boo!' from doorway or curtain, and 'Bobo' she was destined to remain for years, as Princess Elizabeth's nanny, maid, dresser companion, confidante, 'the rapport between them almost telepathic'.

'Bobo' implanted the tactful game of four bears, with Baby as the very little bear, and Lilibet told that nice visiting lady, Cynthia Asquith, her own ideas on naming Margaret Rose. 'I'm going to call her Bud, she's not a real rose yet, she's only a bud.' When the bud at fourteen months took her first tottering steps, Lilibet announced, 'Now we're going to have *real* fun!'

alertly aware that the eternal pastime of horses could soon be played properly, with Margaret in harness. As soon as Cynthia Asquith began writing her series of domestic royal books, she discovered that 'every word must go for approval not only to the Duchess but also to King George V', adding the glitter of truth to stories of childhood that might otherwise seem mere journalistic improvisation.

Lady Helen Graham, the Duchess's early lady-in-waiting, a published author herself, gives us a reliable picture of Lilibet aged five, 'a lively, trim little figure in a green wool jersey and kilt of Royal Stewart tartan, with hair shading from gold, and eyes that were always observing, like those of a bird. She noticed everything; but never thought she herself was being noticed. It just seemed fun to wave to people and to have them wave back. She never could understand why photographers would pick her out for attention and frowned upon them with obvious disapproval.'

According to Cynthia Asquith, Princess Margaret at two could hum the 'Merry Widow' waltz and almost any song she had ever heard, while Lilibet would 'at once notice anything out of place, an unfastened hook, a lace untied, an obtrusive safety-pin, anything she felt was not intended to be seen'. Gazing down from the high nursery windows of 145, she would notice that the mounted policeman had a new stirrup and recognise the hacks from the Knightsbridge riding schools who reappeared through the day with different riders. Lady Airlie found that a Christmas gift of a child's housemaid's outfit led to a passion for housework, vigorously renewed when Princess Margaret was given a set of miniature dust-pans and brushes a year or two later.

Her mother taught her to read, persuasively introducing the Beacon primers – in fact, from an American publisher – and at the age of six Lilibet could read on her own with fair fluency. Her 'Uncle David', the Prince of Wales, solved his annual gift problem with a new Winnie-the-Pooh; her other Uncle David, her mother's younger brother, added to her stock of toy farm animals. And all the world was a stage with the setpiece of Hyde Park Corner, with ambulances pulling in to St George's Hospital with 'more poor sick people', and the constant traffic of red London buses. When covered-top buses were intro-duced, her excited cries aroused the nursery, 'Come and see, quick – a bus with a hat on!' At four years, piano lessons had begun with Mabel Lander, speedily nicknamed Goosey, whose arrival at 145 at 9.25 every morning was regarded as grown-up routine. Occasionally, wet afternoons brought forays into the basement kitchen to help the cook, Mrs MacDonald, to bake scones, first attempts in cookery which Princess Elizabeth later took very seriously, saying that she ought to be able to cook for a husband.

In the adult world of 1931, the economic realities of depression saw the King relinquishing the then not inconsiderable sum of £50,000 from the Civil List and the Duke of York similarly gave up Naseby Hall and sold his stable of horses. 'I am only doing this on consideration of facts, damned hard facts,' he wrote to a friend. Within the glades of Windsor Great Park, however, the young Duchess of York turned her attention to the remains of an old Regency villa, a two-storeyed box of moss-stained grey stucco, which was all that was left of George IV's last rural hideaway, the Royal Lodge of a hundred years earlier.

The Duchess lost no time in persuading the King how beneficial the fresh air would be to the children. As Sir John Wheeler-Bennett has said, inconvenience, dilapidation and decay were the keynotes, but one senses a flurry of urgency in the family correspondence, as if a couple of inexperienced young house-hunters had been warned by an estate-agent that other viewers were interested. 'It is too kind of you to offer us Royal Lodge. I think it will suit us admirably,' wrote the Duke of York to his father, and from Balmoral the King responded, 'I am so pleased to hear that you and Elizabeth liked the Royal Lodge and would like to live there,' and the grace-and-favour lease was as good as signed. For Lilibet there began an enchanted sequence of Saturday picnics, of bonfires and twig-gathering with Margaret looking on from her pram, while Christmas brought the tinselled trees and carols of Sandringham, the season that the Prince of Wales described as 'Dickens in a Cartier setting'.

Old friends recollect the children playing 'night train to Scotland' on their mother's couch, with Margaret acting as coach attendant and sleeping passenger, but this belonged to the summer weeks before going to Glamis or the old Deeside house which the Yorks had made their own at Birkhall. With weekends, from time to time, with her Strathmore grandparents in Hertfordshire, with visits to cousins and friends, such were the changing scenes of Lilibet's childhood, but for five more years 145 was always truly home.

At its heart, side by side, her father's study and her mother's sitting-room overlooked the private green serenity of Hamilton Gardens at the back of the house. Lilibet early recognised that if they were busy or absent it was usually because they were somehow helping Grandpapa England and Granny Queen, as she called her grandparents. Across the park were aunts and uncles, similarly occupied, and elsewhere were innumerable cousins; few children could have had more. Then, in the egality of childhood, there were Alah and Bobo, Catta (the Duchess's maid), Mr Ainslie, the steward, 'Golly' (the sobriquet which fell upon Mrs MacDonald, the cook, for her mass of dark hair) and other fond domestics. There was 'Goosey', too, and Mrs Rankin – otherwise Madam Vacani – who provided dancing lessons; while slightly at a remove there were the Household staff, the elderly Basil Brooke, the Duke's comptroller, and the genial secretary, Patrick Hodgson, whose niece Sonia presently became one of Lilibet's closer personal friends.

In the royal folklore around the Princesses, we need not accept that Lilibet was a lonely child. She made friends with everyone, from the 145 telephone operator to the Prime Minister. The children of the Duchess's girlhood friends, Plunkets and Buccleuchs, came to nursery tea, or else the young Allendales from next door and Elphinstone and Lascelles cousins. Three years younger than Lilibet, the youthful Master of Carnegie was led up to Mr Baldwin one day, with the introduction, 'He's rather nice, isn't he?' An older cousin, 'Sandy' Ramsay, filled an impalpable substitute role as an elder brother, and a nursery canary was named after him, 'A gift from Sandy when he was an egg!' The name 'Aunt Nelly' was bestowed on the Duke of Montrose's ageless daughter, Lady Helen Graham, who undertook to handle the Princess's correspondence, which was gradually increasing from children around the world, although the task was no hindrance to Nelly's occasional contributions to Blackwood's Magazine.

Cynthia Asquith dates Lilibet's 'first public appearance' as a concert for children when, rising four, she accepted a 'large, damp and prickly bouquet' as to the manner born but evidently found the dancing mane of the conductor more entertaining than the music. At five, she rode to the Trooping the Colour ceremony in an open carriage with her parents, raising a small hand to acknowledge the cheers precisely as her mother did. Then she was one of four little bridesmaids at the Sussex wedding of Lady May Cambridge and Captain Abel Smith. Londoners discovered she could be glimpsed going for an afternoon ride or, on a Friday, setting out with her mother to Windsor, and Lilibet for her part more than glimpsed the Londoners. She eagerly watched out for an old couple – the 'very old couple' – regularly to be seen working in the front garden of their little house on the Great West Road, and looked out, too, for 'the Jolly Grocer' and 'Old Mother Newspapers' at her news-stand, characters who never knew of the junior royal attention lavished on them.

As the storm-clouds of the 1930s' recession passed, affairs improved at Royal Lodge, and at weekends the Yorks camped in two redecorated rooms 'safari style'. The old conservatory had vanished, replaced by a bedroom wing, and an exterior of soft rose colourwash unified old and new. With the approach of Princess Margaret's first birthday there arose the problem of finding a governess for Lilibet, 'someone young enough to enjoy playing games and running about out of doors with her'.

Through her elder sister, Lady Rose Leveson-Gower, the Duchess presently heard of a newly qualified Scottish girl, aged only twenty-two, who did prodigies of walking. Marion Crawford was intent on becoming a child psychologist rather than a governess, but she was giving classes to Lady Elgin's young family near Dunfermline, and Lady Rose arranged what seemed a chance social meeting with the Yorks. 'We all ate our buns and drank our coffee without any hint given me of what was coming,' Miss Crawford recollected nearly twenty years later. But the sequel was a charming and friendly letter from the Duchess. 'Why not come for a month, and see how you like us and how we like you?'

As it happened, the royal couple had been called to London on the March evening when the governess first went to Royal Lodge and Alah Knight took her upstairs to meet her future pupil. 'A small figure with a mop of curls sat up in bed. She wore a nightie with a design of small pink roses. She had tied the cords of her dressing-gown to the bed-knobs and was busy driving her team' were the newcomer's first impressions. 'I mostly go round the park once or twice before I go to sleep, you know. It exercises the horses,' the Princess explained, with introductions over, and plied her visitor with questions before Alah unhitched the team and 'laid her down like a doll'. 'Are you coming to stay with us? And will you play with us tomorrow? Will you come to the Little House with us?' Before Margaret was nineteen months old, it was always 'with us', never 'with me', Crawfie noted, and was soon to find that at the Little House endless games of horses and housekeeping awaited her.

'From the start there was always about her a certain amenability, a reasonableness rare in anyone so young. With a high IQ, she was quick at picking anything up, and one never had to do a lot of explaining,' 'Crawfie' has summarised. During her Edinburgh training at Moray House, Miss Crawford had worked in the closes and courtyards of the city's worst slums, mercifully long since vanished, and found with satisfaction that the Princess, like other children, was never happier than when 'thoroughly busy and rather grubby'. 'Until I came,' added Crawfie, 'she had never been allowed to get dirty. I started a few innovations. . . .'

The whoops of Red Indians were heard among the smut-soaked shrubs behind 145, and the Duke of York was pressed into hopscotch tournaments and games of tag. The vast world of commerce was unlocked with visits to Woolworth's in Oxford Street to buy pieces for a model farm or purchase small Christmas presents, until many a Woolies' china ornament nestled in Queen Mary's cabinets among the Fabergé treasures. Jostling with Crawfie among the shoppers, Lilibet was happily never recognised. Inspecting the ducks and rowing-boats on the Serpentine in Hyde Park was infinitely preferable to watching the wildfowl on the lake in the grounds of Buckingham Palace, where there were seldom other small children like herself. 'Other children had an enormous fascination,' Crawfie noted, 'like mystic beings from another world.'

These unconventional adventures met with Alah's thorough disapproval. It was sufficiently democratic in her view that Lilibet went Christmas shopping with her mother at Harrods, where it was customary to clear the aisles for royalty. Once a year, the children went to a pantomime, decorously seated in the royal box, though presently longing before long to sit in the stalls and see better. When Margaret outgrew her pram, the woods of Windsor and St Paul's Walden echoed to her cries of 'Wait for me! Wait for me!' To Alah the two Princesses

31

could now be primly dressed alike on public occasions as if they were twins. But for Lilibet there was always the gentle elder-sister seniority, loving, protective, authoritative in turn, and only presently relaxed for the sisters in sharing the Little House, Y Bwythn Bach.

In retrospect, the Little House risks appearing as an extravagant play house, though at the time it seemed more a shrewd expression of Welsh pride and initiative as well as a gift of loyal affection for its little chatelaine. The making of Queen Mary's Dolls' House in the 1920s had remained in the public mind as a fabulous miniature, and a group of Cardiff business men had put forward the idea that they might similarly build and equip a child-size house as a gift to Princess Elizabeth from the people of Wales.

It was to take the form of a traditional Welsh thatched cottage, exclusively of Welsh workmanship, scaled down to two-fifths of ordinary size. The Duchess was delighted with the proposal, and asked only that the house should first be put on display for a good cause, which in itself precisely fulfilled every Welsh hope. Attended by faithful queues, the Little House was exhibited in Cardiff and other cities, raising considerable sums for hard-pressed charities, and no-one objected if it seemed more contemporary stockbroker or ideal home in style than Welsh traditional. It was not a dolls' house, the publicists stressed, but a royal house 'wherein the little owner can spend many happy hours practising the domestic arts'. The four rooms were some 7 ft square and 4 ft 6 in in height, and at the press preview journalists were seen for the first and only time going round a royal home hunched to their knees.

In the kitchen, the stainless steel sink and make-believe cooker were of correct scaled-down proportions, and in the bathroom a 40 in bath awaited the ablutions of washable dolls. In the living-room a table 19 in high was set with miniature china of proportionate size. Suitably small, the portrait of the Princess's mother over the mantelshelf was by the Welsh artist, Margaret Lindsay Williams. On her first day of royal duty, Crawfie found only one place where she could comfortably stand upright, 'all 5 ft 7 in of me', at the top of the stairs. Visiting giants could, in fact, be comfortably seated. Cynthia Asquith has told of bishops, Cabinet Ministers and army generals squeezing themselves into its hospitality, marvelling at electric lighting and a junior telephone, real water flowing hot and cold, and plumbing that worked.

Ultimately, after a term of practical use, Lilibet noticed that the chimney above the thatched roof was a dummy, linked with neither fireplace or flue. 'One does not need fires in summer,' she excused the fault.

Nor was the youthful and innocent owner told until years later that the odyssey of Y Bwythn Bach on its road journey to Royal Lodge had begun with a fire. Wrapped in tarpaulin and drawn by a steam tractor, busily throwing out smoke and sparks, the timbers proved fireproofed but not the tarpaulin and the thatch with its covering flared like a haystack. It is solemnly on record that the Monmouth fire brigade arrived within four minutes, and *The Times* staidly announced that 'letters and telegrams of sympathy reached the Lord Mayor of Cardiff from all classes of people'.

Fortunately the furnishings had travelled separately; an insurance company paid up nobly on a child-size policy – normally kept in a small table drawer – and the cheque was pleasantly returned by the Duchess for amendment 'as making good will cost nothing like that sum'. Fifteen years later, the coincidence was noted that the Princess's first intended married home, Sunninghill Park, was similarly ravaged by fire before she could occupy it. But the Little House was quickly restored to order, a unique treasure ranking in enjoyment and practical usefulness as Princess Elizabeth's first major personal possession, and still affording pleasure to the most junior royal set of today.

The Duke and Duchess necessarily stooped to attend the inaugural tea, and at every visit, the children themselves opened up the house, cleaned and dusted, enjoyably scrubbing the kitchen floor when needful. When the time came to leave, they wrapped up the silver, put away the linen and blankets, and covered the furniture with dust-sheets, as the staff always did in every royal home. Crawfie at first imagined that a suitably petite domestic kept the place in order, but the only domestic was the Princess herself, mastering the chores of washing up, cleaning the bath-tub and later even listing the laundry.

The Little House also stands in its own yew-hedged garden within earshot of the main house, where the Princesses tended the outcome of their penny packets of seeds, weeded the paths and in due course grew their own potatoes, with the triumph of having them served for lunch. 'What *kind* of potatoes are these?' Lilibet once asked, inspecting a grown-up friend's kitchen-garden. 'We had Epicures today – they are very good.'

Thus were instilled the qualities of tidiness and discipline, method and routine, necessary to a monarch. Not that any shadow of that future as yet crossed Lilibet's mind, although there were inklings, dimly perceived and not wholly brushed aside, that at times troubled the adults around her. 'Sometimes strangers speak to me as if they knew me,' she once said, with a perplexed expression. What did she make of the linen at the Little House, embroidered with an 'E' and a coronet? And what of her shilling-a-week pocket money, the shining new silver shilling embossed with her grandfather's portrait, to be put away in her embroidered purse against the next shopping spree at Woolworth's? It was simple enough that Grandfather England should supervise the coinage of his realm, that larger coins could be won for good work done . . . absurd if grown-ups called one of the largest coins half-a-crown. Grandpapa's portrait on a postage stamp ensured its safe journey, and Granny Queen's picture in a newspaper, with aunts and uncles, indeed made newspapers very interesting to look at. And perhaps there were other nudges of destiny. In collecting the minutiae for a book, Cynthia Asquith was told of when Lilibet, rising eight, was introduced to a lady named Victoria. And the visitor noticed 'a barely perceptible straightening of the child's back, a slight darkening of her eyes, and a tiny tremor in the clear voice, "Victoria? I think I have heard that name before."'

3

The little Princesses

'All I ask is, teach Lilibet and Margaret a decent hand,' King
George V briefed Miss Crawford. 'A hand with some character
in it. None of my children can write properly. They all do it
exactly the same way.' It was the governess's first experience,
as she says, of 'royalty's economy in words'. She had come to
the Yorks on a month's trial and it was more than a year before
she became a permanent member of the Household. 'No-one
ever had employers who interfered so little,' she writes. The
educational pattern of the children in line to the throne was left
largely to her judgment.

A garden room on the first floor, formerly the Duchess's
boudoir, was transformed into a business-like schoolroom.
Crawfie had only to mention her needs to Major Brooke, the
comptroller, and blackboards, globes, dictionaries and primers
magically appeared, while maps on the walls heightened the
school atmosphere. The Duchess's chief concern was that the
desk should be in the best light for teacher and pupil, 'The
desk should look happy, too.'

One could go wrong. A young French lady came in to teach
primary French. Her method, after some elementary conversation, required Lilibet to write out columns of tiresome
verbs. During the session Crawfie played with Margaret in
the next room, where one day hysterical cries from Mademoiselle sent her rushing in to find Lilibet dripping with ink and
Mademoiselle in hysterics. Goaded by boredom, the Princess
had suddenly picked up the silver inkpot and upturned it over
her own head, with the highly satisfactory climax of deluging
her curls, her face and frock.

Mademoiselle did not come again. In due course, Georgina
Guérin, daughter of the Duchess's girlhood French teacher,

appeared at Birkhall to institute a fun-day of speaking nothing but French. Lilibet's general schooling shaped into a curriculum which won Queen Mary's understanding praise, 'wonderfully ingenious, considering how many subjects have to be included'. Transferred to Thursday afternoon, Mabel Lander's music lesson had founded 'a good, firm round touch' and brought her pupil to the popular milestone of 'The Merry Peasant'. Coming every Wednesday, a drawing teacher, Miss Cox, daughter of one of Brangwyn's studio assistants, had elicited 'a very decided talent and plenty of inventive fancy. . . . Princess Elizabeth would make quicker progress if the standards she sets herself were not so high. She is apt to get discouraged by falling short of her own ambition.' But, as children will, Lilibet began illustrating her letters with marginal colour-wash sketches in careful detail. Crawfie received a Christmas blotter decorated with corgis, recognisable lambs and an accurately antlered stag, and within a year or two Queen Mary could gauge progress on receiving a skilful lino-cut of a circus horse.

Drowsiness was inclined to settle, on the other hand, over sessions with embroidery or knitting. Arithmetic was a bane, and a rueful holiday message reached Miss Crawford with love from Lilibet from Balmoral. 'This evening I added up the score for Racing Demon and found that I made a great many mistakes. It took me ages to think it out. Just simple adding!' Later on, finding Margaret similarly afflicted, Queen Mary judiciously pointed out that although 'mathematical exercise makes for accuracy, these two probably never will have to do even their own household books' and the daily hour of arithmetic was reduced to benefit history. On Monday afternoons the drawing-room floor at 145 creaked to a dancing class, and Tuesday was brightened by the singing class which Lady Cavan organised for her own two daughters at her home in Kensington. Not least the weekend at Royal Lodge saw Lilibet's riding lesson with Mr Owen, formerly her father's groom at Naseby. An old snapshot depicts him, a sturdy fortyish man, bowler-hatted, gloved, gaitered, clearly full of reliable lore on burrs and galls and girths, ready to listen companionably to chatter of the latest juvenile pony books but alert to interpose, 'Be on your guard now!' without missing a word. His maxims rose so readily to Lilibet's lips that her father at last cried in exasperation, 'Don't ask me. Ask Owen. Who am I to make suggestions?'

With her eighth birthday the Princess was promoted to luncheon downstairs with her parents. The Duchess always looked back with gratitude at the benefits of lunching at her father's table in the old days, the amusement of improvising conversation with elderly statesmen ten times her age, the unforeseen friendships floating in the wake of such ancient gods as Lord Rosebery and Lord Curzon. No matter if Lilibet made juvenile gaffes, as with Ramsay MacDonald, 'I saw you in *Punch* this morning, Mr MacDonald, leading a flock of geese.' Good marks for trying. 'I mustn't be shy,' Lilibet said, after one over-stiff occasion. 'I *wish* I were more like Mummy!'

With the promotion to luncheon, her mother prepared her for an introduction to the continental royal crowd, all the innumerable strangers awaiting her at the wedding of her uncle Prince George, Duke of Kent, to Princess Marina. 'There are several relations who will be bridesmaids, such as my nieces and cousins,' wrote the bride's father, Prince Nicholas, 'and of course Princess Elizabeth, naturally.' The Abbey wedding was followed moreover by the unfamiliar ritual of a Greek Orthodox ceremony at Buckingham Palace, which saw Lilibet coping with Marina's fifteen-foot swirl of silver lamé 'with dignity and sang-froid' in the view of Lady Cynthia Colville. But it passed unnoticed that a fair-haired thirteen-year-old Greek boy named Philip was among the junior guests and neither Prince nor Princess remember the circumstance.

Crawfie would have ensured that the Kents' Caribbean honeymoon was traced by map and picture. After six months at her parents' table the Princess better understood how intensively her family were concerned with ideals of service to the community. A bank manager managed his bank. A King ruled his kingdom with kindness and justice, with all the King's horses and all his men and the help of his government, an impersonal yet sufficient idea.

In 1935 Princess Elizabeth's ninth birthday fell on Easter Day, which a Windsor guest considered 'the happiest prelude to her grandfather's Silver Jubilee hardly two weeks away'. The King grumbled diffidently of 'all this fuss and expense – what will people say?' and the convincing reality of the wave of national emotion for his twenty-five years on the Throne caught him by surprise. 'A glorious summer day,' he wrote afterwards, 'the greatest number of people in the streets that I have ever seen in my life, the enthusiasm most touching,' and he noted *The Times* report that the two little Princesses rode with their parents to St Paul's Cathedral in an open State landau 'waving to the people and enjoying the spectacle as only children can'.

The thanksgiving service, both the piety and spectacle of the ceremony, could only have deepened the religious faith Lilibet had gained from her mother. Back at the Palace, on the balcony, she continued to wave at the happy crowds when the wearied adults could respond no more, and that evening was allowed to stay up late to hear her grandfather broadcast his thanks to his peoples. 'I am speaking to the children above all,' came that familiar voice from the speaker-cone. 'Remember, children, the King is speaking to you. As you grow up, be ready and proud to give to your country the service of your work, your mind and your heart. . . .' The message was ineffaceable in his granddaughter's memory.

Another day, the Princess accompanied her grandparents on a drive to see the remarkable decorations in north London, where every house was decked with banners and streamers and messages, 'such nice decorations', Queen Mary confirmed, and the King, who was fond of repeating his jokes, no doubt echoed for Lilibet's benefit the jest already tried on his friend Major More-Molyneux. 'I suppose', he said, 'you think these flags are hung out for you? Let me tell you' – with a bow, hand on heart – 'they are for *me*!' Equally the King would not have resisted showing the Princess some of the new Jubilee additions to his beloved stamp collection, and, not least, in a special frame for her to keep, the Canadian one-cent with her portrait.

She had also seen the baskets of congratulatory mail stacked on a table beside her grandfather's desk, and at about this time she first came to read some of the letters written to her by children away in the back blocks of Australia, on farms in Africa and from remote mission stations. 'All breathing loyalty and affection to her as their Princess,' says Lady Helen Graham. 'I think these messages from one child to another brought the first direct revelation that she was of importance to others.'

Fortunately, the burden of Jubilee impressions was eased by closer personal events. 'Do you know,' Lilibet rapturously exclaimed one day, 'I've been to the Military Tournament *and* the Horse Show *and* the Tattoo!' And after his birthday party in June her doting grandfather noted that 'all the children looked nice, but none nicer than Lilibet and Margaret'.

'Grandfather King' was of course permitted few glimpses of the more violent scenes of family life. 'She bites!' Lilibet would cry. 'Look at the teeth marks!' while Margaret would counter, 'She slapped me first!' There was face-slapping and hair-pulling. 'She always wants what I want,' Lilibet would wail. Margaret complained, 'She orders me about!' The elder sister, it was true, underwent much difficulty in her self-imposed task of keeping the younger fairly in order. 'Lilibet was the one with the temper,' Marion Crawford tells us, 'but it was under control,' while Margaret could tear apart the tidy, methodical cocoon of Lilibet's disciplined scene. Their hatred of hats could bring on a scene, with a duel of elastic-snapping and cries of 'You beast!' Margaret quickly forgot and forgave. Lilibet went into her shell of reserve, fretting over the ructions. 'Yet if you once gained her love and affection,' Crawfie says, 'you had it for ever, but she never gave it easily.'

The hat-band battles simmered into the calm of Glamis, with Grandpapa Strathmore, whose carefully-parted whiskers tickled when he kissed, and Grandmama Strathmore, who never failed to find fresh costumes for charades, a ceaseless pastime in the company of Bowes Lyon and Elphinstone cousins. With this crowded setting, it was nevertheless a major diversion to go down to the station to watch the fish express racing through, and then there were the fascinating possibilities of crossed pins stuck together with chewing gum and placed on the railway lines and transformed into miniature pairs of scissors beneath the next train.

The Glamis house-party, that Jubilee summer, was enlivened also by the engagement of Lilibet's Uncle Harry, the Duke of Gloucester, to Lady Alice Scott, third daughter of the Duke of Buccleuch, thus the second of the King's sons to choose a Scottish bride. Lilibet carefully composed a letter of congratulation to the betrothed couple and Lady Alice's choice of both Lilibet and Margaret as bridesmaids at Westminster Abbey was the immediate sequel. Lady Alice elected that a new and comparatively inexpensive young dressmaker named Norman Hartnell should make her wedding gown, and so it came about that the Duchess of York brought her two daughters to his new salon for their dress fittings. Yet the little girls, as Mr Hartnell wrote, 'seemed more interested in the scintillating cars that purred in the mews outside than in their frocks' and he clearly had no idea of the successful years of royal patronage that lay in store.

Sadly, the death of the Duke of Buccleuch shortly before the wedding caused the ceremony to be transferred to the private chapel at Buckingham Palace. The crowds had to content themselves with cheering the bride as she made the short journey from her London home, and again outside the Palace when it became evident she would appear on the balcony. 'The bridesmaids looked charming – Lilibet and Margaret looked too sweet,' wrote Queen Mary predictably. But Hartnell's pink satin little girl dresses were unseen beneath their white fur coats – and no-one dreamed that within a year, a month and a week, their parents would have become King and Queen.

Nevertheless, the Christmas of 1935 turned out to be the first Christmas Lilibet had ever spent away from her mother. The Duchess fell ill with severe flu added to complications of pneumonia and had to remain at Royal Lodge, with her husband and Nelly Graham for company, while the children accompanied their grandparents to Sandringham.

The King found the Norfolk weather too cold to take Lilibet on their usual round of the stables, though the Princesses had the fun of seeing his parrot Charlotte delicately treading among the plates and saucers on the breakfast table. We know that Lilibet gave her grandmother a lino-cut of a circus horse, drawn by herself, and she wrote to a friend of keeping 'Mummy and Papa's gifts until they come. . . . We had lots of lovely presents and a sleigh on wheels but we have only taken it out once.' As a gift to various relatives that year, the Duke and Duchess had commissioned a recording of their daughters singing a carol duet and the two voices echoed repeatedly through the drawing-room, while the girls giggled at themselves or created a quartet. The newly wed Uncle Harry and Aunt Alice were full of fun and the Kents had brought their new baby, Edward, whose christening Lilibet had attended in the Palace chapel only the previous month. Yet the Prince of Wales, who had arrived on Christmas Eve, could not shake off a sense of foreboding in the atmosphere.

'Bertie's two children romped around the twenty-foot tree. Yet in this closely knit fabric of family ties I felt detached and lonely. My brothers were secure in their private lives; whereas I was caught up in an inner conflict and would have no peace of mind until I resolved it. But this was hardly the time or place.' He noticed that his father had grown thin and bent, and yet failed to perceive that the King was in truth killing himself

40

with worry over his son's affair with Mrs Simpson. 'After I am dead, the boy will ruin himself in twelve months,' he grumbled to Mr Baldwin. And to his wife's great confidante, Blanche Lennox, he burst out passionately, 'I pray to God that my eldest son will never marry and have children, and that nothing will come between Bertie and Lilibet and the Throne.'

On Christmas Day, Lilibet heard her grandfather broadcasting to the world from the little room across the hall and, seated at his side for family lunch, she knew the care he took with his annual message. 'It brings me into touch with my peoples,' he had explained (to Dr Lang), 'and that I'm very keen about.' On New Year's Eve she was allowed to sit up late with him and watch the film of *Monte Cristo*, perhaps the first movie she ever saw. Next day, with a powdering of light snow on the shrubs, she went out walking with Queen Mary while the King rode quietly beside them on his old pony Jack.

Three weeks later the Princesses were at Royal Lodge when, in their mother's room early in the morning, they were gently told that they would not see their grandfather again. The King was dead. Lilibet cried in her mother's arms, and then the Duchess had to hurry to Sandringham to comfort Queen Mary.

Miss Crawford was recalled from holiday with the message, 'Please don't let this depress them more than is absolutely necessary. They are so young.' Princess Elizabeth had been encouraged for some months to look at the picture newspapers and inevitably saw the front-page photographs of the coffin watched through the night in Sandringham Church. 'Ought we to play?' she asked.

Later, on seeing the news pictures of the lying in State in Westminster Hall and the endless double line of mourning Londoners slowly moving past, the nine-year-old Princess said of her own accord that she would like to go. The Hall was closed for a few minutes to ensure privacy and, tightly clasping her mother's hand, Princess Elizabeth gazed silently at the catafalque.

Above the bier, hung with purple velvet, the harsh outline of the coffin was softened by the draped Royal Standard. The candlelight shone with the superb poetry of State upon the Imperial State Crown and the Orb, the tall Cross and the bent heads of the four plumed Life Guards keeping vigil with four Yeomen of the Guard. 'Everyone was so quiet,' the Princess said of her abiding impression afterwards, 'as if the King were asleep.'

Youth is resilient and takes its own view, grief quickly forgotten. Princess Elizabeth had come to know the previous year that her joking, genial Uncle David of Wales would one day be King. She had visited his sitting-room at York House, where a portrait of Queen Mary, in silvery evening-gown with diamonds and the Order of the Garter, hung at the chimneypiece, and a red-dappled map of the world, of the Empire, completely covered one wall. Some necessary genealogy had been deftly woven into a history lesson, the shadowy form of great-grandmama Queen Victoria made more distinct.

'If ever I am Queen,' Lilibet had responded lightly, 'I shall make a rule that there must be no riding on Sundays. Horses should have a rest, too.' It seemed a remote contingency, taken lightly and of no importance. Crawfie has written on the then Prince of Wales as 'the most constant visitor . . . devoted to Lilibet . . . playing after-tea games of Snap and Happy Families.' But now he made genial plans with Lilibet by phone which he then forgot, and for her tenth birthday he sent her a set of Beatrix Potter books in a suitably small bookcase to fit the Little House, pathetically unaware that she had outgrown Mrs Tittlemouse and progressed to *Alice in Wonderland*, *Black Beauty* and *Ivanhoe*.

An infrequent appearance at Royal Lodge was one Sunday afternoon when he drove over from Fort Belvedere to show off his new American station wagon, bringing 'a friend or two' who turned out to be, in fact, simply Mrs Simpson herself. 'We all walked through the garden,' the Duchess of Windsor recalls the episode in her memoirs. 'Our conversation was largely a discussion of the merits of the garden at the Fort and that at Royal Lodge.' Returning to the house for tea, 'the two little Princesses joined us, both so blonde, so beautifully mannered, so brightly scrubbed, that they might have stepped from a picture-book. Along with the tea-things was a big jug of orange-juice for the little girls. David and his sister-in-law carried on the conversation.' But Crawfie, who was usually at family lunch or tea, was taken aback at the visitor's 'distinctly proprietary way of talking to the new King. I remember she drew him to the window and suggested how certain trees might be moved and a part of a hill taken away to improve the view.' And yet she seemed 'entirely at ease, if anything rather too much' in delivering these judgments in her hostess's home.

Even the children sensed an uncomfortable atmosphere, and the Duchess drily suggested that Crawfie might like to take them into the woods for a while. Lilibet could hardly contain her curiosity. 'Who is she?' she asked uneasily, when they were away from the house. The governess could only answer that the King, of course, knew many Americans.

It was fortunate, during the summer, that the new interest of swimming lessons under the redoubtable instructress at the Bath Club, Miss Amy Daly, removed the children a little from the sense of adult anxiety and plunged them literally into a new element. Miss Daly had her own unorthodox method of inspiring confidence and encouragement. On her first visit to the pool, Lilibet found a girl poised high on the diving-board who, at a word from the instructress, executed a flawless swallow dive.

'I shall never be able to do that!' the Princess gasped in apprehension.

'Oh, yes, you will, and more easily,' said Miss Daly. 'You see, she is blind and has to trust me absolutely. You can see what you're doing.'

As soon as Lilibet could manage a few strokes, the Duke and Duchess came to the club to watch her, delighted that she could conquer a medium which the Duchess, for one, had never mastered. Margaret was slower and had to be encouraged to strike out from the edge with cries of 'Don't be a limpet!' Some of the other children believed their new-found buoyancy to be due to 'swimming-cake'; offering her young pupils a cup of tea, Miss Daly was unaware of the remarkable properties attributed to the accompanying small squares of madeira sponge. One day Lilibet brought Miss Daly a drawing she had done of herself at diving stance. 'But I drew it before last week's lesson,' she apologised, 'when I didn't know as much as I do now.' The swimming-cake, it seemed, had been asked for at home. Ultimately both Princesses gained their Life Saving Certificate, which involved Lilibet plunging into the pool fully dressed to 'rescue' Margaret.

Contributing another interest, their other Uncle David (Bowes Lyon) teasingly invited them to St Paul's Walden. 'You must come and see my ten thousand babies. I bought them for five pounds,' and the long beech avenues were found to be repaired or replanted with his new family of beech sprigs. At Birkhall, while the intractable King was abroad, cruising with Mrs Simpson in the yacht *Nahlin*, Archbishop Lang noticed the warmth of the Yorks' family life and yet noted also the chill of coming events. 'The kind Yorks bade me come to them. . . . After tea on the second day, the children – Lilibet, Margaret Rose and Margaret Elphinstone – joined us and sang some action-songs most charmingly. It was strange to think of the destiny which may be awaiting the little Elizabeth, at present second from the Throne! She and her lively little sister are certainly most entrancing.'

To keep the true passage of events from the children became, for the moment, joint preoccupations of both family and Household. There was always the hope also that the King's own major preoccupation might blow over. Georgina Guérin again came to Birkhall to immerse Lilibet in French lessons, and her pupil wrote happily of spending another two or three weeks at Glamis. 'Georgina is coming with us too and she is very pleased. I have a tiny cold so I am not kissing Granny.' Back at 145, there were more official visitors, their business such that there seemed more reasons for meals in the nursery with Alah or alone with Crawfie. As the crisis deepened, and the prospect of abdication became more certain, the Duke and Duchess of York seem to have deferred from day to day the task of sketching some explanation to Lilibet. On the Sunday evening of 29 November they travelled to Edinburgh, where the Duke was to be installed as Grand Master Mason of Scotland, leaving the two Princesses with their governess in London. Four days later Lilibet asked for her picture newspaper and read the bewildering headline 'The King and Mrs Simpson'.

Both the children asked questions and, wrote Crawfie, 'some sort of explanation had to be made. . . . Mine was an exceptionally difficult task. I had as far as possible to come between the children and general upheaval', and when the Duke and Duchess returned to London later that morning Lilibet already knew that her Uncle David, the King, had fallen in love with a lady whom England could not accept as Queen because she had a divorced husband still living, a simple moral issue which the Princess could clearly comprehend. But she knew also that her father and then herself were next in line and with a child's logic, according to Alah, she fervently prayed for a baby brother.

On Thursday 10 December, soon after ten o'clock, the King of an eleven-month reign began signing the fifteen documents of the Instrument of Abdication. As he finished, in the uncharted minutes when she became Heiress Presumptive, Princess Elizabeth was quietly passing from her history lesson to her poetry lesson, according to curriculum. Late the previous evening, however, having occasion to leave a note for Miss Crawford, she had selected a sheet of Buckingham Palace notepaper and, ahead of events, headed it ABDICATION DAY. 'Mummy says we may not swim tomorrow as the crowds will be rather big and there are no cars. Hope to be able to on Friday. It's a great pity. Good night.'

Thursday afternoon now usually brought Miss Lander for the music lesson, and the sound of an old upright piano may have been sounding through the house at the hour when Queen Mary called on the new Queen Consort and Empress of India. The new Queen, so lately the Duchess of York, was in bed with a cold, and after Queen Mary's departure, Miss Crawford was summoned to the bedroom to discuss how the children should best be told. Quite by chance, Lady Cynthia Asquith had been invited to nursery tea with the Princesses that same day, as if to give us insight into an hour of history.

'Though Princess Elizabeth still displayed her habitual self-control she would dart to the window when a specially loud cheer went up and excitedly whisper, "Thousands of people outside."' When I rose to go, she escorted me down the stairs. On the hall table lay one solitary letter which she picked up and fingered. She saw the envelope was inscribed to "Her Majesty the Queen" and her face went very solemn. "That's Mummy now," she said, with a tremor in her awestruck voice. Beyond that one remark she made no allusion to the event that, changing the course of history, must so profoundly affect her childhood and confront her with so formidable a future.'

With more privacy, however, both the sisters had many questions to ask of Lady Helen Graham. On being told that she might have to live in Buckingham Palace, Lilibet responded with horror, 'You mean for *ever*?' Princess Margaret, then six years old, got it 'rather upside down'. 'I was Margaret of York,' she complained. 'Now I'm just Margaret nothing.' 'The elder sister', wrote Helen Graham, 'said less because she knew more.'

We do not know whether the King's eldest daughter stayed

up late to hear her uncle's farewell broadcast at 10 p.m. But the crowds still gathered in the lamp-light outside No. 145, cheering from time to time, a tumult conveying some echo to the children's bedrooms at the back of the house.

Part Two

Princess Elizabeth

4

The King's daughter

When King George VI returned home from his Accession Council, his daughters greeted him in the hall of 145 Piccadilly with a curtsey, as their mother had suggested they should. He was mindful that he was within two days of his forty-first birthday and, touched and taken aback, he stooped and kissed them.

The little Princesses had been accustomed to curtseying to their grandparents as King and Queen, but the new King felt that he could not endure the symbolic barrier, and it was the last time they curtseyed to either parent except on formal public occasions. An hilarious family lunch followed. The cares of all the past weeks were cast aside, and when the telephone rang the King said merrily, 'Now who shall I say I am?'

That afternoon the new Queen felt that it would be unwise to go out after her cold, and the two girls privately drove with their father to join Queen Mary at Marlborough House where, from the window of her wardrobe room, they could watch the pageantry of his proclamation across the road at St James's Palace unobserved. Queen Mary noted in her diary that she, too, 'felt a sense of relief that all was settled' and would not have missed explaining the scene to her granddaughters, the duties of the supporting Heralds and Pursuivants, the colourful mace-bearers and State trumpeters, and then the meaning of the rich phrases of sovereignty, sonorously uttered by Garter King of Arms, conveyed a special significance.

'George the Sixth by the Grace of God, King of the United Kingdom of Great Britain and Ireland, and of the British Dominions beyond the Seas, Defender of the Faith, Emperor of India, to whom we acknowledge all faith and constant obedience, with all hearty and humble affection, beseeching

God, by whom Kings and Queens do reign. . . .'

The plans for Edward VIII's Coronation on 12 May 1937 had laid down that the two Princesses should follow their parents in procession into the Abbey. The date was unchanged, with the new decision that they should walk on either side of their aunt the Princess Royal, the King's sister, to their places beside Queen Mary in the royal gallery. The new King and Queen were anxious that Elizabeth should understand as much as possible of the sacramental aspects of the ceremony but, not to set a strain on youthful enthusiasm, the topic was deferred until after Christmas at Sandringham.

With Christmas cards to be painted and presents packed, the two children had their own tasks. Lilibet had caught Queen Mary's fever of saving old ribbon and attractive gift wrapping, and most packages evinced some second-hand use. On Christmas Day itself the birth of Princess Alexandra of Kent occurred in London, and the King's daughters were no longer alone in the younger generation of Princesses. Next day Lilibet helped Margaret to list her gifts and their givers and write her thank-you letters, as well as writing her own. 'I have been given such a lot of books,' she wrote to one friend. 'Uncle Harry and Aunt Alice gave me two pony books. One was called *Little Lass* and the other *Pony Tracks*. Also a little lamp with a colt and cairn playing. Mummy gave me a beautiful racing stud (a toy set). Alah gave me a box of chocolate peppermints and Bobo a tin of toffees. . . . May gave me a wood-cut of herself on her pony. . . .' Queen Mary, too, thankfully considered her happiness at being 'back in the old home, with Bertie, E and their children. . . .'

With the New Year, as if reviewing the aftermath of the abdication, legal pundits expressed doubts as to the position under the Act of Settlement if no son were born to the King. Could the two daughters thus rightfully share the Throne? An argument was advanced that in English law there is no rule of primogeniture among females and all daughters rank equally in dividing an unassigned inheritance and, in the House of Commons, the Home Secretary, Sir John Simon, killed the argument by announcing, 'In the event of her father's death, Princess Elizabeth will succeed to the Throne as sole heir.' Fifteen years were to pass before this contingency drew near. Yet the fanciful may find an undertone of prophetic event in a letter Lilibet wrote in her careful childish hand on 11 January, in her father's Coronation year, edging a piece of Sandringham notepaper with black crayon and explaining that Bobo's father had died the previous day. 'We are all feeling very sad, except Margaret who is naughty and enjoys herself just as much. Georgina arrived safely (for French lessons) which is a pity. With lots of love from Lilibet, in mourning.'

The King and Queen moved into Buckingham Palace on 15 February and Lilibet and her sister followed from Royal Lodge two days later. That first night, with the wind howling in the chimneys, Lilibet said wistfully that it would be nice to have a secret tunnel back to 145. The King had, however, already been working at the Palace for a week or two to be near his secretaries, and the Princess experienced the novelty and strangeness of going there to tea with her father and mother as she had with her grandparents. The usage of the rooms was being changed around and tea was served amid the formality of the Belgian Suite. This might have impressed Lilibet all the more if Crawfie had not sat down on a pink-and-gold chair which thereupon disintegrated with an ominous splitting sound. The cane had not been repaired for thirty years, 'as if someone almost intended the joke', Lilibet laughed. Going with Bobo another afternoon to inspect a bedroom they would share, anxiety had to be allayed that the corridor was broad enough for the troop of toy horses, now thirty strong. Ten years later, they were still there on her wedding day, so little did Lilibet like to see unnecessary change.

In welcoming the new King, the press attitude towards his elder daughter was equally warm and approving. 'Her self-possessed yet perfectly unspoilt and childish deportment when she appears in public with her mother shows that the training of this important little girl is proceeding on the right lines,' said *The Times*, and the *Daily Mail* added, 'This little lady has in her the qualities of greatness.' Reading such effusions, the Princess urged that 'apart from lessons and trying to be good' she could be more helpful. Evidently her mother also felt that the child was not too young to begin and, shortly before her eleventh birthday, Princess Elizabeth helped to receive the guests at an afternoon Palace reception, standing with her parents at the top of the Grand Staircase and walking round the State Rooms afterwards with effective gamesmanship in making conversation. 'I *mustn't* be shy,' she told Cynthia Asquith. 'But I wish I were more like Mummy.'

Queen Mary had once used the same phrase with different emphasis, 'I wish you were more like your dear mother.' But, in settling into Marlborough House, she had found her granddaughter an amusing companion in 'altering small things', judging the new position of a chair or sharing the bitter-sweet diversion of looking through old photographs. The old Queen began taking an added interest in arranging afternoon excursions for Lilibet, one of the first being to see 'Granny's rearrangements' in Kensington Palace, among them the furnishing in Queen Victoria's bedroom, where Queen Mary herself had been born. Suddenly Lilibet's great-great-grandmother came to be realised in the imagination, for here were some of her possessions and toys, and here the very room where, a month beyond her eighteenth birthday, she had learned that she was Queen.

Now it was almost precisely one hundred years later, and a young curator never forgot the emotional impression, in that Coronation year, of seeing Queen Mary, then nearing her seventieth birthday, walking round the old palace with the young Princess, both companionably engrossed despite the three-score years' difference in their ages.

In lighter vein, Princess Elizabeth's name and title were perplexing. No longer Elizabeth of York, she might be properly styled Princess Elizabeth of Windsor, but the newspapers disliked the title for fear of confusion with the abdicated Duke. Dermot Morrah, Arundel Herald Extraordinary, wrote of her as Princess Elizabeth of England, which annoyed the Scots. It was to be eleven years before her wedding certificate gave her as Elizabeth Alexandra Mary Windsor, with her rank or profession as Princess of the United Kingdom of Great Britain and Ireland. And incidentally with 'Margaret' as the smallest and most softly written signature of all on the page of the marriage register.

From her inexhaustible collection Queen Mary now brought out a panorama of King George IV's Coronation, all its marshalled tuppence-coloured figures unfolding concertina fashion in a procession thirty feet long, and Lilibet quickly knew them by heart. 'There's the Lord Mayor with the Crystal Sceptre,' she would say. 'There's Gold Stick – that will be Uncle Algy.' Nelly Graham helped the governess to plan a pre-Coronation course of reading, from the appropriate journal of the youthful Queen Victoria to H. E. Marshall's juvenile history, *Our Island Story*. The Princess thought it a pity that the dramatic challenge to combat flung down by the armoured King's Champion, riding on his horse, should have been discontinued, but she read with compassion of the Champion who fell from his saddle. 'Poor man,' she sighed.

In a more contemporary sense, her father helped to shape the early opinions of monarchy forming in her young and impressionable mind. Early in his study, every evening or so, the King took to discussing the day's events alone with her, drawing some precepts of his own theories of kingship and possibly clarifying his own as yet untried ideas. The weekend after her eleventh birthday saw her at his side watching a march past of international boy scouts. Two days later she travelled down the Thames to Greenwich with her parents, where her father opened the National Maritime Museum. Thus by land and water the King showed his daughter what he had to do, and what the tasks of royalty were in which one day she might play a part. 'It is one of my main jobs in life to help others when I can be useful to them', he later summed up in his diary the credo that he passed on to his daughter with such affection and foresight.

One evening, the Princess emerged from his room to display with excitement 'a very, very special book' he had given her. Bound in beige linen with her name and style embossed in gold, the volume was her private copy of the illustrated *Order of the Service of the Coronation*. She studied it intently . . . the recognition, the symbolism of the swords, the meaning of the Colobium Sindonis, a surplice which her father would wear after his anointing. . . . Every activity soon reflected a Coronation purpose, even tiresome French lessons. It was the Queen's idea that in welcoming President Lebrun of France among the State guests Lilibet should make a little speech in French. The speech was memorised and then read with perfect pronunciation, though with an unexpected sequel. The President complimented her and, to the King's immense pride, she replied impromptu in unhesitant French, telling him laughingly of her rehearsals. 'Quite a triumph', noted her governess, 'for a girl of eleven.'

Queen Mary had taken Lilibet and Margaret to the Royal Mint to see the making of the King's seal, and as the Coronation approached, she drew Lilibet's attention to the intricate details, taking her to the workshop where the jewellers were working on the resetting of the crowns and making the lightweight gold circlets with crosses and fleur-de-lis, the coronets of

King's daughters. No doubt she was also satisfying her own curiosity: the dowager Queen had also set a precedent by deciding to witness the Abbey ceremony, and it is a little known detail that she wrote to the Duke of Windsor in Austria to borrow his diamond Garter Star. Lilibet asked if she could wear 'Grandpapa's pearls', the necklet the old King had given to her shortly before the Gloucester wedding, and then was all but overawed by the lace and silver splendour of her gown and her ermine-lined purple cloak.

'Do you like my silver slippers?' she asked Crawfie, and lifted her skirt to disclose that she was wearing the short white socks of childhood and showing 'a length of honest scratched brown leg'. With Queen Mary she had also discussed as her best possible gift to her parents, *An Account of the Coronation* 'To Mummy and Papa, From Lilibet By *Herself*.' Written in red ink in a government-issue exercise book, it evidences her youthful powers of description, but unfortunately the would-be biographer is still denied access to anything beyond the oft-quoted first page.

'At five o'clock in the morning I was woken up by the band of the Royal Marines striking up just outside my window. I leapt out of bed and so did Bobo. We put on dressing-gowns and shoes and Bobo made me put on an eiderdown as it was so cold and we crouched in the window looking on to a cold misty morning. There were already some people in the stands and all the time people were coming to them in a stream with occasional pauses in between. Every now and then we were hopping out of bed looking at the bands and the soldiers. At six o'clock Bobo got up and instead of getting up at my usual time I jumped out of bed at half-past seven. When I was going to the bathroom I passed the lift, as usual, and who should walk out but Miss Daly! I was very pleased to see her. . . .'

So began a day of days. In the nursery day-room, Princess Elizabeth's cousin and special companion, Margaret Elphinstone, awaited her as a house guest. From Miss Daly on, everyone whom she knew seemed to have been invited to watch 'from inside' or to serve and help in some way. Princess Margaret, though on her best behaviour, inevitably caused her sister some concern. 'I do hope she won't disgrace us all by falling asleep in the middle,' Lilibet said gravely. 'After all, she is very young for a Coronation.'

But six-year-old Margaret had to be nudged only once or twice when she played with the prayer-books, and capably carried the folded tail of her long cloak over her arm. The two children rode to the Abbey with Queen Mary and Queen Maud of Norway in an open State carriage. 'I sat (in the Royal Box) between Maud and Lilibet, and Margaret came next,' wrote Queen Mary. 'They looked too sweet in their lace dresses and robes, especially when they put on their coronets. Bertie and E. did it all too beautifully. The service was wonderful and impressive – we were all much moved. . . .'

Hand in hand, quietly whispering with bent heads, admonition and counsel never better blended, the two Princesses preceded Queen Mary in the ceremonial procession from the Abbey. Then came the tumultuous ride through the great throngs on the long return route by way of Hyde Park and, with little respite, the repeated appearances on the Palace balcony and the tedious 'arranging' for the official photographs, which took nearly an hour. By seven o'clock Princess Elizabeth looked exhausted and was sent early to bed.

The brilliance of the Coronation in 1937 was one of the flashes of sunset in a darkening international sky. Two weeks after the ceremony Mr Baldwin resigned from the premiership for his intended retirement, as he had planned to do. His designated successor was Mr Neville Chamberlain and the era of urgent peace-seeking had begun. The King explained to Lilibet the difference between a change of Prime Ministers and a change of government, and one of his Household was impressed by the way he did it 'as if he spoke to an equal', imparting an interest in politics long before most children would have known what was going on.

It pleased the public when Princess Elizabeth appeared with her parents at the Coronation naval review at Spithead aboard the creaking royal yacht of those days, *Victoria and Albert*. The press contingent noticed 'Uncle Dickie' Mountbatten bending over her and explaining the uses of an anchor, though few saw an inherent symbolism in the incident.

Her parents were torn between their expressed desire to shield her from the formidable future and their wish that she should share the pleasures and pageantry – and indeed the plaudits – of the year. They gave her a cake of her own to cut alongside the cake they would be cutting at a Palace tea for disabled ex-Servicemen. Lilibet's instinctive response was to cut her first slice and then help Margaret with cutting the second slice. After a Garter Service at St George's Chapel, Windsor, they yielded happily to Lilibet's suggestion that she should walk back with Margaret through the people. When the first Courts of the reign were held, a blithe forgetfulness overcame bedtime, and the children were allowed to watch a 'fly's eye view', as Elizabeth termed it, of gleaming cars and befeathered débutantes. On the night of a State Ball they watched the forming of the royal procession like two hidden Cinderellas, concealed in their pink dressing-gowns behind an observation grille.

The discovery that the children often stayed up late to see their father and mother dressed to go out or to receive guests troubled their grandmother. 'The thing that rather distresses Queen Mary is their late, and fluctuating, bedtime,' Lady Cynthia Colville was to write from Marlborough House. 'Yawns in the morning certainly seem all wrong.' In July, moreover, the two Princesses accompanied their parents on the State Visit to Scotland, where they watched 'Papa' invest 'Mummy' with the Order of the Thistle, and Lilibet sent off a frantic letter to Crawfie, 'Please will you write back and tell me what St George is, and St Andrew and St Patrick?' An assiduous apprentice, she had begun acquiring the credentials of her craft question by question. Family praise for her Coronation account had also increased her writing confidence, and she began to chronicle events in a series of five- and six-page letters in a tidy, precise and well-spaced hand.

'When we arrived at Prince's Street it was all very exciting,' she wrote from Holyroodhouse. 'The Scottish Horse was great fun because one company was on riding horses and the other on some of Lord Ancaster's deer ponies, very rough and shaggy and all pulling like steam-engines! The Royal Company of Archers are very picturesque in their green uniforms and big eagles' feathers. . . . The march past of 4,600 soldiers was very tiring because we stood for an hour and dust continually blowing in our eyes.

'At the beginning three horses led the soldiers and they had no band, so the band of the Scots Guards played for them, and that silly drummer went Bang! Bang! Bang! on his drum. One of the poor horses got such a fright. It shied and stumbled and then reared up and leapt into the air! It was frightening to watch it.'

A gleeful weekend was spent with her aunt, Lady Elphinstone, at Carberry Castle. 'I think it is a lovely place,' wrote

Lilibet. 'After tea we had a pillow-fight with Lord Airlie and Sir Ian Colhoun (I don't know how to spell his name), John E., Margaret E. and myself. After that Sir Ian and Lord Airlie had a blindfold fight. Then we had a blindfold race and a crawling race. . . .' The summer stay at Balmoral brought accounts of frying potatoes and sausages at a picnic, of Papa's good shooting, 'beating Gannochy in all the years Papa has been there', together with wistful mention of Winifred Hardinge's 'lovely time at camp . . . they threw Captain's niece down from the top of a house into a blanket!'

At Glamis the Princess was impressed by her Strathmore grandmother's 'delightful bird table . . . my grandfather was collecting all the scraps during lunch and he told me that all sorts of birds came and one day a green woodpecker came. They are very shy birds and rarely come near a house. . . .' Her gift for assimilating and setting in order is clear in these letters. Back again in London Lilibet continued to do well in the sunny classroom overlooking the gardens where seven-year-old Margaret also now applied herself to her lesson-books. Latin was placed on the senior agenda and we find Queen Mary complimenting the governess for even giving a walk in the garden and the names of the flowers, 'a profitable turn'.

Still in her twenties, the governess felt the extreme responsibility of teaching the heir to the Throne. 'But no-one seemed to be perturbed on this score except me,' she tells us. 'No new instructions were given, no suggestions made.' In November, at the tender age of eleven, Lilibet – and Margaret with her – attended the State Opening of Parliament, watching that ineffable pageantry from the Royal Gallery, and the historic import of the ceremony impelled Miss Crawford to consult Queen Mary. No-one knew better of the pressures on the new Queen or the preoccupations and programmed activity encouraging her to leave educational problems to Crawfie.

Queen Mary's guidance lay in asking tactful questions. 'Do the children ever learn poetry by heart? Rather wonderful memory training, and doesn't it help to get through a good deal of first-rate interesting stuff which otherwise they will never read? Genealogies, historic and dynastic, are very interesting to children, and for these children really important. Can such things be worked into history? Of course old-fashioned geography is hopelessly out of date. But for them all the same a rather detailed knowledge of physical geography might be valuable, and also of the Dominions and India?' Such were the questions she urged through Lady Cynthia Colville, and Miss Crawford was relieved to learn that special tuition in constitutional history would come later. Meanwhile, she walked on air with Queen Mary's assurance that Lilibet's education was in 'wonderfully capable hands'.

Queen Mary nevertheless experienced a new satisfaction in steering Lilibet through a further programme of excursions, to the National Portrait Gallery to talk of ancestors and to the museums, 'so many different departments that one always finds something interesting'. Showing them the bullion stacked like bricks in his vaults, the governor of the Bank of England invited the Princess to take any bar of gold she could carry . . . only to prove that gold is heavy stuff, and they were not to be budged.

One of Queen Elizabeth's – the present Queen Mother's – few reported comments on her daughters' education was that she wished them to have a trained appreciation of the arts. The National Gallery, the Tate, the Courtauld and Wallace collections became natural allies. With the advice of Kenneth Clark, then Surveyor of the royal pictures, Miss Crawford borrowed a picture a week for the schoolroom easel, affording an intimate progress through the family collection, particularly the smaller paintings, to improve the Princesses' knowledge. King George V had enjoyed guiding his sweet little Lilibet around the pictures in his rooms, Frith's *Ramsgate Sands*, Wilkie's *Penny Wedding*, a jovial Mulready or two, his own boyhood favourites. Crawfie is said to have begun with a Gainsborough portrait of one of George III's sons, but the smallest canvas of the royal collection, Gerard Dou's *Maidservant Cleaning a Pan*, six inches square, aroused Lilibet's special interest and protection, a treasure she regarded for a while as peculiarly her own.

On occasion the young Princess accompanied her grandmother on shopping forays into Bond Street. There exists at Windsor a Zoffany portrait of George III and a copy in needlework by the eighteenth-century Mary Knowles. One afternoon Queen Mary acquired a self-portrait in needlework by Mary Knowles depicting her at work on the George III, and the Queen today sometimes displays it to visitors as 'one of Granny's bargains'. It ranked as 'a nuisance' that Miss Crawford's more venturesome excursions were brought to an end by the new phenomenon of IRA bomb-planting. The terrorist was as active then as now, less skilful but necessitating equally watchful royal security.

The King used to joke that his mother needed protection against herself. Early the following year, he and Lilibet had badly poisoned hands, ivy-poisoning caused, as he told Osbert Sitwell, 'by Queen Mary making us pick it off walls at Sandringham', and they took a few days' convalescence at Eastbourne. Supposedly incognito, the two Princesses rode ponies on the sands, paddled and built sand-castles, pleasures hitherto only for half-day Sandringham picnics to the beach near Hunstanton. Their two detectives, however, were vigilant and Lilibet took it for granted that there was no possibility of making temporary seaside friends as other children seemed to do.

At twelve Princess Elizabeth 'bothered Papa' into allowing her to take the salute before a gathering of 5,000 children at a daylight rehearsal of the Aldershot Tattoo, which was rather the opposite of his intentions at the time. The King wanted his daughters to feel that they were members of the community, rather than exposed in juvenile leadership, and early in their reign the King and Queen began to welcome weekend invitations for Lilibet to help to strengthen friendships beyond the immediate family circle.

'Uncle Dickie' Mountbatten's elder daughter, Patricia, was only two years older than Lilibet, and it created a special affinity that she, too, had a sister, Pammy, a year younger than Margaret, and no brother. Visiting Adsdean, then the Mountbattens' home near Chichester, there were ponies to see and ride, and an astonishing menagerie to inspect, the souvenirs of Lady Mountbatten's travels, a wallaby, a lemur, two miniature kangaroos, a lion cub that 'slept at first on Mummy's bed'. Patricia moreover was a Girl Guide, heroine of exploits which Lilibet enviously retailed in letters to others, 'One day Mary and Patricia made a horrid mess by mixing up their ration of food all in one and they had to eat it themselves.' Patricia, too, first suggested forming a company of Girl Guides at the Palace and her idea was seized with enthusiasm.

Miss Violet Synge, later Guide Commissioner for England, who inaugurated the scheme, has told of her early Palace problems. The minimum Guide age was eleven, and all Guides at the time wore long black stockings. 'Need we wear stockings when we have uniform?' Lilibet asked. 'Because Mummy says we needn't.' 'Quick thinking was needed,' wrote Miss Synge, 'and we compromised on socks to the knee.' Commanded by Lilibet 'to show a fine pair of hiking legs', Margaret was successfully enrolled as a Brownie, but the first enlistment of Guides from among cousins and friends, the children of Court officials, threatened a fiasco. As Miss Synge has said, the Palace doors were flung wide to the troop by scarlet-coated footmen; and nannies treated the affair as they had the dancing classes, bringing their charges in party frocks with white gloves. Lying on her tummy in the summer-house, Princess Elizabeth said in scornful tones, 'They won't be able to roll about and get dirty!'

When the group was presently enlarged to some thirty children, the sisterhood improved and nannies were discouraged by being put to use in first aid. 'Are second-class emergencies nearly finished?' piteously complained one of their number, while vigorously thumped between her shoulder blades. 'It's so very painful, being treated for choking!'

Soon two patrols were formed, Robins and Kingfishers, with Patricia Mountbatten mysteriously a Second Leader of the one while Lilibet was chosen as Second of the other. Although Miss Synge suspected unfair diplomacy, Patricia was reassuring. 'No, we really want her. I think she'll be awfully good', and epic adventures arose from Miss Synge's determination that a Guide must always have her wits about her if she is to rise to sudden emergencies. Scotland Yard telephoned (as it seemed) to report two intruders in the Palace gardens and 'the Guides were off like hounds on the trail'. A gangster, looking remarkably like Crawfie, experimented with kidnapping but what chance had he against the Guides? 'We became detectives or cowboys or Red Cross nurses, and our lives gained depth and colour from the romance brought to them,' wrote Miss Synge, and recorded with satisfaction that Princess Elizabeth put on a very sulky face when sent to try on a dress 'until she remembered she was a Guide and put on a cheerful one'.

The Princess admirably reconciled these games and gaucheries with more adult concerns: a share in the State Visits of King Carol of Rumania, the smiles and dignity of presenting winning rosettes at the National Pony Show and her eager following of her father's racing interests. Lord Wigram called her a very good racing Guide. The King's mild interest in his racing string was more a gesture of support to the British bloodstock industry in maintaining his father's stables until he found amusement in Lilibet's partisanship. It made her day when a horse in his colours called Cosmopolitan rightly defeated another horse named King of the Air. On the October day in 1938 when Mr Chamberlain flew to Munich, Cosmopolitan ran in the Hopeful Stakes at Newmarket and the twelve-year-old Princess was glumly disappointed that the colt did no better than second. But at about this time, week-ending with her Harewood cousins at Egerton House, Newmarket, she saw beneath the arch of the stable yard the panel commemorating in letters of gold the triumphs of her great-grandfather, Edward VII.

> 1893 – two races won – amount £ 372
> 1894 – five races won – amount £3499

and so on through eighteen years to the impressive total of 106 races won for £134,687. Looking back, that moment amid the familiar stable smell of hay and soap and fodder may have seen the first stirring of her Turf ambitions.

Watching her father and mother's tennis prowess at Royal Lodge and their matches at Luton Hoo may have tempted her into tennis lessons, until her coach despairingly reported, 'The Princess will never succeed until she forces herself to run after the ball.' Her friendship with the Wernher daughters, Myra and Georgina, at Luton Hoo, was more stimulating, and the Wernher papers may one day disclose encounters with their cousin Prince Philip a year or two earlier than the well-known Dartmouth meeting.

A 'young people's dance' at Windsor indicates Lilibet's widening social circle on nearing her teens. The eldest of the three Ogilvy brothers (the present Earl of Airlie) was only a month her junior, though his younger brother Angus tended to be more in evidence. The thirteen-year-old Earl of Dalkeith (the present Duke of Buccleuch), the young Master of Carnegie (now Duke of Fife) and Fergus Bowes Lyon figure increasingly in later childhood letters. Fergus, the present Earl of Strathmore, provided the happy Sandringham coincidence of a birthday on New Year's Eve. But boys tended to disappear to school and were seen only on holidays. A year younger than Lilibet by a year, Libby (Elizabeth) Hardinge became a more constant girlfriend. She was moreover the Queen's goddaughter. 'That makes us almost sisters,' Lilibet said. Then there were the three Plunket brothers, sons of one of Mummy's earliest boyfriends and even more intriguing with their tales of an American grandmama, Fanny Ward, who was on the stage and successfully pretended never to grow a year older. Of the three, Robin was closest to Lilibet in age and Patrick closest in temperament, very much enjoying being guided around the Palace pictures when an opportunity offered.

It was among the earliest deep emotional shocks of Lilibet's life when she chanced to read in *The Times* that his mother and father had both been killed in a Californian air disaster, and could hardly restrain her tears. Never before had she known anyone to suffer the tragedy of losing both parents. Like George Hardinge and young Dalkeith, Patrick was at Eton, and there began a custom of inviting him to Royal Lodge for Sunday lunch or at mid-term which strengthened the foundations of a life-long friendship.

Lilibet was seldom inclined to mope, but she passed through a phase of sorrow with her mother, with the sudden death of her grandmother, Lady Strathmore, shortly before the King and Queen's State Visit to France in July 1938. 'But suppose poor Mummy should need to break down?' she had asked. In the following year there came her parents' visit to Canada and the USA which had been under discussion for two years. 'If you bring either or both of the children with you they will also be very welcome and I shall try to find one or two Roosevelts to play with them!' President Roosevelt had written invitingly. Attractive as it sounded, the King had to reply, 'I am afraid that we shall not be taking the children . . . they are much too young for such a strenuous tour.'

The royal couple were to sail on the chartered liner *Empress of Australia*, and on 5 May the two Princesses went down to Portsmouth with Queen Mary to inspect the ship and say goodbye. The children could never remember being separated from their parents for as long as seven weeks and tears were expected. On the contrary, they were 'enchanted by the train journey' and 'seeing the ships' as Crawfie noted, and that night Queen Mary entered up her journal with some relief. 'We took a tender farewell and landed. The ship left punctually at three, a fine sight from the jetty, and we waved handkerchiefs. Margaret said, "I have my handkerchief," and Lilibet answered, "To wave, not to cry," which I thought charming.'

5

In the teens

'The King was amusing at lunch, talking of sending Princess Elizabeth to Eton, feigning ignorance that it is a boys' school. She accepts his teasing in good part' . . . 'When so many are gawky, Lilibet is enchanting, with her long slim figure' . . . 'An air-raid precautions exercise was held at Windsor Castle today, with sirens, bells, whistles. The King and Queen and the Princesses joined in, little Margaret rushing from group to group, making piggy noises through her gas-mask.' 'Sitting for the sculptor, Strobl, Lilibet was quite prepared to pose motionless for an hour, but much relieved to find she could move about'. . . 'The Princess enjoys her singing lessons with Miss Longman, chiefly for the pleasure of participating with other children in part-songs.' Through a paper-chase of such jottings Princess Elizabeth approached her thirteenth birthday at Windsor Castle.

At Sandringham also, over the New Year of 1939, Queen Mary noted that she watched an ARP exercise in the morning and 'we ladies put on funny hats for dinner'. Early in March the Princess enjoyed the novelty of visiting Broadcasting House with her parents, a pleasure dissolved a day or two later with the grim news that Hitler had invaded Czechoslovakia and so destroyed the Munich Pact. For the first time in her father's reign, Princess Elizabeth was mentioned in the *Court Circular* on 6 April as a guest at the luncheon party at Windsor Castle given for Colonel Beck, the Polish Foreign Minister. Historically it must be set down as an unpropitious occasion, for as a result of the bilateral agreement against aggression made that day Britain was at war with Germany within five months.

Events both grave and absurd marked that transitional

phase of early adolescence. Crawfie recorded that Lilibet had ceased biting her nails but 'became almost too methodical and tidy', as if determined to keep her world in good order. 'She would hop out of bed several times to get her shoes quite straight, her clothes arranged.' Margaret's gift of mimicry in an hilarious session of Lilibet preparing for slumber helped to laugh her sister out of this fever.

At Royal Lodge, only plump little Margaret now could walk comfortably through the Little House, demonstrating the awful fate of a giantess growing out of her abode. The following evening saw a party at Windsor Castle for one hundred boys and girls, as the newspapers put it. Crawfie clearly knew nothing of events occurring while she was on leave, and one suspects that behind the screen of royal privacy a seventeen-year-old Dartmouth cadet named Philip might have been seen doing the Lambeth Walk with Lilibet three months before they first met in public.

A few days after the King and Queen had sailed for Canada, the Princesses made their own voyage of discovery on the London Underground. Margaret is said to have insisted that since Papa and Mummy were having an adventure, they too could have one. Playing up to her sister, Lilibet enquired of her elders whether escalators were quite safe for eight-year-olds and which was the best way of stepping off a moving stair. Scottish-born Crawfie, it turned out, had never travelled by Underground, and Lady Helen Graham was almost equally vague. The departure, accordingly, was from a District Line station, like the subway or Metro, involving nothing more subterranean than a stairway, but the thrill of 'the train rushing out of the tunnel and the sliding doors opening as if by magic' was authentic, as Nelly Graham recollected, and two stations later the unaccustomed travellers changed to the deep-level Northern Line.

'Few people at first noticed the children,' wrote Lady Helen Graham, 'but there came a time when an old gentleman suddenly became conscious that for some reason he was the target for all eyes right down the compartment. It took him a few bewildered minutes to realise that it wasn't himself but two demure passengers next to him, holding their tickets very ostentatiously.'

So obvious now was public interest that, at Tottenham Court Road station, their detective had to help them to reach the YWCA for tea. At the self-service counter, Lilibet left their teapot behind. 'If you want it, come and get it!' bawled the tea-lady.

In more serious mood, without her sister, Elizabeth paid her first visit to the Royal Academy, as if she significantly found herself the first lady in the land and was at pains to select a duty fitting the first engagement undertaken in her teens. James Gunn's unsatisfactory State portraits of her father and mother dominated the summer exhibition, while the sculptures were grouped about the proposed memorial figure of her grandfather. Gunn's exceptional portrait of Hilaire Belloc may have been remembered ten years later when she took pride in hanging the sketch of his conversation piece of Belloc, Chesterton and Maurice Baring in her sitting-room at Clarence House. And certainly she seemed impressed by another painting of the year, Lawrence's *Queen Elizabeth Visits her Army at Tilbury* and recognised it in an Essex town-hall twenty years later when she was Queen Elizabeth herself.

Further visits were paid to the London art shows in that last childhood summer of peace, perhaps the strangest involving a visit of the two sisters to their old home at 145 Piccadilly to see an exhibition of historic treasures. 'To find the familiar old rooms stripped of all the dearly remembered things, to see the old doorways newly labelled *Their Majesties' Dining-Room, The Queen's Boudoir* . . . and then to move through whispering throngs to find their old dolls displayed on the nursery floor, a bizarre ordeal to them both,' wrote a sympathetic observer.

Then in June the Princesses experienced the 'terrific vibration' aboard the destroyer taking them to be reunited with their parents aboard the *Empress of Britain* in mid-Channel; and a month later they felt steeped in nautical atmosphere when they embarked on the old royal yacht *Victoria and Albert* for that never-to-be-forgotten visit with the King and Queen to the Royal Naval College at Dartmouth.

Cadet Prince Philip was Captain's 'doggie' that day, messenger, helper, royal escort and guide. Usually under the impression that this was Philip and Elizabeth's first meeting, the story has been told and retold. Yet apart from the brief encounters of royal weddings and the Coronation festivities, visits to Coppins and with the Wernhers at Luton Hoo had cemented acquaintance, as we have seen. On 2 May the *Court Circular* had ineffaceably reported that Prince Philip with his mother, his Milford Haven grandmother and his eldest sister Margarita had gone to tea with Their Majesties at Buckingham

Palace, an interesting event not forty-eight hours before he officially entered Dartmouth as a special entry cadet.

The difference, we may observe, was the presence of Crawfie as a recording angel, with her fingernail impressions of the fair-haired sharp-faced boy, 'rather offhand . . . at a boy's most unattractive age', unguarded phrases deleted from her published reminiscences. At Dartmouth, Lilibet 'never took her eyes off him', and his uncle, Lord Louis Mountbatten, 'rather encouraged him to show off'.

'How good he is, Crawfie. How high he can jump!' the Princess enthused at the tennis-courts, though Philip recollects only a dull game of croquet. When he came aboard the royal yacht, Lilibet lost her shyness, plying him with plates of shrimps, cakes and a banana split.

In the evening, the royal yacht departed with every available College boat following like an armada, steam and sail, motorboats, rowboats, until gradually they turned and receded leaving only one lone oarsman, audaciously rowing alone. 'The damned young fool,' said the King. 'It's ridiculous and most unsafe.' 'Lilibet took the glasses', says Crawfie, 'and had a long look at him.' That weekend Elizabeth had seen hundreds of boys, boys in cadet uniform, boys in white sweaters, boys marching and sailing. Now there was only Philip, as he turned to row back at last, a speck on the evening sea. The following weekend they met again, when the Queen gave a Saturday night party at Royal Lodge, with the Kents and Wernhers, Mountbattens and Bowes Lyons, and doubtless Lilibet and Philip among the younger guests. It was the last such gathering before the war, and within a few months the fourteen-year-old girl and the eighteen-year-old midshipman had begun a flow of cousinly correspondence.

Friends and relatives noticed that Princess Elizabeth evinced a marked literary bent. If Margaret was the actress of the family, Elizabeth was the author, ready to compose a nursery serial story or describe a Coronation. Cynthia Asquith indeed tells us of the Princess's early interest in 'a magazine entirely organised and run by children', to which she was a regular and spirited contributor, an interesting prospect for research and speculation, but the Queen says she can remember nothing of it after all this time, and one surmises at merely a pleasant juvenile pastime between cousins. In her teens, her descriptive five-page letters betray a sharp eye not dissimilar to the Queen Victoria who published her *Leaves from the Journal*. . . . History, as Sir Henry Marten has said, 'provides an admirable background for English composition. . . gives to the young mind a vast storehouse in which to wander at will . . . a vehicle for the training of the memory, the cultivation of the imagination, the development of balanced judgment. . . .' If King George VI had not read these words in Marten's book *On the Teaching of History*, he had heard of him as the staple of history teaching at Eton. In his mid-sixties, round-faced and benign, Mr Marten in 1939 had been Vice-Provost of Eton for eight years, and behind the King's jest of sending Lilibet to Eton there lay a shrewd decision that Marten would be the best man to give Lilibet personal lessons in British constitutional history.

The friendship between the young Princess and this wise Pickwickian figure was no more that of Stockmar and Victoria than Crawfie was Lehzen. As joint author of *The Groundwork of British History*, Marten had mentioned Victoria in only three of the hundred pages devoted to her reign. But the book, as the preface explained, was striving 'to encourage the faculties of understanding and reason . . . and to make boys think why things happened'. Thus we may see the objective picture, untinged by family reminiscence, which his first girl pupil now received of her great-great-grandmother.

In Mr Marten's words, 'The increasing knowledge and experience which Queen Victoria possessed and her close family connection with most of the crowned heads of Europe were assets of great value in the conduct of foreign policy. We know that she insisted on seeing all the foreign dispatches, and being informed and consulted on foreign affairs. . . . It is however in times of crisis that the need of the Crown is greatest. An alteration made by Queen Victoria in a dispatch probably saved us from a war with America in 1861 . . . the part played by the Crown in our national affairs was much greater than was popularly supposed.'

But the text-books remained unopened, the Princess nervous as any new boy when she first entered the Vice-Provost's study, awed at the books flowing over from shelves to chairs. Mr Martin for his part, charmed by the young girl, believed in exercising vivacity to prevent a pupil becoming bored, no matter the cost of an element of caricature. He would chew a corner of a handkerchief while thinking and gaze blankly at the ceiling or suck lumps of sugar from his pocket. At one stage he produced a curious-looking umbrella. 'No ordinary brolly. . . . One may open it indoors without fear of misfortune', and the umbrella turned out to be a portable globe of the world with which to elaborate some point of international law.

He began his royal pupil gently, it appears, with a game of royal lotto, with counters coloured red for Kings, blue for Queens, brown for Princes, to pattern the lineage of the Royal Family through the centuries, and before long he was taking Princess Elizabeth in history twice a week, amid the clatter of schoolboy footsteps at Eton or at Windsor or the Palace as convenient. In the archives are a set of green Eton notebooks which the Princess kept in good order, learning the usage of indented headings and abbreviations; the methodic flow of sustaining disciplines which carried her into adolescence as the world turned from peace to war.

When war broke out between Britain and Germany on 3 September 1939, the two Princesses were at Birkhall, that pleasant secluded Jacobean house at the foot of Loch Muick on the Balmoral estate. The nation had blacked out every window and every street-lamp, and the King and Queen had hurried to London, leaving Sir Basil Brooke, the former Household comptroller of the old Piccadilly days, in charge. The Queen had given instructions that the girls should be alarmed as little as possible, but on the sunlit Sunday evening the two sat together to hear their father's broadcast to the nation.

'To every household of my peoples,' he said, 'I speak to you with the same depth of feeling for each one of you as if I were able to cross your threshold and speak to you myself. Over and over again we have tried to find a peaceful way out of the differences between ourselves and those who are now our enemies. . . . We are called, with our allies, to meet the challenge of a principle which, if it were to prevail, would be fatal to any civilised order in the world. . . the principle which permits a State, in the selfish pursuit of power, to disregard its treaties and its solemn pledges. . . .'

The quiet woods of Birkhall seemed remote from challenge, but the morning newspapers, with their news of the bitter fighting in Poland, brought out Elizabeth's sisterly concern, 'I don't think we should talk about battles in front of Margaret. We don't want to upset her.' Fortunately nine-year-old

Margaret was going through a writing phase, and the two 'just sat scribbling'. Elizabeth resumed her correspondence. 'What dreadful things have been happening lately. Really the Germans are brutes the way they go on, sending messages to the German people that they have taken Warsaw. . . . Have you any evacuees in your house? We have hundreds all round from Glasgow. . . .'

'Princess Elizabeth wrote me a charming letter, telling me of all their activities and their work for the Red X and the working party,' Queen Mary acknowledged, while settling into her wartime home at Badminton. But the young writer selected her themes for the separate recipients. 'More history for children to learn in 100 years!' she wrote consolingly to a younger friend. In the Birkhall schoolroom, when Red Cross sewing parties were organised, Lilibet prided herself on knowing all about the sons and husbands in the Forces. Margaret's contribution was being in charge of the gramophone: her apt favourite record for the sewing ladies was Gigli singing, 'Thy tiny hand is frozen'. Some of the Glasgow children had gone home already, Lilibet soon reported, omitting to add that they had been scared of the woods and afraid of the deer. With the local Girl Guides she proposed hikes along the loch 'to help show them there's nothing to fear, and the children won't miss their parents too much'.

Soon there were vivid descriptions of the Newfoundland lumberjacks near Ballater, their axes heard for miles, their chainsaws screaming like dragons, and the men stopped work to smile and wave at passers-by (in particular, the Princesses). Rehearsals began for a Christmas play at the local school, where Lilibet blushed with pleasure at being cast as one of the Three Kings, but unluckily one of the 'vaccies' caught mumps and the play was cancelled. Then one evening the wireless news announced the sinking of the battleship *Royal Oak* with heavy casualties, and Lilibet leapt horrified from her chair. 'Crawfie, it can't be, all those nice sailors.'

Her tragic, tearful concern was among the causes that prompted the King and Queen to bring the girls home so that they could all unexpectedly spend Christmas together at one of the smaller houses at Sandringham. 'Perhaps we were too happy,' Lilibet wrote wistfully, 'I kept thinking of those sailors and what Christmas must have been like in their homes.'

Meanwhile, Mr Marten's history lessons continued by post. The Princess mailed an essay each working week for comment and correction, and her mentor occasionally ringed a word for misspelling or his Z showed need for a new paragraph, but his Ns for nonsense were rare. Miss Crawford felt that his lessons had heightened Lilibet's interest in people and politics, with which history is so basically concerned. Mr Marten, on his side, noticed that the essays were never without a personal letter or message or some youthful mention of everyday events which she felt might be of interest. Her letters to her cousins, Patricia and Pammy Mountbatten, at school on Rhode Island, were regular but contained 'nothing much', in one view, so strict was her regard for the wartime slogan 'Careless talk costs lives' and the admonition 'Keep It Dark'. It was safe to mention that her Christmas cards had included one from Philip, and one finds her badgering her father not to forget to send a return card. 'Papa had told me yesterday that he had not send off Philip's card yet! I was rather disappointed but as long as he gets it I don't mind.'

It was Princess Elizabeth indeed who made the running in those early days of pen friendship with Philip. No sooner was he posted to the convoy battleship *Ramillies* than she made sure he was on Queen Mary's knitting list for woollen scarves, unaware that the *Ramillies* was sweltering in the Indian Ocean. The Princess tried her hand at knitting socks 'with perplexing results' and was admittedly better at compiling what were called 'comforting letters of home news' for her serving cousins of the Bowes–Lyons, Lascelles and Abel Smith families, young men five or six years older than herself.

In the lull of the 'phoney war', the 'war of words and propaganda', as the King summed up, the two Princesses did not return to Scotland. 'The blossom is coming out on the tree outside the schoolroom and the forsythia is very pretty. Bragger has pruned the roses in the sunken garden. . . . We have found lots more old iron in a covert in the park,' Elizabeth wrote from Royal Lodge in April 1940. On her fourteenth birthday, she is said to have spent two hours writing letters to friends. Three weeks later the full force of the German paratroop attack was unleashed on the Netherlands and, following a prearranged plan, the Queen telephoned Miss Crawford at Royal Lodge to say that the Princesses should be taken to Windsor Castle 'at least till the end of the week'.

'The two girls clung to me apprehensively,' Crawfie remembered. 'About the stone passages the shadowy figures of servants and firemen loomed. I remember one old man remarking, "By the time we've blacked out all the windows here, it's morning again."' The Castle furnishings everywhere had been partly dismantled, pictures and chandeliers banished, glass-fronted cupboards turned to the wall. Many walls were thickened with sandbags, and choice pieces of the Regalia were lodged in the vaults, where Sir Owen Morshead once showed Princess Elizabeth her mother's crown safe in an old hatbox stuffed with newspaper.

After the first air-raid red alert, when everyone spent a sleepless night in the dungeons, beds were put down there and, later, bathrooms were installed improving on the buckets which the Master of the Household, Sir Hill Child, called 'improvisation'. Officially ex-secretary Lord Wigram was Governor of the Castle, but now Elizabeth sat at the head of the table at Household breakfast, lunch and dinner, deciding who should sit next to her left or right, placing everyone with celerity while Margaret enjoyed the same latitude at her end, and two or three Guards officers came to meals when free of duty rotas. The following year Princess Elizabeth was formally appointed a Colonel in the Grenadier Guards, and the cameras show another side of her personality. She stands rigidly to attention at a march past, her figure still plumpish and juvenile in pleated skirt and woollen jacket, but her features taut, every muscle tense, as if seeking to embody all the discipline of regimental tradition in her small person. Crawfie took note of the social development of her pupil. The rather shy girl was becoming 'a very charming young person, able to cope with any situation'.

At another level, she befriended the local anti-aircraft gunners, the Bofors boys, as she called them. When the Windsor sirens gave warning of an enemy daylight plane one day the two Princesses took shelter in one of George III's pebble-lined Gothic catacombs in the hillside, shushing one another to listen for the Bofors' ack-ack, only to be disappointed that no sound penetrated their chalk refuge. Mysteriously one morning the air quivered with distant gunfire, and Lilibet delayed a riding lesson for the few minutes until she had telephoned her mother at the Palace to be reassured that all was well in London. The far-off thuds were the guns and explosions of Dunkirk in the week when the King chronicled that 335,000 troops were brought back from the beaches.

After the fall of France, there came 'a moment of dread quiet before the storm of fire and blast was to break over Britain'. While the new-formed Home Guard literally drilled with broomsticks, ordinary life went on much as usual, the anxieties of war measured and accepted equally by every family. The Princesses made gardening expeditions to Royal Lodge, where the house was opened up to enable the King to snatch a few hours' relaxation from London, and the sisters hoed the cabbages outside their little Welsh cottage. One weekend the King made a game of fire-fighting, spraying water hilariously, while making sure that his daughters could both understand and use a stirrup-pump. The laughter and the sense of purpose, the everyday acceptance, precisely embodied the national mood on the eve of the Battle of Britain. 'The children used to be swimming about in the pool with the drone of enemy planes overhead,' the Queen recollected those summer afternoons.

With enemy forces not fifty miles from the English shores, the substantial threat of invasion was envisaged. With all her courage, Queen Wilhelmina of the Netherlands was convinced that she would have been taken hostage by the Germans but for the rescuing British destroyer *Hereward*. King Haakon was pursued the length of Norway before boarding the cruiser *Devonshire*. In London and at Windsor a special unit from the Brigade of Guards and the Household Cavalry, known as the Coates Mission, stood ready for surprise attacks on the Royal Family, and the Princesses kept small packed suitcases beside their beds in case they had to be hurried to the West Country.

'The raids are tiresome but Windsor is an armed camp,' wrote Queen Mary, and Lilibet zealously described her grandmother's rare visits in the latch-and-key diary she entered up every evening. In her letters she wrote of 'climbing ladders to pick damsons for a jam factory', and Hubert Tanner, the schoolmaster of the cottage school in the park, came in for youthful appreciation, his classrooms crowded now with East End children, and Elizabeth contributed the ideas of pony-trap rides, sports days, tea parties and singsongs to help bind the Cockneys into the community and lessen their sense of loneliness, of being away from home. More often than not, the Princess drove the pony-and-trap mutely unrecognised.

A restless conviction of insufficiently doing her bit, an anxiety to do still more, became more persistent. 'It makes me *very* angry when I think of those poor homeless people with nowhere to go,' she wrote, after south-east London was bombed, and her 'vexatious and tiresome' knitting-needles were taken up again to provide woollen headgear for Civil Defence stocks. Then the shattering onslaught of heavier air-raids, with her mother's memorable broadcasts to the women of France and to women at home – and the shock to her of Buckingham Palace being bombed – evoked a practical idea. Of her own accord, Elizabeth proposed that she might make herself useful in a broadcast, in her phrase, 'to the children of the Empire'. In seeking the King's permission, she lacked nothing in persuasive argument.

Here was her first sketchy conception of herself in a tangible role of leadership as the representative of her own generation. She wrote the first draft script herself and pencilled a final revision to enable Margaret to join in saying 'Good night, children' so that she 'shouldn't feel left out'. Her mother took pains to help her with the 'endless rehearsals to get her phrasing and breathing right' and as always Lilibet was a responsive pupil. Listening to one of the engineers' final rehearsals from outside his study, the King was struck by the microphone resemblance to his wife and burst in excitedly, 'She sounds exactly like her!'

Derek McCulloch of the BBC Children's Hour recalls that the Princess experienced nervous difficulty with the tempo and the Queen sat at her side in the studio room at Windsor during the transmission, beating time gently. Given as it was while 'Lord Haw Haw' was boasting on the German radio of a force of 450 Luftwaffe planes attacking London, the broadcast held emotional significance. 'I can truthfully say to you that all we children at home are full of cheerfulness and courage. We are trying to do all we can to help our gallant sailors, soldiers and airmen, and we are trying, too, to bear our own share of the sadness and danger of war. We know, every one of us, that in the end all will be well. . . .'

At Badminton, Queen Mary was moved to tears as she listened. 'Excellent, so natural and unaffected,' she described the broadcast. Archbishop Lang considered it 'quite admirably spoken – her first address, strange to think, to what may be her future subjects!' In South Africa, ironically with no hint yet of the future republic, the novelist Sarah Gertrude Millen noted, 'It was perfectly done. If there are still queens in the world a generation hence, this child will be a good queen.'

The broadcast produced an avalanche of mail, first from

children in Britain, then messages smuggled by a roundabout route from the German-occupied Channel Isles; and presently a flow of letters from overseas provided the Princess with a daily stimulus for months. As Lady Helen Graham remarked, 'Princess Elizabeth had embarked on a time of serious preparation to qualify herself for the position of heir', and everyone around her was familiar with her capacity for taking pains. Across the river at Eton, lectures were resumed with her tutor, and the schoolboys politely gave her minimal attention, though several acquaintances, old and new, were invited to Household lunch, and some were enveigled into joining Crawfie's madrigal-singing group.

For the bleak Christmas of 1940 the discarded Birkhall play *The Christmas Child* was revived and, down in the reinforced air-raid shelter, the Princesses passed the time studying their lines, while the enemy thrummed overhead to Coventry and their other objectives. Staged in the medieval atmosphere of St George's Hall at Windsor Castle, the actual performance, before an audience of relatives and friends of the performers, was happily uninterrupted by enemy alerts. For the first time, Princess Elizabeth wore a crown, a make-believe leftover possibly from an Edwardian fancy-dress ball, in her role as one of the Three Kings. Princess Margaret played the Child, the shepherds were schoolboys with scarves for turbans and, overwrought as he was by his visits to the devastated air-raid centres, the King was intensely moved by the tender pathos and charm of the spectacle. 'I wept through most of it', he confessed to his journal that night.

The New Year again found the Princesses at Sandringham with their parents, this time at Appleton House, 'a dear little house', cushioned in deep snow to Elizabeth's joy. The war was no longer reflected in her letters, except that 'Papa and Mummy and everyone are looking much better' and that she had irretrievably grown out of her skating boots. Another picture is also afforded us by the Canadian Prime Minister, Mr Mackenzie King, of Balmoral in high summer when he first met the Princesses at their mother's two-room picnic cottage on the moors. 'They had arranged the table inside with lettuce leaves for decoration, pleased with everything they had done to make things look nice. There were no servants. . . Princess Elizabeth very sweet in the way she talked . . . very natural in some further conversation we had together.'

If her tutorial studies that term included 'The Evolution of a

Self-Governing Dominion', though she did not noticeably intrude Canadian affairs as a topic, she had now closely read Trevelyan's *English Social History* after a term devoted to 'The Colonies', and had progressed to reading Elton's *Imperial Commonwealth*. At Windsor Mr Marten would sometimes clap a book for dust, explaining that it was a dusty subject. A swarm of bees near the library window made him digress into the laws of ownership. 'If they have any owners, those owners have rights. I think we ought to know about those rights, don't you?'

In due course Princess Elizabeth devoted a term to studying 'the national exchequer in war and peace' and was taken step by step through the laws and liberties of England, the growth and apparatus of the monarchy and its relationship to the Church, Parliament, the Cabinet and the evolution of the British Commonwealth. In lighter vein, her studies were leavened by an interest in her fathers racing affairs, particularly the two-year-old colt Big Game, victorious in every race he ran. The future of the British bloodstock industry, though curtailed, was borne in mind amid ration-books and blitzkreig.

More for Margaret's sake, and for the children at the royal Windsor school, the Girl Guides company got off to a new start, with Elizabeth as a Patrol Leader, perhaps pretending to be a little younger than she really was. 'I think I have forgotten how to sweep a room now,' she had comically confessed in a letter to Miss Synge. 'Cook, Needlewoman and Child Nurse tests are holding me up but I hope to pass soon.' The cookery class in the Windsor housekeeper's kitchen saw Elizabeth enthusiastically busy with baking-board and rolling-pin every Thursday afternoon, and stews and soups and cakes were sent up to the ARP (air-raid precautions) men on watch on the Castle rooftops. The following year equally found the Princess involved with the Sea Rangers, encamped beside the Frogmore lake, where she learned to handle a sail and earned a bosun's badge. When Horace Smith at the Holyport stables was invited to coach her in side-saddle riding, he found her whisked away with an equerry after every lesson 'as if she had not a moment to spare'.

6

War and peace

Shortly before Princess Elizabeth approached her sixteenth birthday, the Rev. Stafford Crawley, Canon of St George's Chapel, Windsor, prepared her for her Confirmation. Without this, it is arguable that she could not have reigned, for the British Constitution requires that the Sovereign should be a communicant member of the Church of England. She approached the ceremony with the reverent and simple faith which she shared with her parents. 'I'll have to try and be good, won't I?' she said lightly to Crawfie, recalling the 'I will be good!' of the young Queen Victoria. But Crawfie comments, 'She said least of what she felt most deeply.'

The Archbishop of Canterbury, Dr Cosmo Lang, visited the Princess at Windsor on 28 February, the eve of the ceremony. He had assisted at her grandfather's Coronation, had wedded her parents, crowned her father and presided over her baptism, and now wished above all to bless 'one who may be Queen' as his last act before retirement. 'I had a full talk with the little lady alone', he recorded, 'and though naturally not very communicative, she showed real intelligence and understanding. I thought much, but rightly said little of the responsibilities which may be awaiting her in the future, this future more than ever unknown. The Confirmation itself was very simple – in the ugly Private Chapel.'

Queen Mary thought that her granddaughter 'looked so nice with a small veil and quite composed'. Her friend, Lady Airlie, saw the Princess for the first time for three years. 'I saw a slender figure in a plain white woollen frock, a grave little face under a small white net veil. The carriage of her head was unequalled, there was that indescribable something which Queen Victoria had . . . although perfectly simple, modest and unselfconscious, she gave the impression of great personality. Yet it seemed so short a time since she had toddled round Queen Mary's sitting-room holding on to one of my fingers!'

The Princess's birthday the following month also saw a small family gathering, while in public she inspected her new-gained regiment in a march past of 600 men. Her appointment as Colonel of the Grenadier Guards was a matter of great pride and pleasure to her, and the Command took pains to render her due honour, sending small detachments to represent every battalion. It was less well known that she afterwards gave a party for all the officers and men who had been present.

Accepting her mother's view that she might still look too young in uniform, she had undertaken the review wearing a pleated skirt and woollen jacket, but in the afternoon she donned her Girl Guides dress to visit the Labour Exchange in Windsor town and register under the preliminary youth scheme of the National Service Act. Cameras flashed as she signed the registration form. If a hint of naïve comedy lurked in the specially scrubbed and polished room, if other girls of her age group cast sceptical as well as admiring glances, she was however totally sincere. At tea with Lady Hardinge a few days later, she plied her hostess with questions on her daughter Winifred's progress in the Wrens and shrugged at her own mere inauguration of a local savings week. The King's private secretary, Sir Alec Hardinge, responded by sending her a remindful newspaper mention that 'the Princess really became liable for National Service, of a very special kind, at her birth'.

She could plead with her father that her cousin, Lady Mary Cambridge, barely eighteen months her senior, was working with a voluntary aid detachment in blitzed dockland, while Patricia Mountbatten (two years older) was 'already' in the Wrens. Evidently the King adopted a convenient attitude of parental vagueness. The Princess interested herself in her Grenadiers with such zeal that she taxed the ingenuity of her brother officers to devise duties suitable to such youthful top brass.

Pursuing her imaginary ideal of what a Colonel of the Grenadier Guards should be, she considered it just to express rightful criticism as well as praise. After one young subaltern had smarted under the cold glance and ringing voice, a major diplomatically mentioned to one of her elders, 'You should perhaps tell the Princess quietly that the first requisite of a really good officer is to be able to temper justice with mercy.' After that, there were no longer wry smiles in the mess, for Elizabeth was quick to learn.

These were the days of the raging battles around El Alamein when the casualties within the family or among her friends shadowed her with the harsher facts of war. Some seventy young officers passed through Windsor in the course of the war. A list was kept of their names and, if one was notified killed, the Princess took it upon herself to write to the bereaved mother, expressing her appreciative memories of her son at Windsor. Whenever she faced this task, Crawfie or Helen Graham noticed signs of strain, but it seemed to Elizabeth the least she could do.

Deeper personal anxieties had to be subdued, though seldom absent. A favourite Bowes-Lyon cousin, the young Master of Glamis, was killed in action at Halfaya Pass. The Werners' only son, sometime her tennis partner at Luton Hoo, gave his life in the western desert. Elphinstone and Lascelles cousins were taken prisoner, and among her younger friends Lilibet was greatly concerned when Lord Plunket was reported wounded, the Eton boy whom she had befriended after his parents had died in a pre-war air-crash. And what of Philip, on destroyer patrol in the North Sea, never far from her thoughts and prayers, in peril on the sea?

He had suddenly shown up at Windsor the previous autumn, entertaining the King – and assuredly Lilibet – with his comical account of adventures at sea: the fish blown up with small depth-charges, the shell on the laundry which blew washing everywhere. . . . 'I believe they fell in love that first time he went down to Windsor,' Queen Mary was to tell Lady Airlie. On 4 August 1942, there was no news of Philip – from King George of Greece or other guests – when the Royal Family gathered at Windsor for the christening of Prince Michael of Kent. Three weeks later Elizabeth was at Balmoral when her father was called from the dinner table and she underwent the terror of bracing herself for a shock. The King returned with the tragic news of the death of the Duke of Kent, her popular 'Uncle Georgie', whose plane had crashed on a Scottish hillside.

But the Princess was, as ever, 'reserved and quiet about her feelings'. As Marion Crawford has said, 'only once did she walk into my arms, thinking of nothing but that she had to have a little comforting. She came into my room, very white and wide-eyed. "Grandfather Strathmore is dead," she said, and burst into tears.' And this was when Elizabeth was already a young woman, aged eighteen.

In the darker days, it was as well that the Windsor Christmas pantomimes had been started, as light relief, interludes of happy excitement to the sisters in the otherwise unvarying pattern of their lives.

It was Margaret who discovered that Mr Tanner, the Windsor Park schoolmaster, had been a Gilbert and Sullivan actor and could agreeably write the script for a pantomime. *Cinderella* was the first obvious choice, chiefly because Margaret had made up her mind to play Cinderella opposite Elizabeth as principal boy. From then on, a pantomime was an annual event which, to the King's amazement, raised the then not inconsiderable sum of £850 for the Queen's Wool Fund.

Elizabeth was astonished at a proposed admission of seven shillings and sixpence (35 pence). 'No-one will pay that to look at *us*!' she protested, to be capped by Margaret's 'Nonsense! They'll pay anything.' The Queen suggested that the back seats should be only a shilling. At rehearsals, the King was taken aback on first seeing Lilibet's costume, a minilength tunic worn over buckled satin breeches. But revealing the knees was permitted the following year for *Aladdin* when Prince Philip was in the front row.

'I have never known her more animated,' wrote Crawfie. 'There was a sparkle about her none of us had ever seen before. Many people remarked on it,' and this time it was Princess Margaret's turn to indulge in publishable correspondance. 'On Xmas eve we all had dinner together, nine of us only. . . .' Next evening Philip's cousin and future best man, David Milford Haven, joined the group. 'We and Philip went mad,' the letter continued. 'We played charades, clumps and then we danced and danced. It was the best night of all . . . we danced four nights running!'

In private a new note of true gaiety, optimism and even romance was unmistakable. With Rommel in retreat, the King incautiously entertained the prospect that the war might be over by the next Christmas. The Queen, too, had noticed the unmistakably developing situation between Lilibet and Philip which, as parents, they thought it best to soft-pedal. 'We both think she is too young,' the King wrote to Queen

Mary at Badminton, to put his mother in the picture. 'I like Philip. He is intelligent, has a good sense of humour and thinks about things in the right way . . . but P had better not think any more about it for the present.'

He had also been astonished to discover that in legal and constitutional terms Lilibet was considered even younger, more immature and less responsible, than he had supposed. Speaking to Winston Churchill of his wish to visit his victorious armies in North Africa and his heroic and much-bombed people in Malta, he had found his Prime Minister favourably disposed to the idea. Temporary authority at home would be delegated to five Counsellors of State, and the King mentioned his conviction that his elder daughter would soon be ready and of age for the task. But in Parliamentary fact the position was still regulated by the Regency Act of 1937 which made her ineligible until attaining the age of twenty-one; and the fifth place had to be filled by King Edward VII's grand-daughter, the Countess of Southesk, far less qualified in training and then only a step less remote in succession than King Haakon of Norway.

The absurdity annoyed the King. However, on his return, the difficulty was solved by an amending Act, passed un-opposed, enabling Princess Elizabeth to become a Counsellor of State at eighteen 'in order that she should have every opportunity of gaining experience in the duties which would fall upon her in the event of her acceding to the Throne'.

That possibility appeared remote, yet in 1944 when the so-called 'Hitler's secret weapon', the flying bomb, was launched on south-east Britain, every man, woman and child was placed under fire, their lives entirely at chance hazard in the random explosions. Within three weeks 2,500 people were killed, 8,000 wounded and 250,000 houses damaged. No relief was possible against the indiscriminate robots except the number destroyed by the defence forces. There was a day, according to Violet Synge, when the missiles droned over ceaselessly; and the Princesses were cooking sausages with the Guides in the park when the unmistakable thrum of a 'buzz-bomb' was too close for comfort. The girls fell flat, as they had been taught. The Guide Captain flung herself across Elizabeth, Crawfie across Margaret. 'Mercifully, it kept going. It cut out and dropped on Windsor racecourse,' Crawfie records. Throughout the war 200 bombs fell within the King's estate, with few corresponding casualties, though tragically a Royal

Lodge gatekeeper and his wife lost their lives when their cottage was destroyed.

One morning, when the Princesses went to London to their dentist, a pattern of flying bombs was mapped along their route and a friend remembers that the Queen was 'in torment' until she knew that they were safely back at Windsor. Yet perhaps the worst ordeal was on a Sunday while the Royal Family were at Windsor, and the news came through piecemeal that a bomb had destroyed the Guards Chapel near Buckingham Palace during the morning service. More than 120 of the congregation were killed, among them many family friends and acquaintances.

Ahead of these sombre events, during a congenial phase when Philip was on standby for the trials of his new destroyer *Whelp*, the thin paper-rationed British newspapers were enlivened with rumours that Princess Elizabeth would shortly be created Princess of Wales. The stories, as so often, created an atmosphere of favourable public opinion, even to agitation that the House of Commons should petition the King to grant her the title on her eighteenth birthday. Churchill favoured the idea but found 'a conflict of thought' with His Majesty.

'I argued that it is a family matter, and that the Dominion Prime Ministers could suggest that she should have a Dominion title,' wrote the King in his diary. 'He agreed to put it before the War Cabinet and let me know.' Four days later it was officially denied that he contemplated any change in 'the style and title of the Princess Elizabeth', and as usual he wrote to his mother, Queen Mary, with his own common-sense reasons. 'How could I create Lilibet the Princess of Wales when it is the recognised title of the wife of the Prince of Wales? Her own name is so nice . . . and what name would she be called by when she marries, I want to know?' What name, equally, one may ask, would Philip as her husband have had except Prince of Wales? And what titles would have awaited Prince Charles and his wife today?

Her eighteenth birthday was nevertheless embellished with a decorative flourish close to the King's heart. 'Colonel Prescott handed her the Colonel's Standard, which will be used for her future inspections,' he noted. 'Officers and guardsmen of the Training Battalion Grenadier Guards were present. We gave a family lunch to which Mama came. A lovely hot day. Lilibet can now act as a Counsellor of State.' A few days later, the Princess attended a dinner of Dominion Prime Ministers at the Palace, her first official dinner, as if in recognition of 'coming out'. Seated between General Smuts of South Africa and Mackenzie King of Canada, the latter thought she 'looked very pretty and very happy and graceful, very natural, not in the least shy'. Together with Churchill, the assembled Premiers signed their names in a birthday-book, the King's gift to his daughter. According to Queen Alexandra of Yugoslavia, Lilibet's happiness perhaps lay in two family pages, clipped together to hide another signature, *Philip*.

Lady Helen Graham also gave an adulatory broadcast talk as if to introduce her to the public. 'She is worthy of your love,' 'Nelly' assured her listeners. 'But she never mentioned my faults,' said Elizabeth.

The Princess would hardly have failed to remind her father that eighteen was the call-up age for the Services, while he was bound to advocate the importance of Home Front duties. The Palace dinner was soon followed by her first solo official visit to the City of London, where she was installed as the new President of the National Society for the Prevention of Cruelty to Children. 'I trust that in the days to come we may hope that every child's life may be a free and happy one,' she concluded her presidential speech, the first speech of a future Queen.

No-one at the Palace had foreseen how rapidly other goodwill societies would jump on the bandwagon to enlist her interest and possible patronage, and from Windsor Lady Helen Graham had to remind the Queen that Lilibet as yet had no private sitting-room of her own, nowhere in readiness to receive official visitors. In general she uncomplainingly divided her time between her bedroom in the Lancaster Tower, the nearby nursery as a sitting-room and the map-studded schoolroom, and was delighted when the Princess Royal's former pink-tapestried sitting-room was rearranged for her, 'her first real breakaway from nursery and school-room life', in Crawfie's view.

The growing pressure of 'official' correspondence was managed as yet by a Palace clerk, and the urgent need of a suitable young lady-in-waiting was solved, on her Uncle David Bowes Lyon's recommendation, by the appointment of twenty-three-year-old Lady Mary Palmer, whose father, the Earl of Selborne, was David's colleague at the Ministry of Economic Warfare. The war had made her a capable private secretary, and any preference for a married Lady was settled by Mary's own forthcoming marriage and, as Lady Mary Strachey, she remained the Princess's effective working companion for several years.

At this stage, the Princess consulted the Queen on all her draft patronage and presidential speeches but gave much thought to conscientiously writing and re-writing and re-writing her scripts, and amendments were rare. The King, who had regarded himself as 'dragged up, shy and unprepared', derived ever more satisfaction with her progress. Lisa Sheridan, the photographer, watched them sharing a working session at Royal Lodge one Saturday afternoon when the King was busy with his boxes. 'I noticed that he drew the Princess's attention to a document and explained certain matters very earnestly. The Queen and Princess Margaret meanwhile sat silently with their books and knitting. . . . There is a particular bond of understanding, and the King makes a point of explaining everything he can to her personally.'

Elizabeth's awareness of what the royal tasks involved was as yet a precocious view. She knew that Windsor Castle was stripped to a trainee unit in preparation for 'Operation Overlord', the storming of the Normandy beaches as a first step in the steadfast liberation of Europe, and thus the continuous need of discretion. Her illusions on the prestige of kings, of all monarchies, took the form of concern for the prestige of Margaret. Rationing limitations on the sheet size of newspapers often caused her sister to be margined out of royal action photographs, a mortifying process to a fourteen-year-old, and Lilibet suggested a round robin to the editors, 'Please do not cut Princess Margaret out of pictures.' In one way or another, the caution got home.

At the critical height of the Normandy invasion, it also preserved Margaret's peace of mind not to know that her father wished to watch the forward attack, and encourage his armies, in a joint expedition with Churchill. The hazards of the enterprise indeed rightly appalled Sir Alan Lascelles, who had just succeeded Alex Hardinge as Private Secretary. By way of dissuasion, he posed the question whether advice would be prepared for Princess Elizabeth on her choice of her first Prime Minister in the event of her father and Churchill being killed simultaneously. The King slept on it and the plan was shelved.

Certainly Lilibet was relieved to hear it. Ten days after

D-Day, moreover, the King was able to visit Normandy on what might be called 'a long day-return', a thirteen-hour tour involving no delegation of royal authority. On 23 July, however, the King absented himself for eleven days to visit his armies throughout the battlelines of Italy, watching actual fighting and artillery bombardment with General Alexander, and on that day Princess Elizabeth first assumed royal functions – with the Queen, the then Duke of Gloucester, the Princess Royal and Princess Arthur of Connaught – as a Counsellor of State.

The lawful business of the Counsellors, on being appointed by Letters Patent, are narrowly defined, but two of the needful five may form a quorum to sign routine documents of State. Thus Elizabeth's hand was at the tiller of the monarchy. One paper was a reprieve of a death sentence for murder, drawing from the Princess her sharp cry of response to sordid reality. 'What makes people do such things? One ought to know. There should be some way to help them. I have so much to learn about people.'

On balance, it was nevertheless an ecstatically happy Princess who graduated into duty during that summer of liberation. She was in love and thought that no-one knew her secret. She was mistress of her own affairs more than ever before, and enjoyed a sense of fulfilment in at last fully devoting her services to the community she had long regarded herself as dedicated to serve. She moved through a London more ruinous and smoke-begrimed than since the fire of 1666. Wild flowers were growing again in the rubble around St Paul's, as when Wren was working there. The affairs of charities, hospitals, orphanages, philanthropic institutions, flowed across her new-furnished desk, the very stuff of graduate royals, and during the Balmoral holiday it was appropriate to visit Edinburgh for her first solo official ceremony in Scotland, receiving purses for a YMCA appeal.

On 1 December, she went to John Brown's shipyard on Clydebank, unannounced and with the necessary secrecy of war, to launch the battleship *Vanguard*, then the newest and most powerful capital ship in the world, and her Personal Standard or banner of arms was raised for the first time from the flagstaff in the shipyard. 'May God bless her and all who sail in her,' said Princess Elizabeth, smashing the traditional bottle over *Vanguard*'s bows, unaware that she was launching the ship in which she would one day sail for her first visit to one of the great territories of the British Commonwealth, by deep irony one of the first countries destined to sever its Commonwealth ties.

The exasperation remained for Lilibet that she had not been allowed to join one of the Services of her own accord. Even her honorary colonelcy in the Grenadiers could not compensate for missing the discipline of going through what other girls had to go through. There were tough arguments, said the biographer Dermot Morrah, for father and daughter alike had inherited a rich measure of Hanoverian obstinacy. But a compromise was found and, early in 1945, Senior Director Leslie Violet Whateley of the ATS, the women's Auxiliary Territorial Service, was summoned to the Palace to discuss the prospect of Princess Elizabeth enlisting and training as a driver.

The King could resist his elder daughter's persuasions no longer. The time was ripe, moreover, and in March 1945 entry as Second Subaltern, ATS, was granted to No. 230873, Elizabeth Alexandra Mary Windsor. Age: eighteen. Eyes: blue. Hair: brown. Height: 5 ft 3 in. The move was popular and it hardly mattered if a newspaper lacked precise accuracy in reporting that 'The heir to the Throne will be plain ma'am to her subordinates and will share sleeping quarters with her sister officers. She will sleep in a camp bed like any other ATS girl.' Lilibet had slept under canvas with the Sea Rangers, although, as a close friend recollects, 'tactful as she was, there always seemed to be some good reason why she should not do so. She was getting older, and had been brought up so much alone. Margaret, on the other hand, was extremely proud of her own sleeping-bag.'

In fact Elizabeth did not sleep in barracks but returned to Windsor every night, and at dinner 'talked of nothing but sparking plugs'. The arrival of her uniform was a cause of great excitement and pride, though Princess Margaret, on seeing how unbecoming khaki could be, felt satisfied that this was one outfit which clothes rationing would not cause to be passed on to her. None other than Elizabeth Windsor's company commander, Commandant V. E. M. Wellesley – a descendant of the great Duke of Wellington – briskly arrived at Windsor to welcome the new recruit and drive her to the Mechanical Transport training centre at Camberley. But, once there, Elizabeth changed into dungarees and was pitched into the NCO's course in the theory and practice of heavy mechanics. She had never driven a car and an instruction truck awaited her, jacked up, minus its wheels. The course was designed to whisk her to an ultimate 'pass' in night driving and the repair of heavy vehicles. Within a few days, so it must have seemed to the nervous but willing beginner, she was flung into the driving seat of a Bedford truck and ordered to drive it along the training road. The instructor at her side had been ordered to treat her 'like any other'.

The discovery that Lilibet faced the same rigours as any greenhorn when in the instruction pit intrigued Princess Margaret. 'How do you stand to attention', she enquired, 'when under a bus?' She went to tea one day in Lilibet's mess, amused 'to see how hearty all the lady officers were, drinking sherry and smoking cigarettes'. Elizabeth has never smoked. Sure enough, No. 230873 Windsor satisfactorily observed the unit routine and within a few weeks was seen driving the fifth lorry in a learner's convoy through the narrow streets of Windsor town. The engine of the leading vehicle stalled on Castle Hill, the convoy was held up and subjected to a difficult re-start on a slope. But Driver Five was seen to 'get away to a fine start'.

Queen Mary, too, presently went to see for herself the phenomenon of her granddaughter's proficiency, which also proved 'an eye-opener' to Lilibet of the absurdities of army spit and polish. 'You have no idea what a business it has been,' she wrote, 'everyone working so hard. Now I realise what must happen whenever Papa and Mummy go anywhere. It's something I'll never forget.'

Soon enough it was the Princess who was driving Commandant Wellesley to Camberley in a Wolseley staff car. The mornings were scheduled for lectures, from map-reading to maintenance, studies in admin. and military law and so forth, and driving practice over routes, so the tyro drivers thought, chosen for their disconcerting qualities.

Across one of these devil roads, one day, Driver Windsor found herself miserably stranded with her lorry broadside, helpless in face of a policeman with his demand, 'What d'yer think you're doing?' 'I couldn't tell him,' she said afterward, 'because I didn't know. But' – triumphantly – 'he never recognised me.' In the later opinion of one of her detectives, the course turned Elizabeth into one of the best drivers within his experience. And working in the workshop alongside other young women from every walk of life was not the least of the factors assessed as valuable in her own view.

The King and Queen came down to Camberley to see one of her tests, a publicity occasion with army photographers and reporters, and found their elder daughter almost unrecognisable in oil-smudged working gear under a car, 'very grave and determined to get good marks'. 'What, not got it going yet?' the King remarked jocularly, after returning from watching other girls. When the Princess climbed into the driving seat and switched on the ignition, nothing happened. Her father had surreptitiously unclipped the distributor cap.

Before the war ended, the Princess was reported to have triumphantly driven an army lorry up to London through the blackout and via Piccadilly and the Mall into the forecourt of Buckingham Palace. Commandant Wellesley was able to report, 'Her Royal Highness is a very good and extremely considerate driver.' But not to embroider one of the news reports, the alleged 'heavy truck' was in reality a staff car and the journey occurred in daylight. Exaggeration of moderate achievements was often one of the less palatable fruits of national affection.

The demands on the Princess's time were fast becoming more intensive than anyone had anticipated and the ATS training had gradually to yield to other activities, although the full course occupied a great part of her attention for a year, and more personal interests went by the board. Her music teacher, Miss Lander, was greeted with the regretful cry, 'Oh, Goosey, I haven't got on at all!' For her nineteenth birthday an additional lady-in-waiting was needed to relieve Mary Strachey and the Princess proposed the post to Mrs Jean Vicary Gibbs née Hambro, whose husband was killed in action soon after the battle of Arnhem, leaving her a widow of twenty-two with two small children. From this appointment flowed the happiest consequences in the following year, for she was only three years Elizabeth's senior, and the following year, she married Elizabeth's cousin, Andrew Elphinstone, with the Princess acting as bridesmaid.

The birthday itself was celebrated in the tranquillity of Appleton, when the family was in private sadness and official mourning for President Roosevelt. Ten days later the imminence of Germany's surrender recalled the King and Queen to London, and the two Princesses returned to Windsor. Then suddenly the war in Europe was over.

Heedless of Lilibet's protests, Margaret swept her German study books to the floor, claiming that she would never learn another word. The girls dressed for church as usual, when a phone call asked them to return to town at once. At the Palace the King had made a film of a speech he was to broadcast, but the speech was delayed and the film unshown until the Powers could agree on timing their announcement of victory. 'A terrible anti-climax,' wrote the King. 'The press had worked everybody up that VE day would be today. Placing of loud-speakers and flood-lighting at Palace, etc. The PM wanted to announce it but Pres Truman and Ml Stalin want it to be announced tomorrow.'

There ensued a day of hiatus and indecision while people gathered outside the Palace with a curious restraint, as if determined not to cheer too soon. Then, on 8 May, after Churchill had lunched with the Royal Family, his formal announcement of victory boomed over the radio. The roar of the multitudes for the King and Queen had the sound of rapture. Though decked in blue and gold, the Palace balcony was notoriously unsafe, the adjacent stonework cracked by bomb damage, and there were jokes on whom should go out first. To a tremendous ovation, the King and Queen first appeared, with the Princesses, and then Churchill was brought forward. Princess Elizabeth had made a point of wearing her ATS uniform. 'We went out eight times altogether during the afternoon and evening,' the King recorded. 'We have only tried to do our duty during these five long exacting years. . . . I have found it difficult to relax, there is still so much hard work ahead.' But as night fell he surrendered to young Margaret's eager insistence that she and Lilibet should go down and join the crowds. Four young Guards officers were deputed to escort them as, with no more disguise than scarves and old country coats, they went out into the singing, cheering, dancing throng of revellers. 'Poor darlings, they have never had any fun yet,' the King added in a footnote to his diary.

In the crowds they cheered with everybody else every time the King and Queen appeared on the balcony. They cheered the footmen who finally came out to close the doors and then they went dancing down the Mall to Whitehall, ducking under the 'fun fences' formed impromptu by chains of linked hands. 'It was absolutely wonderful,' wrote Princess Margaret. 'Everybody was knocking everybody else's hats off, so we knocked off a few, too. Everyone was absolutely marvellous. I never had such a beautiful evening.'

Elizabeth must have dearly wished that Philip had been there. He was having fun in Melbourne, where his destroyer *Whelp* had docked for a refit and the Princess's sole correspondence next morning is said to have been a long commentary to him. The next two jubilant days saw the Princesses sharing in the State Drives through the bedraggled streets, where long-stored bunting could nowhere conceal bomb scars but helped mask the lack of paint. A National Service of Thanksgiving in St Paul's was followed by a visit to Edinburgh for a similar service in St Giles's Cathedral. Next day, after a night of train travel, the two sisters accompanied their parents to Westminster Hall, where the King received and replied to addresses from both Houses of Parliament.

Considering that the carriage of the royal procession horses had spent years in the country carting farm crops, Elizabeth delighted in their exemplary behaviour, never once put out by the cheering crowds. The secret, she discovered, was that they had been drilled in the stables by weeks of listening to 'the noisier wireless programmes'.

A side-effect of the enthusiasm was the appearance of sackloads of mail addressed to Princess Elizabeth and the appointment of a third lady-in-waiting to cope with the avalanche. In June the Princess went to Wales to inspect 3,000 Girl Guides drawn from every part of the Principality, and a similar ceremony occurred when she briefly visited Northern Ireland with her parents. It seemed appropriate that she once more wore the dark blue Guides uniform of her girlhood. On VJ Day (for Victory in Japan) on 15 August, peace – after six lost years – once more reigned around the world, and it caught the fancy of the public that Princess Elizabeth, repeatedly appearing on the balcony with her parents and her sister, again wore a girlish summer frock. And this time Elizabeth hastily wrote that 'the celebrations really were terrific. I have never seen so many people all at once.'

7

Peace and Philip

In Princess Elizabeth's private life, one of the first events of total peace was a letter from Prince Philip, with his own account of the frock-coated Japanese surrender aboard the Flagship *Missouri* in Tokyo Bay, and perhaps the pleasant inference that his destroyer *Whelp* might be bringing home rescued prisoners of war. With this delectable prospect, in the euphoric new dawn, the Princess had no difficulty in coaxing her parents to take her to the first post-war race-meeting at Ascot, her first visit to the races.

They received a jubilant welcome and, as Dorothy Laird says, the Princess was an immediate recruit to racing. She went down to the paddock with her father, climbed with Margaret Elphinstone to the roof of the stand to see the view, was permitted in the weighing room and begged to stay on for the last race. She thus saw the first winner of an Ascot race trained by a woman, with Mrs Florence Nagle's Sun Up. Women trainers were then prohibited under Jockey Club rules but a polite fiction covered training by a head lad, a moral not lost on the royal enthusiast. Three weeks later she watched her first Derby in the exiled Newmarket edition, and by October her father's thirteenth race win of that exciting year had permanently involved her in the stimulating personal decisions of the Turf.

At Balmoral, still under the rapture of release from war, the talk was 'of nothing but stalking and antlers and points'. On 3 September, with the sixth anniversary of the outbreak of war sealed in final victory, the King suggested that his nine guns should try to fill the game card with samples of everything that Deeside could provide; and wearing an old pair of her father's plus-four trousers, Elizabeth went off with Margaret

Elphinstone and soon shot a stag. The King was pleased that she showed proficiency, and on his next birthday the guests gave him a silver table-mat engraved with their names that henceforth always stood beneath his breakfast plate. Indeed, the erudite *Shooting Times* was eventually to list the present Queen as securing one of the five best deer shot by women in Scotland, her stag being a 'royal' of 12 points, the left antler measuring 27 in, the right $27^{15}\!/_{16}$ in, and a plaque in a Balmoral corridor similarly testifies to the Queen once taking five stags in a day.

Elizabeth was of course passing through a phase of experiment, possibly even making amends for the lack of a brother. Among her autumn duties, each more advanced than the last, a smooth progress to major events was seen. Taking the salute at the Sandhurst passing-out parade progressed to an Army Cadet review in Hyde Park. That autumn, she also sponsored her first godchild, the infant son of young King Peter and Queen Alexandra of Yugoslavia, who was christened in the Chapel Royal of Westminster Abbey. No sooner was the baby in her arms than he 'commenced to kick and wriggle so much that poor Lilibet looked thoroughly scared, but she never faltered', wrote the fond mother. Faltering can be dangerous at the font.

Shortly before her twentieth birthday, the Princess was sufficiently experienced to undertake the major ceremonial of a three-day visit to Northern Ireland, not only to launch the aircraft carrier *Eagle* but also to help launch another baby at a christening. The Princess sailed from Greenock in the new cruiser *Superb*, her own banner of arms at the masthead, with the escorting destroyers *Fame* and *Hotspur*. The newspapers noted this as her first voyage in her own right aboard a warship and her first solo journey beyond the mainland. With HMS *Eagle* duly launched from the Belfast shipyard of Harland and Wolff, the baby Lavinia Osborne-King was also baptised, daughter of that special friend of her childhood, Sonia Hodgson. 'First a boy and then a girl as godchildren,' a friend reminded the Princess some years later. 'Did it strike you?'

On the systematic two-day tour of Ulster, the Princess was probably not too preoccupied to consider the fun of telling Philip of her own naval experience, her own life at sea. As all the world knows, Philip's photograph, clean-shaven, in naval uniform, had appeared on her dressing-table, to be replaced on older advice by a more discreet likeness splendidly camouflaged by a nautical beard. One morning, early in February 1946, Elizabeth intercepted Miss Crawford and said quietly, 'Someone is coming tonight.'

Philip, Elizabeth and Princess Margaret, all three, dined at the Palace that evening around the small serving table in Elizabeth's sitting-room and it was remembered that they 'later romped in the corridor'. Not yet recovered from the wartime dismantlement of pictures, cabinets and ornaments, the Palace corridors afforded more space for youthful high jinks than now.

If some of the conversation was inevitably romantic, there was the engagement of Jean Vicary Gibbs to Andrew Elphinstone to announce, and the possibility that Lilibet might be a bridesmaid. Philip settled into the Mountbatten household in Chester Street, and the observant Crawfie noticed that 'Lilibet began to take more trouble with her appearance. It seemed to matter more to her what she wore at this evening party or that. Then I would find that Philip had been there.'

In this early phase, fifteen-year-old Margaret was aware of the difficulties. 'He isn't English,' she asked; 'will it make a difference?' Her governess reassured her that Prince Philip had lived in England all his life 'as English, really, as you or I'. In his haste to become British by naturalisation, Philip consulted a Mountbatten solicitor, although the hurdles were found at a higher level. With his meticulous sense of correct conduct between heads of State, the King felt that formal approval should first come from the King of Greece, whose post-war status was not assured until after a Greek plebiscite on the Constitution. Clearly, a slur on the new monarchy might arise if a Prince of Greece changed his nationality so soon after King George II of the Hellenes had returned to the throne. At tea-time, in that monarch's suite at Claridge's, a royal hunt for a missing pot of home-made jam created a confusion, as the Greek-born Queen Alexandra of Yugoslavia put it, 'about as difficult as finding a way for Philip'.

In the fastness of Royal Lodge the King and Queen found it hard to believe that their eldest daughter had fallen in love so decisively with practically the first man she had ever met. 'They feel she is too young to be engaged yet,' Queen Mary described the situation to Lady Airlie. 'They want her to see more of the world before committing herself and meet more men. After all, one is very impressionable at her age. . . . I think they are right to make her wait.' Parental advice against haste was emphatic, and at one stage the couple went with friends to see a play *The Hasty Heart* as if it might afford a moral or offer a solution.

In 1946 Princess Elizabeth celebrated her twentieth birthday in the sunshine of Easter Day. The previous afternoon had seen an excursion with her father to Hurst Park races, hoping for a win by his filly Hypericum. In the event the horse preferred a disastrous dance at the starting gate, but there was the excitement of seeing the King's four-year-old Rising Light as a neck-and-neck third in the Paradise Stakes.

Was it all as promising and hopeful as the all-white bouquet delivered that Sunday at Windsor Castle? Or had the Princess's anniversary been best observed while Prince Philip was on leave earlier in April and arranged a theatre party 'to celebrate just about everything'? The play *The First Gentleman*, with Robert Morley as the Prince Regent, was a success of the season and, as Princess Margaret put it, they really had fun afterwards 'supping at the Savoy'.

The two Princesses were recognised only when the house lights went up in the interval. Only one chance observer knew the four young men – Andrew Elphinstone, Peter Townsend, Prince Philip and Lord Rocksavage. Of the two other ladies, Jean Gibbs was soon to wed Andrew Elphinstone, and Lavinia Leslie married Lord Rocksavage the following year. It would be eighteen years before he succeeded his father as Marquess of Cholmondeley and hereditary Lord Great Chamberlain, one of the high officers of State weddings.

In the play, Wendy Hiller was the high-spirited Princess Charlotte, and, if Philip was disconcerted by the scene of her death in childbirth, it was surely difficult to be otherwise when seated next to the Princess in line to the throne. But then two years elapsed for the next scene, and the final curtain came down with pealing bells and glasses raised 'to the next Queen of England, Victoria'.

At the time, it seemed comically propitious to the eight playgoers that Mary Pickford 'the world's sweetheart' was seated nearby, and the royal group went on to the Savoy in high spirits. The hotel publicist, Jean Nicol, records that their table, 'the round one in the second alcove to the left of the restaurant stairs', was decorated with red roses and became

Elizabeth's favourite table there for ever after. The Princess proposed a toast to 'the happy pair', Jean Gibbs and Andrew Elphinstone, and Philip responded with, 'Sophie and George!', his widowed sister Sophie and Prince George of Hanover, whose wedding he attended at Salem the following week.

At about this time, realistic efforts were made to extend Elizabeth's social life, and the records disclose a string of theatre and supper parties with a number of young people. Posted soon after to HMS *Glendower*, a naval training shore establishment in North Wales, Philip lived for a time in a Bangor hotel and, evidently finding no virtue in concealment, often gave letters to the night-porter to mail addressed openly to HRH The Princess Elizabeth.

On four separate occasions through 1946 and into 1947 Elizabeth's engagement was rumoured in print and four times denied by Commander Colville, the Palace press secretary, the word 'engaged' making the denials precise if misleading. If Philip remained unknown on his visit to the aptly titled 'First Gentleman', he could hardly avoid involvement in rumour after Jean and Andrew's wedding at the Chapel Royal, St James's. At the reception Elizabeth looked shyly bride-like herself, with her bridesmaid bouquet and diadem of flowers. Naturally, the one photographer roaming among the guests seized his opportunity, and his unposed picture of Elizabeth and Philip side by side became a world best seller the following year.

The Princess's public duties, her initiation as a Bard of Wales, her days of factory and patronage visits, were brightened by the pleasure of his snatches of leave. Unknown to press and public, Philip spent a three-week interlude as a guest at Buckingham Palace. Breakfasting in the Household dining-room, 'he would come in hurriedly, eat his food and hurry out, having exchanged not more than a dozen words', according to one of his table companions. 'Older officials considered it unfair to the boy to be around so much, if there was to be no engagements.' The atmosphere bore conflicting elements of chill and warm sympathy. Miss Crawford felt that Lilibet was being given an opportunity of seeing 'how she liked him in large doses'.

On the day after Philip's twenty-fifth birthday, a paragraphist reported a party for fifteen at the Bagatelle restaurant – given by Mrs Graham Hodgson, mother of Mrs Osborne-King – at which the Princess supposedly asked the dance-band to play the tunes from *Oklahoma*, whereupon the song-title 'People Will Say we're in Love' clung to the couple like an official announcement.

At Balmoral, Elizabeth glanced with interest at the King's entry of a grouse drive in his game book mentioning Philip for the first time: '19 August 1946. Philip, Eldon, Cranborne, David L. Althorp and myself. Fine, NW wind. Saw a nice lot of young birds, 12 hares, 1 snipe, 1 black game, 210 grouse.' Lord Eldon and Cranborne (the fifth Marquess of Salisbury) were old friends of the King's generation. David was the Queen's younger brother. Viscount Althorp, then only twenty-three and unmarried, commands our interest as the future father of Lady Diana Spencer.

During the Balmoral holiday, some thought that an implicit understanding had been reached, possibly at Birkhall, during one of those pleasant walks along the banks of Loch Muick. 'Beside some well-loved loch, the white clouds sailing overhead and a curlew crying out of sight . . .' was a phrase the Princess wrote into a Scottish speech rather out of context the following year. Nothing would happen until the naturalisation, Queen Mary assured Lady Airlie.

The King had accepted an invitation to visit the Union of South Africa with the Queen and his daughters early in 1947, and Elizabeth urged her father that she should be at least engaged beforehand but without effect. 'I was rather afraid that you had thought I was being hard-hearted about it,' the King was to write after the wedding. 'I was so anxious for you to come to South Africa as you knew.' The Princess was 'quiet and subdued, her brightness shadowed' as she collected her frocks for the journey, and one day she returned from a factory visit almost in tears. The girls in the crowd had shouted, 'Where's Philip?' heedless of the embarrassment and hurt. 'Poor Lil. Nothing of your own. Not even your love affair!' sighed Princess Margaret, and within four years these words in turn appeared in print in Crawfie's reminiscences.

In happier vein, soon after Philip's decision to bear his mother's maiden name in its modern equivalent of Mountbatten, he was transferred as instructor to the naval school at Corsham, Wiltshire, barely two hours from London or Windsor in his little sports car. The South African tour plans, on the other hand, appeared to toughen. 'My heart rather sinks,' wrote Elizabeth, within family privacy, on seeing a third typing of the programmes. 'It is absolutely staggering how much they expect us to do and going for so long at a stretch. I hope we shall survive, that's all.'

The royal party sailed on 1 February on the same battleship *Vanguard* which Princess Elizabeth had launched two years earlier, but the King considered that 'it would not do at all' for Philip to go on board for the farewells, and the family leave-taking took place at the Mountbattens at 16 Chester Street two nights earlier. Much to her annoyance, Princess Margaret was laid up with a chill, and perhaps her subsequent isolation in her cabin sufficiently explains a photograph taken as the battle cruiser drew away from the quayside, showing Elizabeth standing at the ship's rail, 'forlorn and alone'. It would be more than three months before she saw Philip again, a cause indeed for being disconsolate, a last phase of 'separation to make sure'.

Decked with rosebud chintz, the Princesses' cabins had assumed a homely feminine atmosphere, but Elizabeth's calm crossing to Northern Ireland had ill prepared her for the February seas of the Bay of Biscay. 'I for one would willingly have died,' she wrote, on 15 February, 'I was so miserable. I wasn't actually seasick but everything hurtled about so much. I found my eyes gave out and it was exhausting trying to keep one's feet! However, as soon as I could stand upright without too much effort, I was perfectly all right, and now with the sun we all feel much better.'

The King travelled with a court in miniature: Sir Alan Lascelles as private secretary; Michael Adeane, the assistant secretary; Tom Harvey, the Queen's secretary, and 'the two Peters', the equerries, Wing Commander Peter Townsend and Lieut-Commander Peter Ashmore, now Vice-Admiral Sir Peter Ashmore, Master of the Household. When the seas abated, and the sun came out, it was 'liked being stroked' the Queen said to Peter Townsend. Games were organised on deck, and among the naval officers 'one or two were real smashers', wrote Elizabeth. Only the news from home daunted the travellers as the ship ploughed southward. The hardest winter experienced in the British Isles since 1880 had to be endured in the teeth of a coal shortage that caused constant fuel cuts, while the post-war food rations remained at little above subsistence level. . . . 'We hear terrible things about the weather and the fuel back at home. While we are scorching in the tropics, it makes it difficult for us to imagine exactly what is going on,' commented Elizabeth. 'Yet sometimes we feel – I say we but I really mean I – rather guilty to be right away from it all and that we should be enjoying ourselves so much.'

Father and daughter spoke with one voice. 'I am very worried about the extra privations all of you at home are having,' the King had similarly written to Queen Mary.

In the next two months, at the heels of their parents, the two Princesses were to experience all the kaleidoscopic wonders – and all the physical rigours – of a royal tour of the post-war modern pattern. Cheered always to the echo, welcomed everywhere, they were offered such enormous meals after the lean years of war that the Queen felt it necessary to request smaller menus, and they were rushed through a sustained schedule over thousands of miles that finally left them thin and worn out with fatigue. The hospitality and generosity shown them could not have been more lavish. On 3 March, Princess Elizabeth broke away from her parents' programme to open a new graving dock at east London and found herself grasping a gift-box filled with diamonds. In Kimberly the De Beers Company presented the sisters with two large blue-white diamonds of the highest quality. In Southern Rhodesia the people subscribed to a birthday cheque of £10,000. In Cape Town another casket of diamonds greeted Princess Elizabeth's coming-of-age. And the Princess, for her part, for her first experience of the larger Commonwealth, discovered a country of unimaginable greatness: Table Mountain, the Drakensberg and Victoria Falls were like punctuation marks in the crowded pages of the African scene.

It was less than a year since Elizabeth had ridden on a bus for the first time in her life, a single decker hired for a motor-coach outing with the Sea Rangers from Dartmouth to Brixham. Now, for the first time, she freely experienced the swift new interest of flying, in a bush-hopping trip to the Free State Game Reserve and then on a longer flight from Johannesburg to Rhodesia. It was perhaps a convention that the two Princesses should don white dustcoats and head-scarves and ride on the footplate of their ivory-and-gold 'White Train', with its fourteen coaches, the longest, heaviest and yet most luxurious train that had ever run on the South African railways. Reading as much as she could beforehand on South Africa, steeped during her Eton studies in its racial and political history, Elizabeth anticipated the duality of a nation with two capitals, two flags, two national anthems, two separated groups of cheering crowds, one white, one of darker skin. Less envisaged were the swirling dust-clouds that enveloped the royal party at the native meeting-grounds, the fresh beaches of the Indian Ocean, the wood fire barbecues, the sight of thousands of tethered native horses, the immense gathering of some 70,000 Basuto tribesmen, the incredible depths of the Crown goldmine, the salute of the hooded cobras at Port Elizabeth, dexterously compelled by their keeper to poise erect, the alternative view of grandeur and glimpses of squalor.

To the native mind there was an incident of propitious significance at the hill-top of Cecil Rhodes's grave, when, the Queen Consort being unable to walk in high heels, Elizabeth took off her sandals to give to her mother and thus walked symbolically barefoot on African soil. Inspecting Basuto Girl Guides, the Princesses did not fail to notice and to sympathetically visit a group of lepers sitting apart from the rest in a bus, a royal gesture against superstition that gained wide and deeply appreciated praise. Arriving at Stellenbosch, the deliberate silence of the onlookers sharply reminded the royals that opposition to the idea of monarchy remained a political tenet of the Afrikaans population. But the natural charm of the Princess could not but melt republican hearts and the atmosphere softened. That evening King George made the happy gesture of returning the Family Bible of President Paul Kruger which had been sadly removed to London after the Boer War, and an unexpected and informal visit was paid to his eighty-two-year-old widow.

With such incidents reported, broadcast, photographed and reiterated, the 1961 withdrawal of South Africa from the Commonwealth has not annulled the memory of what was accomplished. The two per cent majority on the white referendum for the Republic might otherwise have seemed more positive. At the time it had seemed fitting that the Heiress Presumptive should celebrate her coming-of-age in Cape Town as a climax of the tour, a shift from national to wider considerations. In the morning, she inspected a great parade of the South African Army with Field-Marshal Smuts. In the afternoon she attended a huge rally of youth organisations. In the early evening, speaking from a room in Government House, the Princess made her memorable twenty-first birthday broadcast to five hundred million of her father's subjects, and to many others throughout the world attracted by the drama and pathos of the occasion. 'I am 6,000 miles from the country where I was born,' she said, 'but I am certainly not 6,000 miles from home.'

Great pains were characteristically taken with the speech. There is a story that after the Princess read the draft manuscript she returned it to Alan Lascelles, saying, 'It made me cry.' If we smile at this picture of the young Princess in a pose of romantic melancholy, the finished polished speech also provides phrases unmistakably her own. 'I declare before you all that my whole life, whether it be long or short, shall be devoted to your service.' The memory-training trick of glancing back at the previous year's entries in her journal may have recalled the fate of Wendy Hiller's Princess Charlotte.

Throughout the tour, in the phrase of the King's biographer, Sir John Wheeler-Bennett, the demeanour of Princess Elizabeth had been remarkable for its youthful dignity, commingled with her spontaneous gaiety and enthusiasm. In March 1947, the root cause of the gaiety was equally evident in the list of 817 naturalisations announced in the *London Gazette*, among them No. 808, Mountbatten, Philip: Greece; Serving Officer in His Majesty's Forces. An added enthusiasm was also evidenced by Peter Townsend. 'At most stops, horses were waiting for those who felt like a gallop before breakfast. With the Princesses, we sped in the cool air, along the sands or across the veldt. These were the most glorious moments of the day.'

But Princess Elizabeth's solemn act of dedication, her promise to devote her whole life to the service of the great Imperial family, the patent sincerity of her girlish voice, could still shine inspiringly in memory thirty years later: 'But in our time we may say that the British Empire has saved the world first and has now to save herself after the battle is won. . . . It is for us who have grown up in these years of danger and glory to see that it is accomplished in the long years of peace that we all hope stretch ahead.

'If we all go forward together with an unwavering faith, a high courage and a quiet heart, we shall be able to make of this ancient Commonwealth which we all love so dearly an even grander thing – more free, more prosperous, more happy and a more powerful influence for good. . . .'

Returning on 11 May to the land of her birth, Elizabeth

danced a little jig of joy on the *Vanguard*'s deck. Philip was awaiting her at the Palace, and before the evening was out the King had given his agreement to an understanding.

A family story is that Prince Philip had first arranged to see the King before greeting Lilibet, and after that momentous interview the King asked Elizabeth to fetch something he had left in his study, 'a present for you'. There she found Philip, and their happiness can hardly be imagined. But their understanding of an engagement, their betrothal, had to remain a secret while the Commonwealth governments were consulted. Engagement rumours were at once rife and were denied. Ironically, the breathing space was a boon. The voyage home had not made up for illnesses and lost sleep and, as Lady Margaret Egerton said, 'the family was worn out'.

The Princesses nevertheless drove through London with their parents to the then customary welcoming ceremony at the Guildhall, and a month later Elizabeth repeated the drive in her own right to receive the freedom of the City of London. On 10 June one of the débutante presentation parties vexatiously fell on the unseen Philip's birthday. On 12 June, the King's official birthday, Princess Elizabeth rode at his side for the ceremony of Trooping the Colour, taking up the once traditional role of the Prince of Wales. The sight of her small slim person, impeccably uniformed as Colonel-in-Chief of the Grenadier Guards and mounted side-saddle, made a great impression on the public, who had never seen her mother in military uniform nor suspected that the Princess could produce such representative military style.

June slipped into July, and a small green sports car was not infrequently parked outside Buckingham Palace beyond the screening wall of the private entrance. But otherwise, I think, the one clue to an engagement beyond the speculation was the presence of the widowed and reticent Princess Andrew of Greece, Prince Philip's mother, who had taken up residence with her sister-in-law, the Marchioness of Milford Haven, at Kensington Palace.

Apart from the forgotten encounters of childhood, Elizabeth first met her future mother-in-law at lunch at Royal Lodge, a lady in the grey dress of a nursing order, her sombre deep-set eyes so often apt to twinkle unexpectedly with a hint of Philip's merriment. Deaf and dumb in infancy, Princess Andrew's disabilities had with training and pertinacity long since been cast aside. The loving relationship between Philip's mother and his future wife was immediate. When speaking, Lilibet thoughtfully always turned her face to enable her lips to be read, and often impulsively took Princess Andrew's hand as they talked, 'conveying so much reciprocal feeling', as a friend noted.

One afternoon, in her grey sisterhood costume, Princess Andrew called at the second floor showroom of a trusted jeweller, and asked if the stones of a ring given to her by her late husband could be re-set to her own new design. There were practical difficulties in the original pattern but her wishes were closely followed, embodying a solitaire diamond supported by diamond shoulders set in platinum. This was to be Princess Elizabeth's engagement ring, and if when first slipped on her finger it seemed slightly too large it was readily modified.

'Something is going to happen tonight,' Elizabeth told a confidante on 8 July. 'He is coming tonight,' and at midnight, the long-desired announcement was released, 'It is with the greatest pleasure that The King and Queen announce the betrothal of their dearly beloved daughter The Princess Elizabeth to Lieutenant Philip Mountbatten, RN, son of the late Prince Andrew of Greece and Princess Andrew (Princess Alice of Battenberg), to which union The King has gladly given his consent.'

In her journal eighty-year-old Queen Mary noted, 'I must say the young couple look very happy. I trust all will be well. . . . They both came to see me after luncheon looking radiant.' With felicitous timing, a royal garden party was being held at the Palace the following day and the couple could thus immediately appear together in public.

The Princess had fondly expected that a demonstration of cheers and applause would greet Prince Philip, and the guests wished to show approval but could find no opportunity until the Royal Family moved towards their private tea marquee, when an inhibited croak of cheering and some timid clapping occurred. Scotland happily afforded a more vociferous welcome when the Family took up residence at Holyroodhouse two weeks later and the engaged couple appeared at a race-meeting at Hamilton Park. 'It was delightful to see that the handsome Lieutenant Mountbatten bent over Princess Elizabeth, but not too attentively, and that they laughed a great deal together, talking like conspirators and sharing private jokes,' was the view of a press spectator. Yet Elphinstone cousins thought it a pity that Lilibet's pleasure in Philip's company was matched by an unforeseen need of restraint. They could rarely link hands, public duty and private thoughts never walked arm in arm.

After all the exasperating delays, it amazed the Princess that any perplexities remained for discussion. The Archbishop of Canterbury wrote to the King, for instance, with 'a matter upon which I think I should consult your Majesty. . . . Lieutenant Mountbatten was baptised into the Greek Orthodox Church . . . he remains formally a member of the Greek Orthodox Church. . . .' This was decidedly news to the bride and groom. At Cheam school, at Gordonstoun and in the Navy, Philip had put himself down as 'Church of England', thinking no more about it. 'There would be an advantage if he were officially received into the Church of England,' Dr Fisher concluded. 'It can be done privately and very simply.'

On this point irreverent friends provided their own suggestions. Would he need to be baptised again, his cousin, Alexandra, wished to know? And could one undergo religious naturalisation? The questions went unanswered, and the difficulties smoothed with an announcement that Lieut Mountbatten had been received into membership of the Anglican Church in a private ceremony at Lambeth Palace.

Not without dismay, the Princess had to come to terms with the pangs of intense preparation around her, the butterfly emergent from the chrysalis. After a brief posting to Mr Attlee, Winston Churchill's youngest assistant secretary was seconded from 10 Downing Street as her first private secretary. Jock (John) Colville was to handle all Elizabeth's practical affairs, while his cousin, Richard Colville, was simultaneously appointed press secretary at the Palace, his fearsome initial task being to organise all the news facilities of the wedding.

In their different fields, both the Colvilles were concerned with Elizabeth's hopeful plans and her ultimate bleak disillusionment in seeking to create a married home of her own at Sunninghill Park in the Crown lands belt of Ascot. Like many another old mansion it had been sadly damaged by army occupation during the war and the gardens were littered with derelict Nissen huts 'informally occupied by squatters', as a tactful friend put it. On the other hand, the current house and garden magazines were full of encouraging descriptions of ruinous properties lovingly restored and renovated by enterprising young couples.

With this encouragement, the royal house-hunters walked round Sunningdale Park to find dilapidated ravaged rooms, the ceilings scarred and plaster peeling, and the main roof damaged by fire, the ornamental lake choked by debris. The Windsor rural council had been offered this forlorn property for rehousing the bombed homeless and had prudently declined it. Crown surveyors nevertheless advised the King that – as a beginning – a wing could be readily renovated with proper economy in labour and materials. 'Whither the storm carries me, I go a willing guest,' Philip once summed up his feelings in a visitors' book, though pessimistic that the work might take years. But within a month fire mysteriously broke out one night and the place was gutted.

Queen Alexandra of Yugoslavia has given a highly coloured account of royal comings-and-goings watched by jealous eyes, and rumours of malicious arson swiftly spread. 'How *could* it have happened?' wrote Elizabeth. 'Do you really think someone did it on purpose? I can't believe it. People are always so kind to us. I don't for one moment believe it was the squatters.' In a briefer private memo Philip wrote off the fire as a blessing in disguise. 'And a good job, too!' he noted with asperity.

8

The bride

Within the shores of society, that nucleus of position, wealth and gossip, it became widely known that the royal wedding would quietly take place in the private chapel of Windsor Castle, so widely was it thought that the King would be deterred from an Abbey ceremony by the bearing reins of austerity. London was scruffy after eight years' lack of maintenance. Fabric for street decorations and banners, even millinery materials and shoes were rigidly rationed. A district Trade Union Council resolved against 'the use of quantities of scaffolding and timber in view of the serious housing shortage'. The Quarter-Master General's office proposed only a khaki processional turnout. The gremlins of gloom gibbered in every direction, and for two months Hartnell heard no decision on a wedding dress. 'Someone in the Government apparently advised simplicity, misjudging the English people's love of pageantry and a show,' raged Chips Channon to his private journal. 'A great opportunity has been missed – when else in history has the heiress to the Throne been married?'

Princess Elizabeth said little of her own point of view. She was amused that Crawfie suddenly produced a young Scottish bank manager who had secretly been in the offing for years, and married him on her summer leave. 'Governess beats Liz to the Altar' ran an American headline. The Princess was startled that London Transport proposed to display photograph posters of Philip and herself outside every tube station and asked that the scheme should not proceed. Nothing mattered, except that no details of her wedding gown should be made known until after the wedding, one small secret she wished to keep to herself. Westminster or Windsor – what would truly be for the best?

Happily the wider public choice prevailed, and the wedding was fixed for 20 November at Westminster Abbey. 'Millions will welcome this joyous event as a flash of colour on the hard road we have to travel,' boomed Winston Churchill. The War Office announced the full pageantry of a full dress Captain's Escort of Household Cavalry for the bride and bridegroom and a Sovereign's Escort for the King and Queen. Sentiment was served by a gift of a Welsh-mined gold from the people of Wales, with enough to spare for Princess Margaret, and indeed unknowingly for Princess Anne and Lady Diana Spencer in the remote future. With the help of ingredients presented by the Commonwealth, twelve firms offered wedding cakes. A Florida hotel proposed to provide a honeymoon. After a cautious ruling against wedding gifts from unknown individuals – 'Her Royal Highness does not wish to deprive you' – the avalanche broke all barriers and ultimately a grand muster of 2,660 gifts were shown for charity at St James's Palace.

In printed order they ranged from the sapphire and diamond necklace and earrings from the King to the beaver coat from the Hudson's Bay Company, from personal gifts such as the picnic set from Princess Margaret and the wastepaper basket from Bobo, from official presentations – the RAF's grand piano, the Diplomatic Corps' thirty-piece dressing-table set, the thirteen pieces of Sheraton furniture from the City of London, the hundreds of pairs of nylons – and perhaps not least poignant a pair of hand-made evening shoes from a displaced group of Latvian nationals. Swamped with packages, everyone helped to unpack the presents: the Princess and her sister, Palace staff, a volunteer troop of Boy Scouts. Lilibet hoped 'to wear everything, use everything', but thought better of this later.

She was, wrote a friend, 'bewildered by it all . . . often touched almost to tears by the accompanying letters. She read every one of them. . . .' Thoughtful and considerate, it troubled her to have so much when, in those difficult times, many had so little. Some kindly people even sent clothing coupons to help with her trousseau, precious gifts in that threadbare era, when every coupon represented part of an item of clothing, though these had to be returned with a letter of thanks, since gifts of coupons were illegal.

Chosen herself, with her mother's approval, the wedding gown was, after all, the most elaborate of the designs Norman Hartnell had offered. Ten thousand small white American costume pearls were utilised for the embroidery motifs of rose-like white blossoms, trailed with jasmine and smilax. The eight bridesmaids wore dresses of ivory tulle, with embroidery of pearls and crystal matching the bridal train. The fabric was spun and woven in the Scottish town of Dunfermline, but the wilder absurdities of patriotism still flourished two years after the war, and Hartnell found trouble in the nationality of the silkworms originally providing the silk for the dress itself. Were they ex-enemy Japanese worms or Italian? Hartnell put through a phone call to Scotland and was reassured. Their worms came from friendly Nationalist China!

The problem of Prince Philip's rank and title greatly exercised the King. To his mother, so expert in dignities and precedence, he explained that he was bestowing the Garter upon Lilibet eight days before giving it to Philip, thus ensuring her seniority. He was also creating him a Royal Highness and conferring a peerage with the titles of Baron Greenwich, Earl of Merioneth and Duke of Edinburgh: 'It is a great deal to give a man all at once,' the King added, 'but I know that Philip understands his new responsibilities.'

Even so, the King slipped up for, although the bridegroom came to be popularly known as Prince Philip and received the dignity of Royal Highness, he was not in fact created a Prince, an anomaly not corrected until ten years later when the Prime Minister of the day, Mr Macmillan, advised the Queen that the style of a Prince of the United Kingdom was legally permissible. But evidently no appropriate local definition exists for the husband of the Queen of Canada or the Queen of Australia.

On one of the memo-pad slips used for his dispatch-boxes the King pencilled two other decisions, 'Photography and broadcast commentary, yes. No filming or television. GR.' But the Princess persuaded him to change his mind on filming, and TV cameras were eventually permitted up to the Abbey door.

There were other changes. The London department stores had intended to open on the wedding morning but suddenly announced a staff holiday. Less fortunate employees played truant in thousands. While the newspapers revelled in the host of royal and regal heads, the engaged couple played a running match of thinking up new wedding guests: Philip's old nanny and the schoolmistress from Birkhall, the Hartnell workgirls who had made the wedding gown and kept its secret, a girl from the Scottish silk factory, and even the Sandringham station-master.

The day before the wedding was oddly quiet, except for the throngs in the Mall. The Princess Elizabeth alertly watched the carriage rehearsal from the Palace windows. An outrider's horse called Angela showed slight lameness and was withdrawn from the return procession, and the partnering horse, Lilian, returned alone. 'What happened?' the Princess asked the Royal Mews superintendant. 'There was Lilian puffing herself out on the way home and trying to make herself look like *two*.'

'Lilibet went to bed very early,' Miss Crawford recorded. 'She came up to her room, singing. In the morning I went along to Lilibet's room very early and found her in her dressing-gown, peeping excitedly out of the windows. "I can't believe it's really happening," she said. "I have to keep pinching myself."' It was like her parents' Coronation morning all over again, peeping down through her curtains at the crowds. At 8 a.m. the three Hartnell ladies arrived with their soft bundle wrapped in muslin, her wedding gown. 'Pale as a lily,' Madame Germaine was to describe the bride. 'So pale, silent, solemn, that we were almost alarmed, but when we had smoothed the last fold into place she came out of her dream. "It is really lovely, so lovely,"' she said.

There seemed reason for both pallor and alarm, for Elizabeth was confronted with almost every bridal crisis that could occur. As the hairdresser was setting her mother's sunray tiara on her head, the frame snapped, but the jeweller rushed it away and was back with effective repair within minutes. On the spur of the moment the Princess decided to wear her parents' wedding gift, the double necklace of pearls which were among the presents at St James's Palace and the secretary sent to fetch them unaccountably failed to return, or so it seemed while the minutes sped away. Jock Colville was wearing his Flight Lieut's RAF uniform, and has given his account of the episode. '"Take any car!" the Princess called after me. I looked at my watch. I ran towards a large Royal Daimler . . . "You seem in a hurry, young man," said King Haakon of Norway, "but do let me get out first."' At St James's, where Colville thought it would be simple to confirm his identity by telephone, the line was dead. There were frantic arguments, with vital minutes passing, before the police believed his story. Not least, the bridal bouquet could not be found, until at length traced from the porter's lodge to a cupboard where it had been placed to keep cool. In the final ten minutes reserved for emergencies, Elizabeth resumed her watch at the window, 'with a little smile, her head in the clouds'.

In the Abbey the King considered that his daughter looked 'calm and composed'. Jock Colville thought her 'radiant and entrancing'. Queen Victoria's granddaughter, Alice of Athlone, who was to live another thirty-three years through her life and reign, marvelled at her youthful calm. The impression upon General Smuts was of a bride 'beautiful but sad . . . sad, because she is serious and wise beyond her years'. Archbishop Garbett of York emphasised that the marriage rite was 'as it would be for any cottager who might be married in some small country church'. To each his view. It was noticed that Elizabeth elected to promise to 'love, honour and obey', that she chose the twenty-third Psalm, 'The Lord's my Shepherd' to the Crimond descant that she knew and had rehearsed with the Abbey organist at the Palace. She went to her wedding as gravely and reverently as in the mood of her birthday dedication earlier in the year.

One last oversight remained. The newly-weds had intended to take a favourite young corgi, Susan, on honeymoon with them to Broadlands and at the last minute the dog appeared to be forgotten. Noticing her, a footman just had time to place her, snug under a corner of blanket, on the floor of the open landau in which, on that chilly foggy November night, the couple were riding to Waterloo, the bride herself warm in a nest of hot-water bottles. All the warmth of South London however seemed to focus at Waterloo Station and out from the landau in a shower of confetti tumbled Susan. 'For about fifteen years the faithful companion of the Queen', she is commemorated on a small inscribed stone at Sandringham.

Strangely, Broadlands – the late Lord Louis Mountbatten's home in Hampshire – is open to the public, and the endless file of visitors drop their voices as they enter the erstwhile honeymoon suite, and see the chintz-curtained four-poster bed, the substantial writing desk at its foot. In joint charge with Frank Randall, the butler, Charles Smith recalls that the main dining-room was made cosier 'by a small circular table in front of the log-fire and settees arranged to give a closed-in effect'. The scene of the honeymoon had been announced beforehand, and the Romsey police were augmented to out-wit the world's press photographers, some of whom attempted a stealthy flanking approach to the house through the bracken. The Princess wrote a number of 'happy little letters', as one friend said, reporting the misadventures of a puppy sent as a wedding gift, and the optical illusion of a new dark hedge which turned out to be a glimpse of public highway black with cameras and binoculars. And there was a welcome 'letter from Papa':

'I am so glad you wrote and told Mummy that you think the long wait before your engagement and the long time before the wedding was for the best. I was rather afraid that you had thought I was being rather hard-hearted about it. . . . I have watched you grow up all these years with pride under the skilful direction of Mummy, who as you know is the most marvellous person in the world in my eyes and I can, I know, always count on you, and now Philip, to help us in our work. Your leaving us has left a great blank in our lives but do remember that your old home is still yours and do come back to it as often as possible. I can see that you are sublimely happy with Philip which is right but don't forget us is the wish of your ever loving and devoted – Papa.'

Yet public interest could not be switched off to allow uninterrupted happiness. The press siege of Broadlands was reduced only when the couple agreed to a special session to the photographers. When the honeymooners attended Sunday morning service at Romsey Abbey, sightseers wildly scram-bled over graves and tombstones and carried chairs, ladders and even a sideboard into the churchyard as viewing stands. The young couple were at pains to devise a suitable acknow-ledgment to the public and their message of thanks was deft and full of fun: 'Before we leave for Scotland tonight we want to say the reception given us on our wedding day and the loving interest shown by our fellow countrymen and well-wishers have left an impression which will never grow faint. We can find no words to express what we feel, but we can at least offer our grateful thanks to the millions who have given us this unforgettable send-off in our married life.'

Their honeymoon was in reality in two parts, with a sur-reptitious visit to Buckingham Palace for a dog-lead for the puppy, and then Hampshire was followed by the Highlands and the unbroken privacy of Birkhall, entrenched in deep snow. Philip caught a severe cold and Elizabeth ruefully had cause to write that she supposed most wives nursed their husbands as she was already nursing Philip. Returning to London, they made brief and unexpected appearances at both the Palace and Windsor Castle Christmas staff balls and then simply moved as a married couple into the Princess's three-room suite. Philip's valet divulged that the Duke had no more than a bedroom and bathroom adjoining his wife's sitting-room. 'Living with her parents' was a commonplace phrase of young marriages of the time, but the public wish that the Princess should have an official establishment removed from that of the King was not long in finding voice.

'When I die, Lilibet, you will have Marlborough House,' said Queen Mary, with her youthful memories of the Marlborough House set in the era when that Wren pile had been the home of the heir to the Throne. 'Oh dear, we don't at all want Granny to die, we hope she'll be here for a very long time. We must have a London home before that!' The solution lay in salvaging the royal white elephant of Clarence House, next door but one along the Mall, formerly the home of Queen Victoria's third son, the Duke of Connaught, but for years seldom occupied except for wartime use by the Red Cross and St John organisation. The Edinburghs explored it with sinking hearts – the sheer absurdity of thinking of living there. The only bath was contained in a cupboard. Much of the lighting was by gas, the roof and upper floors were bomb-damaged and, as at Sunninghill Park, stout hearts were needed to explore the warren of corridors and the scarred and derelict rooms.

Parliament had however voted £55,000 towards providing electricity, central heating, the remodelling of kitchens, service quarters and Household offices. The house possessed some admirable Nash ceilings, chimneypieces and doorways; the rear Household wing was of mingled Tudor and late Georgian origin, and optimistic surveyors felt that everything could be put into good order within a year. In the end, it was to take half as long again. But Elizabeth saw the place through her mother's eyes, what it could be rather than what it was, and ultimately the Princess took great pride and careful interest in watching the house emerge from squalor to a new contemporary beauty and comfort.

Any residual cost was to be disbursed from private royal funds. But where were the Edinburghs to live in the meantime?

Many relatives felt that the couple needed more time to themselves and perhaps especially 'getting away from Mother'. A close friend hinted at the need of becoming self-reliant as one grew older. 'Lilibet continued her childhood habit and always went down to the Queen to ask "Shall I do this?" or "Do you approve of that?"' wrote Crawfie, happily ensconced with her husband in a little grace-and-favour cottage in Kensington.

Then Princess Alice, the Countess of Athlone, mentioned that she was wintering as usual with her husband in South Africa, where he had once been Governor-General, and generously invited the royal newly-weds to 'make themselves at home' in her house adjoining the clock tower at Kensington Palace. This opened an idyllic phase in Princess Elizabeth's life. Philip was given a desk job at the Admiralty in Whitehall, and the Princess asked the Kensington Palace police-box to telephone through to her when his returning car was sighted in the evening so that she could greet him at the door. The Athlones' invaluable steward, Mr Bennett, guided the young wife through the perplexities of housekeeping. She closely questioned friends on the possibility of her visiting Harrods' provisions hall undetected but – so far as I know – prudence prevailed and the expedition was never made. Pleasant little dinner parties were given; the King and Queen came to lunch or dinner once a month, and Princess Margaret stacked up a wish to similarly live as a young married in the house exactly opposite, an ambition fulfilled after her marriage to Lord Snowdon twelve years later.

The Athlones gave their staff a regular day off, a custom the Princess needed no encouragement in following. The servants disappeared after breakfast, the Princess prepared the evening meal and then husband and wife did the washing-up, leaving the kitchen 'as they found it', tidied to the last coffee cup. 'We are having a run of luck, and kindness, too,' Elizabeth had said, in beginning this phase of married life among the tiger-skins, stuffed lion heads, paintings of the veldt and other Africana of the Clock House. Before the Athlones returned, another chapter in the story had fitted into place, precise as a jigsaw piece. Not far away from Windsor, a house called Windlesham Moor stood in the pine-and-azalea belt of the rich Ascot mile, and the widow of its former owner, the financier Philip Hill, had suggested that it might be rented. Newly appointed the Princess's comptroller, Sir Frederick Browning included house-hunting on her behalf among his duties and urged with surging enthusiasm that the Edinburghs should view.

The fifty-acre grounds embraced a lake remindful of Sandringham, rose gardens akin to Luton Hoo and rhododendron glades resembling those of Royal Lodge. In the midst of this stood a modern house faced with white-painted stucco, together with a level region of lawn which Prince Philip at once visualised as a cricket pitch. What was more, with paint direly in short supply, the house had been miraculously decorated and put into order and was being rented sufficiently furnished for early occupation. This in itself solved a problem, for the Princess did not like to think of her wedding-gifts lying wrapped and useless in store, and was anxious to put them into use as quickly as possible.

If the decor of Windlesham Moor was over-lush, with the green marble of the reception hall, the fifty-foot drawing-room, there was the tempting array of main bedrooms, each with a bathroom, the principal bedroom suite equipped with built-in dressing-tables fit for a princess. And everywhere were mirrors, illuminated mirrored recesses, mirrored wardrobe doors, mirrored table tops, a useful but unexpected decor for Elizabeth, who rarely bothered to study herself for long in a looking glass.

Consulting her mother, the then Queen remarked that it was 'more palatial than a palace', and Mrs Hill was amenable on the terms of the lease. The upkeep was another matter. Parliament had voted £10,000 a year to Prince Philip with £40,000 to the Princess as heiress presumptive, both sums subject to income tax, but the money was slow to materialise, and needful Household expenses were mounting. The £10,000 contrasted with the £30,000 voted to Prince Albert (as husband of a reigning Queen) in the very different economic circumstances of a century earlier. Philip's philosophy is that you don't worry about money until there isn't any: it sufficed that he was determined to foot all the domestic bills and overheads of the Moor. 'We don't want footmen,' he told Mr King, his steward, who had come to him from King George of Greece. 'John (the valet) can help with extra guests.'

There are several clues to Elizabeth's concern that Philip was paying for everything and that she wanted to pay her own share. Her husband arranged for bills to be cleared through the comptroller's office at Buckingham Palace but, for a month or two, she kept the bills herself and sent off her own Coutts' cheques to the tradespeople. The bills were found returned duly receipted, but Frederick Browning found that some of her cheques were never cashed. Signed Elizabeth P., several tradesmen preferred to frame them as curios.

From bath-towels to her superlative crystal, silver and porcelain, the Princess enjoyed installing her wedding gifts in her new setting. A magnificent Hepplewhite breakfront bookcase had been subscribed by a group of forty-eight royal kinsfolk, and the theme of her first cocktail party was to enable them to see how fine it looked embellished with personal treasures in the drawing-room.

Next day the Princess enquired how many bottles of whisky and gin had been used, not in parsimony but because 'one should know these things'. When the King and Queen first came to dinner, she was uncertain whether her father should be seated as a guest or placed at the head of the table. Her steward solemnly advised that since Windlesham was a private house and not an official residence the King could be placed as guest. 'You were quite right,' the Princess reassured him afterwards. 'The King said nothing about the placing.'

In early March the young couple became aware of one precious piece of knowledge that they kept to themselves for a month or two. 'We shall probably read about it in the newspapers before we really know ourselves,' Lilibet had said ruefully. This nearly proved to be true, for rumours came in print a few weeks later when Philip began a staff course at Greenwich where he lived-in between weekends at Windlesham and frequent visits home to the Palace.

Nearly six months after his daughter's wedding, it was the King's happy inspiration that she should be invested with her insignia of a Lady of the Most Noble Order of the Garter on St George's Day, 23 April – two days after Elizabeth's twenty-second birthday and three days before the celebration of his own silver wedding. The day was further to be marked as the 600th anniversary of the founding of the Order, so far as scholarship could tell of the most ancient Order of Chivalry in the world. The capital letters are not fortuitous; they enhance the distinction of an honour which the Queen today takes with the utmost seriousness: the commentator who once described the Garter ceremonies as a noble pantomime for the benefit of tourists could have scarcely committed a greater error.

In 1946, as a girl of twenty, Princess Elizabeth had followed her father through every move in his wish to restore the Order to its status as a high non-political honour in the gift of the Sovereign, a step in an earnest personal campaign to maintain honours in high repute if they were to remain an embellishment of the monarchy. Father and daughter had long discussions on the Garter, the Order of Merit and other distinctions, so anxious was the King for her to thoroughly understand their ceremonial dignity.

The full pageantry of the Garter had not been seen at Windsor for nearly fifty years, and the King revived it brilliantly, not only prescribing the dark blue velvet mantles with their cordons and collars, the attendance of Heralds, Pursuivants and King of Arms in their rich habiliments, but soberly addressing his knights to remind them that the ancient Admonitions were of Christian purpose. The Princess's investment in the Throne Room of Windsor Castle bore a heightened significance which she has never forgotten.

The festivities of her parents' Silver Wedding were also no sooner over than the Princess and her husband undertook their first State mission abroad by paying a visit to Paris, ostensibly to open an exhibition of British Life in that capital. Among other whimsical exhibits Elizabeth found herself gazing at her great-grandfather's top-hat, preserved under glass, but there was otherwise nothing glazed about the French welcome. As one Parisian said, 'It was the day of liberation all over again,' and the Princess divined that the spirit of freedom was being freshly welcomed as well as herself, 'so imaginatively aware of what the French had suffered that she drove up the Champs Elysées with her eyes brimming with tears', as one witness noted. Overwrought by her reception, she felt faint during the wreath-laying at the Arc de Triomphe and had to summon all her resources to carry on.

Prince Philip's solicitude told the people all they wished to know and guesswork about the baby was in *Paris Soir* that afternoon. Next day Philip showed symptoms of the jaundice liable to affect him under emotional strain but refused his wife's worried persuasions to rest at the Embassy. Like actors going on a stage, both went through the programme their hosts had laid down: morning service, the races at Longchamps, dinner at the Tour d'Argent, Sunday activities that caused a Scottish Sabbatarian to fulminate on 'a dark day in our history'. The visit, in fact, sealed a popularity to be renewed and dramatically demonstrated on each of Elizabeth II's subsequent visits to the French capital. The Mayor of Paris indeed spoke of his citizens with the popular tribute. 'We in Paris loved Princess Elizabeth because she became *tout à fait Parisienne.*'

With so much known, the official Palace announcement that the Princess would 'undertake no public engagements after the end of June' was with curious timing issued from Buckingham Palace on the eve of Derby Day. The next day saw an affectionate multitude at Epsom massed so firmly around the Princess's car that mounted police had to clear the way. The admiring cry of 'Good Old Liz' and the Aga Khan's popular win with a horse named My Love characterised the day.

In chatting with the owner, Elizabeth was a model of royal tact. As a wedding gift the Aga Khan had given her a then unnamed filly duly registered in the 1948 yearling lists as Astrakhan. Yes, she said, the little chestnut had been settled into Freemason Lodge under Captain Boyd-Rochfort and was very well, and the topic was neatly turned. The more horrid truth was that the filly was a dud, her forelegs weak, with an uneven muscular pull evident and a kneecap liable to slip. 'She will never see a racecourse,' said the forthright Boyd-Rochfort, which may have strengthened the Princess's determination to prove the weakling a winner and so reward the donor.

Astrakhan was in fact the first horse registered under the present Queen's ownership, and, on Lady Zia Wernher's recommendation, she consulted a young physiotherapist, Charles Strong, who believed that horses could be treated for rheumatism and sprains as well as people. Astrakhan's subsequent performance on the course persuaded the Aga Khan to offer an alternative choice from four other horses, but the Princess persisted in the unorthodox treatment until two placings and a win in a selective career of four races vindicated her judgment before she retired the filly to stud.

9

Wife and mother

As Prince Philip has remarked, a man does not marry only his wife; he also acquires in-laws, including usually a mother-in-law and a host of new friends. Conversely, Princess Elizabeth acquired three sisters-in-law, an active sharing interest in three or four new family groups, with nephews and nieces sufficient in 1948 to make her an Anglo-German aunt fourteen times over. In all the years of getting to know Philip, 'getting to know all about you', as the song goes, few personal topics fascinated her more than the sisterhood, essentially as British as their Battenberg-Mountbatten mother, who was born in Windsor Castle and regarded as one of the royal family, British in upbringing as Philip himself.

Sixteen years older than Philip, the eldest sister, Princess Margarita, had seemed more like an aunt in his boyhood, and more like an aunt than a cousin to Lilibet in her early teens when they occasionally met at Buckingham Palace. Next came Theodora – 'Dolla' within the family – who had influenced the turn of his education from Salem to Gordonstoun. (Originally there had been Cecilie, who died with her husband, George Hesse, in 1937 in an air crash.) Then Sophie, seven years Philip's senior, always the closest to him in care and companionship.

Bridesmaids together at Lord Louis Mountbatten's, their Uncle Dickie's wedding at St Margaret's, Westminster, they had cherished a wish of being brides together and indeed were all married in 1931 within nine months of each other, all to German princes of similar descent from Queen Victoria. 'When I was only five', young Lilibet sighed. It made the inward vexations in her marriage situation, the thorns among the roses, all the more hurtful, even *obnoxious*, when Prime

Minister Attlee tendered advice to the King that it would be impolitic and unacceptable for the sisters, who were German nationals by marriage, to take part in her wedding festivities so soon after the war.

It was an affront as ludicrous as the Battenbergs' enforced change of princely name in 1917, but Princess Elizabeth's indignant protests – to her father and others – were of no avail. Her letters to the sisters and Philip's brothers-in-law were full of regret and distress. Few realised that the Margravin of Baden, mentioned among the royal donors in the list of wedding gifts to the bride – a diamond and ruby brooch – was in fact Dolla. Or that the unpublicised gold fountain-pen with which Prince Philip signed the Abbey register was his joint wedding present from the three absentees.

Privately Philip cogently pointed out that his sisters were wedded two years or more before Hitler came to power, that Margarita and Dolla's husbands were retired for their anti-Nazi sympathies, that Sophie's first husband, Prince Cri of Hesse, was killed in the Luftwaffe, leaving her a widow with five children, while in contrast his brother, 'the other Philip', had been lodged in a Gestapo prison, and the wife of Philip of Hesse had tragically perished in Buchenwald.

Happily, Princess Sophie had remarried, hence Philip's memorable night out at the Savoy with Lilibet 'to celebrate just about everything', the week before Sophie's wedding to Prince George of Hanover, and she was one of the first house guests at Windlesham Moor in company with two of her teenage Hesse daughters, the princesses Christine and Dorothea. Not only was 'Tiny', as he called her, Philip's favourite sister, but no-one could have been more reassuring or welcome to Lilibet just then. With her five Hesse offspring, and her year-old Hanover baby son, Sophie's matter-of-fact attitude to maternity drew away its fears. 'It's what we're made for,' Elizabeth said just then, and the phrase surely echoed Sophie. The two sisters-in-law went shopping un-recognised for layette needs in Bond Street and Knightsbridge, and Sophie's total lack of fuss preserved them from recognition.

With a touch of Queen Mary's frugality, Elizabeth brought out her old pram, re-sprung and repolished, while Philip risked family laughter and opened a case of his old baby clothes, only to find them too old-fashioned and discoloured for use. His young wife meanwhile gave way to her parents' wish that the baby should be born at Buckingham Palace rather than Windlesham, but remained firm that the event should be in her own room, 'among the things I know'.

While at the Clock House, Elizabeth had so continually turned to her mother for every kind of advice that an older married friend felt it needful to counsel her, 'Really, you must stand on your own feet. Consider your husband's feelings. You can't go to your mother every two minutes.' The Princess considered this very seriously, as she has done with criticism throughout her life.

Finishing his course at Greenwich, Philip feared he was putting on weight, and his remedy was to don layers of sweaters and jog round the Windlesham grounds. Laughing as he ran past, Elizabeth would say, 'I am sure he is mad!'

Princess Margaret wanted to cosset her sister with cushions, but at the end of May Chips Channon detailed a surprising picture of the mother-to-be at a dance at Marina of Kent's home at Coppins. 'The Edinburghs were enchanting. She was in black lace, with a large comb and mantilla, as an Infanta, and danced every dance until nearly 5 a.m. I am beginning to doubt the supposed pregnancy. . . . Philip looked worn out but was the success of the ball with his policeman's hat and handcuffs. He and Princess Elizabeth seemed supremely happy, often dancing together. Towards 3 a.m. we danced the Hokey Cokey hilariously.'

Philip, for his part, intensely enjoyed playing Windlesham host. Prince George of Hanover joined his wife, and Lilibet found his family likeness to her father so striking that she warmly declared he could have been perhaps her older brother. The resemblance could have descended from as far back as George III, although Queen Mary, on coming to tea, detected rather a Sonderburg-Glucksburg (Danish) strain. It was all perhaps a tactful way of welcoming George back to the family, reminding him of student days in Wiltshire, over-conscious as he was of the official attitude of post-war distrust. One day Elizabeth proposed that they should all visit the races at Ascot Heath and, as her steward Ernest King has put on record, Prince George demurred, thoughtful of public opinion. 'Do you think that's possible, Philip?' he asked. Philip responded, 'I'll ring up the King and find out,' and consent was given.

To heighten the Edinburghs' hospitality, Philip's naval confrère, Mike Parker, with the actor and wildfowler James Robertson-Justice and David Milford-Haven were apt to arrive at weekends for cricket on the wide expanse of lawn.

Then 'Dolla' arrived, with her sixteen-year-old daughter, another Margarita, from Cranborne Chase girls' school in Dorset, and her fifteen-year-old son Max from Gordonstoun, fair-haired and engagingly like the schoolboy Philip.

Although undoubtedly enjoying her 'retirement', Elizabeth absurdly complained at times of neglecting her duties, mingled with satisfaction that Jock Colville was sedulously building up further tours of Lancashire, Wales and Northern Ireland for the following year. As a pivot in establishing an Edinburgh Household – Sir Frederick Browning, the remarkable 'Boy' Browning, formerly of the first Grenadier Guards, the first Airborne Division and Chief of Staff with Mountbatten in South-East Asia – revelled in regarding himself as the Princess's faithful henchman. With so many family reunions, food rationing caused problems, and 'Boy' approved mysterious extras from Windsor Castle – milk, eggs, vegetables, pheasant and the like – with the bill then passed to him. Such are the mysterious ways of comptrollers. Known as 'Tommy' to his wife, he was soon Tommy to the Princess also, the first of the new-style warrior courtiers and friends whom she began to gather round her.

With a marked sense of physical well-being, and her sense of fitness, too, in the timing of events, Princess Elizabeth had thought that her baby might not arrive until 20 November, the first anniversary of her wedding. On the evening of 12 November, she drove with her husband to dine with his cousins, the Brabournes and Pammy, at the Mountbatten house in Chester Street. The Princess was in her most cheerful and animated mood, reassured that her father had successfully undergone a minor operation at the Palace that morning to relieve a blocked artery of his right leg.

She was convinced also that her midwife, Miss Rowe, was fussing unduly, yet Miss Rowe's mere reported presence at the Palace had brought an eager throng to the Palace gates. For the first time a traditional heralding of a royal birth was no longer available. The King had discovered that the customary attendance of a Minister of the Crown at such an event was neither laid down by statute nor could be properly claimed as a constitutional necessity, and after consulting the government it had been abolished in a phrase, 'It is merely the survival of an archaic custom, and the King feels that it is unnecessary to continue further.' After three centuries the Home Secretary was therefore spared his customary vigil, in this case of two days.

Like his mother twenty-two years earlier, Prince Charles was born on a night of London mist and rain. On Sunday 14 November, the Palace forecourt lamps came on, the police estimating that a crowd of 4,000 had gathered. As she had wished, the Princess awaited the event in her own room but, in light anaesthesia, she was presently wheeled to the Buhl Room on the Mall side of the Palace which, cleared of its formal furnishings, had been fitted as a surgery for the operation on the King two days earlier. So it chanced that a crucial episode in the latter days of George VI, the first of his three operations, was linked within sixty hours with the advent of the probable next king, his grandson.

Shortly before ten o'clock, the King's press secretary, Commander Colville, wrote out the first bulletin and took pride in carrying the framed notice across the forecourt to see it fixed to the railings: 'The Princess Elizabeth, Duchess of Edinburgh, was safely delivered of a Prince at 9.14 p.m. Her Royal Highness and her son are both doing well.' In the crowds, Robert Menzies – shortly to become Prime Minister of Australia for the second time – happened to be larking with his family, shouting 'most lustily and senselessly' for 'Philip' and 'Grandfather'. In the Palace, Philip had been feverishly playing squash with Mike Parker all evening, and now toasted 'a lovely 7 lb 6 oz boy'. From Marlborough House, despite the lateness of the hour, eighty-one-year-old Queen Mary drove over as the baby's first visitor 'delighted at being a great-grandmother', as she noted in her diary.

Within the week the Princess also began not the chore but the personal pleasure of writing to the many friends, who had offered congratulations. 'Don't you think he is quite adorable?' she wrote to a visitor who had seen the baby at four days old. 'I still can't believe he is really mine, but perhaps that happens to new parents. Anyway, this particular boy's parents couldn't be more proud of him. It's wonderful to think, isn't it, that his arrival could give a bit of happiness to so many people, besides ourselves, at this time?'

Each letter was separately slanted to its recipient. Among the princes and prelates, the monarchs and celebrities, was a message from her old music teacher, Mabel Lander. 'The baby is very sweet and we are enormously proud of him,' replied the Princess. 'Actually he has an interesting pair of hands for a baby, rather large but fine with long fingers, quite unlike mine and certainly unlike his father's. It will be interesting to see what they will become. . . .' Evidently the young parents found it amusing to read each other's letters for their actual self-confessed impressions. Cecil Beaton also noticed 'the remarkably long and pointed fingers' during the baby's first professional photo session at about a month old. Throughout the afternoon, Beaton recollected, the Princess sat by the cot, holding that interesting infant hand, 'watching with curiosity, pride and amusement'. To an elderly friend in Paris Philip described his son as 'bouncing with health and looking at present like a plum pudding', and Philip's benevolent god-father and uncle, old Prince George of Greece, was told the weight at birth with the comment, 'every ounce a treasure'.

The christening at the Palace on 15 December saw the King undertaking the longest walk since his doctors had advised him to rest, the brief distance from his apartments to the Music Room, 'tired and bored with bed', as he had written. As the youngest godparent, eighteen-year-old Princess Margaret held the baby Prince, 'quiet as a mouse', to present him to the Archbishop of Canterbury and announce the names Charles Philip Arthur George.

It now seems a remarkable link that no fewer than four of Queen Victoria's granddaughters watched the ceremony, among them Prince Philip's Milford Haven grandmother, vastly enjoying being the eldest sponsor at the age of eighty-five. With the King and Queen, the godparents included Lady Brabourne, David Bowes Lyon, the elderly Prince George of Greece as a figure from Philip's boyhood, and King Haakon of Norway, whose family name was Charles. The elderly ladies vied with one another in choosing christening gifts of long family tradition but 'Granny's cup' was surely best of all. 'I gave the baby a silver gilt cup and cover which George III had given to a godson in 1780,' Queen Mary triumphantly recorded, 'so that I gave a present from my great-grandfather to my great grandson 168 years later. . . .'

In including her husband's name, more than one guest felt that the young mother may have imaginatively conjured up a King Philip for the mid-twenty-first century. Nearly two years later, in christening their daughter Anne, it was thought that the Edinburghs were consciously reviving Stuart names. Philip said that the idea had not occurred to them. They had chosen merely the names they liked best, though giving some thought also to compliment the greatest number.

Prince Charles's christening heightened the Princess's impatience to get into Clarence House. She urged her Windlesham steward, 'Please call there tomorrow. We'll never get in unless we hurry them up,' and he returned with disgruntled tales of the service arrangements. 'Never mind, let's get in first', said Prince Philip, 'and put things right afterwards.'

Soon after Christmas the Princess fell ill at Sandringham with measles, and could go nowhere near the baby for three dismaying weeks. The new nanny seconded from the Gloucesters' household, Mrs Helen Lightbody, was fully at home in the old Sandringham nursery, and later in February the baby Charles was cradled in a make-do Palace guest-room. Then there was rejoicing. The Princess found Clarence House echoing with 'dozens of workmen hammering and sawing, all keen as mustard', a stack of pine mouldings in her sitting-room were suddenly assembled into a charming pine chimney-piece, and a corridor lined with gloomy panelling looked twice as wide with palest paint.

Husband and wife carefully watched the detail. Elizabeth one day discovered an effervescent craftsman embellishing a door-frame in florid gold, praised the quality and successfully persuaded him to try a softer gilding. In the dining-room, she wished for a certain delicate apple green, and obtained the exact shade by mixing a sample paint herself. The Queen, the present Queen Mother, mischievously enquired whether any finishing touch was missing from the drawing-room. Mystified, the couple could find nothing absent. A day or two later two chandeliers of eighteenth-century Waterford lustre glass appeared, the Queen's extra gift to the furnishing of the house.

The official move was at last made on 4 July, 'Independence Day', as Philip pointed out, though there was still much to be done. Elizabeth satisfied her exacting eye with the precise placing of clocks and mirrors, lamps and vases. Philip concerned himself with the hanging of pictures, including a corridor furnished with his new collection of original modern and mainly royal cartoons and caricatures by Lancaster, Giles, Strube and the like. Would the War of Independence have occurred if George III had thus hung Gillray?

Among the wedding presents, unexpected cheques provided

cash to commission a series of sixteen London drawings from the little-known Alan Carr Linford, an array of Topolski sketches and other arts expenditure. Early visitors to the new homestead noticed the absence of pictures borrowed from the Royal Collection: the emphasis was on contemporary landscapes and seascapes, and paintings by Duncan Grant, Paul Nash, Rowland Hilder and John Piper heightened the fresh and youthful atmosphere. 'The foremost impression is of a charming and quite informal home, of the sun streaming through large windows, with glimpses of flowers in the garden,' wrote Christopher Hussey that summer, 'the rooms themselves gay with colour and glints of gilding and crystal sparkling among walnut and mahogany.'

The personal expression of the Edinburgh's taste, indeed, drew enthusiasm from every visitor, and the Princess perhaps naïvely wished and felt it her duty to share the enjoyment with the people. No television at that time could satisfactorily display her home as the documentary TV series *Royal Family* and *Royal Heritage* were to do twenty and more years later. But one of the best-known descriptive writers of stately home literature, Christopher Hussey, was invited to describe and picture the house in detail, from the array of photographs and papers on the Princess's desk to the electric pastry-oven in the basement, the simple chintzy nursery and the Nash elegance of the drawing-room. Book or magazine readers could wander vicariously. Some measure of precious privacy was to be sacrificed to the camera. Never before had affectionate public curiosity been so generously gratified.

With weekends at Windlesham, further visits from her sisters-in-law, her increasing racing interests and a new programme of provincial tours, Elizabeth's married life assumed a pattern that appeared to extend indefinitely into the future. Philip had launched himself with energy into his usual presidency of the National Playing Fields Association, putting in regular working mornings at the Playing Fields offices in Buckingham Gate as if he had been a professional entrepreneur devoted to the business of providing or improving playing fields through the length and breadth of Britain.

When the Princess deputised for her father at the Trooping the Colour ceremony, her 'Clarry' staff were invited to gather in the hall as she came down the stairs dressed in the gold-braided cap and full riding skirt of her Grenadier Guards uniform. 'Do you like it?' she asked, like any girl showing off a new outfit. 'Now you see how I look on duty.' She looked grave, composed and unfamiliar, quite unlike the young mother sitting on the lawn with her baby on an afternoon off, 'carefully folding up the rug and collecting the toys when it was time for tea'.

If there were suggestions, carried forward from the emotional wear and tear that the couple had not been 'ready for Paris', the King now watched his daughter on the Horse Guards Parade with pride and satisfaction. Storm flies plagued her police horse, Winston, but she handled the golden chestnut with just sufficient rein and firmness. The refresher course in side-saddle technique had not been wasted.

Elizabeth was happier on a fractious horse than she was to be in vicious seas on the battleship *Anson* that same month when visiting the Channel Isles. She was violently seasick and General Browning doubted whether she was fit to land on the isle of Sark and went ashore to explain the situation. A doctor was summoned but, realising what was happening, the Princess roused herself. This was the first time any member of the Royal Family had ever visited little Sark officially. 'Of course I'm going,' she said, in that familiar phrase, 'I *won't* disappoint those poor people.' Again the motor torpedo-boat made its passage through the squally sea. Now in the trough of a wave, now on the crest, the Princess stumbled at last on to the quay. Yet she made her tour of the island, smiling, in a jolting horse carriage, 'enchanting in a summery lemon dress', as the Dame of Sark recorded, and the islanders little knew what the effort had cost her.

In this dukedom of Normandy, the Princess had undergone her baptism as a sailor's wife. Is she normally a good sailor? Conflicting reports suggest that 'it all depends'. But with the autumn of 1949 another separation was approaching. Philip had always planned to return to sea, arguing that he could not receive promotion without earning it, and early in October he left for Malta posted as first lieutenant to the destroyer *Chequers*. If his wife at heart hated this parting, friend Crawfie ventured to put in a reasoning word to reassure her. One could not expect the honeymoon to last for ever. A man has his own interests, a good wife realises that. The Princess had 'listened attentively'. But in November she waited only for Charles's first birthday and the orderly sequence of her engagement-book before flying out in good time for Christmas.

Malta was a new experience. The vine-hung terraces of the

Villa Guardamangia, where the Mountbattens were her hosts, the sunshine on the lemon trees, the narrow streets with their old palaces and churches seemed painted stage scenery, the street cries operatic. Elizabeth felt that she was playing at being a princess, visiting the local hospital, admiring the babies, flowers in her arms. A small world, for whom should she meet in one hospital but the sister who had nursed Margaret through appendicitis, and an air hostess who had belonged to her troop of the Sea Rangers. There were afternoons when she watched Philip playing polo, coached by Uncle Dickie, and evenings when they dined and danced at the Phoenicia Hotel. New adventure lurked even in having her hair done in a salon in the Prince of Wales Road.

Back at home again, Margaret listened eagerly to her exploits. In Philip's absence, the two sisters were flung together again, sharing public events and family intimacies. Elizabeth piloted Margaret to a debate in the Commons, a murder trial at the Old Bailey. After all, one should *know*. They went to Aintree together to watch the fortunes of Monaveen, Elizabeth's steeplechaser, and had the satisfying excitement of seeing him take every fence and come in fifth, when all but seven horses had fallen.

With Margaret in her twentieth year against her sister's twenty-three, the disparity in their ages had disappeared. Margaret was now pipeline to the parochial news of the Palace, the first to realise that Peter Townsend might be appointed Master of the Household, that he hoped to pilot an entry in her name in the King's Cup flying race, and in a different sisterly way the first to know that a baby had been conceived in Malta. Elizabeth ardently hoped it would be a girl.

Princess Anne was born at Clarence House on the sunny Monday morning of 15 August 1950. The accustomed doctors and the same Sister Rowe tended Elizabeth, and again the same crowds laid affectionate siege to the gates. The private secretary now was Martin Charteris, gleefully improving on the courtesy of Buckingham Palace in drafting the bulletin, 'Her Royal Highness the Princess Elizabeth, Duchess of Edinburgh, was safely delivered of a Princess at 11.50 a.m. today. Her Royal Highness and her daughter are both doing well.' The first three words had been omitted from Commander Colville's royally experienced bulletin on the advent of Prince Charles the previous year.

On leave from Malta, the Duke of Edinburgh telephoned the King at Balmoral and then called his grandmother and mother at Kensington Palace. 'It's the sweetest girl.' The baby weighed 6 lb. Seven days later the Duke was at Balmoral, rabbiting over Tulloch with the King, Elizabeth having insisted he should not waste his leave. Seven days more, and he was back in London to register the birth of 'Anne Elizabeth Alice Louise' and to receive her ration book and identity card, still the necessary perquisites even of a Princess of the Welfare State five years after the Second World War.

When Princess Elizabeth went to Scotland with her sturdy son and tiny daughter in mid-September, the Duke had returned to Malta to take up his command of the new frigate *Magpie*, but he flew back to London – bringing his Maltese steward Vincent Psaila – for the christening on 21 October. These minutiae of travel merit chronicling to illustrate how the speed of flying and increasing informality of royal train travel were heightening the easy freedom of royal movement. Prince Philip's eldest sister, Princess Margarita of Hohenlohe-Langenburg, was also an important visitor as a godmother at the christening, sharing the responsibilities of sponsorship with the Queen, Princess Alice (of Athlone), Earl Mountbatten, and Andrew Elphinstone. The miserable rifts of war were pleasantly lessening. Elizabeth was increasingly to welcome her sisters-in-law at Clarence House, and with them a happy coming and going of nephews and nieces. In particular, Princess Sophie of Hanover, now had a second son, Prince George, divided by only a month or two from Princess Anne.

Again, it was Cecil Beaton, not shy but nervous and engaging, who took the first photographs of the baby, with the Princess 'a monument of serenity and patience', as he said later, now holding the baby on her lap, now on a sofa, moving about the room and presently suggesting, 'Put her on this arm. I think this arm would be happier.' At one moment small Prince Charles wriggled within focus, kissing his sister and creating an enchanting photograph. 'Delicious! Most fortunate in every way!' the Princess rhapsodised on seeing the proof.

A State Visit by Queen Juliana and Prince Bernhard prevented a second wedding anniversary in Malta, but the Edinburghs were in Valetta within the week. Windlesham Moor having been relinquished, the Villa Guardamangia was directly leased in the Princess's name. Plate and linen were shipped out; Brigadier Stanley Clark, the Sotheby's adviser, noted 'a car, forty large cases of clothes and personal effects, and also a new polo pony'. To Queen Frederica of Greece the Princess described the new plan as 'like having a flat in London and a house by the sea'. No sooner was Christmas celebrated than Philip inaugurated another romantic adventure. His new command, the frigate *Magpie*, offered no convenient accommodation for Elizabeth but the despatch vessel *Surprise* made a suitable royal yacht, and off they sailed to Athens at the invitation of Queen Frederica and her beloved husband King 'Palo'.

The voyage shines in memory and anecdote. *Surprise* by radio to *Magpie*, 'Princess full of beans'. Message from *Magpie*, 'Can't you give her something better?' The Princess interposed with a Biblical quote, 'One Samuel 15', 'What meaneth this bleating of the sheep?' She had found her sea legs this time, untroubled by the 'short, steep and nasty seas' during a heavy storm, and even enjoying the excitement. In more placid waters Mike Parker suggested she should on no account miss the dawn over the crags of Patras. Sunrise however was miscalculated by an hour and the Princess came up to the bridge in pitch darkness, contentedly brewing tea before the show.

The visit to Athens had been envisaged as unofficial, but the city turned out to be decorated *en fête*, with cheerful crowds forming a welcoming avenue to watch their King Paul driving his guests to the Palace and then, more privately, to family lunch at Tatoi. Days of delicious tourism followed: the climb to the creamy vision of the Parthenon, the steps to Philip's mother's house on the steep slope of the Lycabettus, and then an expedition unrecognised to the old taverna-filled quarter of the Plaka. Another day, a glimpse of the white marble temple of Poseidon on its lonely sea headland, and then an expedition farther afield to Delphi, so that Elizabeth of England walked the slopes of Parnassus and paid her tribute of admiration to the temple of Apollo. At every turn Philip delighted in recalling his boyhood scenes to his wife and it may be accounted a kindness that the Oracle revealed nothing of the future confronting them within a year.

Princess Margaret had spent a few days with her sister at the villa before Christmas, amused at Philip's work-and-play precepts of the ideally managed life. Early in February, Elizabeth flew home to find Martin Charteris ready with a two-month package of engagements perfectly demonstrating the theme, complete with a Malta weekend for the carnival. 'We are living like gypsies,' she wrote gaily, and in April celebrated her twenty-fifth birthday with her husband in Rome. Driving out to Tivoli, they energetically clambered about the staircases and fountains of the Villa d'Este, lunched happily on the terrace of a local restaurant and spent the drowsy afternoon exploring Hadrian's villa. It was an ideal day.

After the scramble around Margaret two years earlier, cameramen were not too troublesome. Staying at the British Embassy, the couple wandered in the Forum with minimum fuss. There was more criticism at home of a brief private visit to Pope Pius than of hours spent in St Peter's, exploring the narrow walks within the dome and the newly discovered street of ancient tombs in the foundations. A weekend was spent with Philip's aunt, Queen Helen of Rumania, at her villa near Florence, seizing an opportunity to visit the Pitti Palace and Uffizi. And then again the return to a working itinerary on which Martin lightly chaffed her as 'never a wasted minute'.

Early May saw the centenary of Prince Albert's Great Exhibition of 1851 celebrated by the no less constructive brio of the Festival of Britain, the south bank of the Thames embroidered by the temporary marvel of the Dome of Discovery and the pencil-thin temporary Skylon. The King inaugurated the Festival from the steps of St Paul's, and had seemed to be recovering in health. But towards the end of the month he fell ill with influenza and the Princess was an effective deputy during the State Visit of King Haakon of Norway. Amid the magnificence of the State Banquet at Buckingham Palace, her great-uncle listened to her speech of welcome with grave demeanour and twinkling eyes. Upstairs, coughing in his bedroom, her father needed no reassurance that she had handled it all superbly.

A day or two later, the King watched by television as his daughter again acted for him at the Trooping the Colour. The decision that she should take the salute had been made months beforehand. This was the occasion when the Princess dramatically appeared in her Guards scarlet jacket and dark riding skirt, as Grenadiers Colonel-in-Chief, the details

Edmund Brock: Princess Elizabeth aged five (The portrait from the morning-room at 145 Piccadilly)

Stella Marks: The Duchess of Edinburgh (Prince Philip directly commissioned this miniature portrait of his bride)

Alfred Lawrence: A pastel study of about 1950

Sir James Gunn: State Portrait of The Queen in her Coronation Robes

Timothy Whidborne: The Queen as Colonel-in-Chief of the Irish Guards, 1968

Douglas Anderson: A portrait of the Queen aged thirty-seven, commissioned by the Royal Scots Dragoon Guards from the Scottish artist. Her Majesty holds an invitation from her Regiment

Wallace King: A portrait by an American painter, 1972, presented to the State of North Carolina

Terence Cuneo: The Queen with some of her favourite dogs, l to r, her corgi Windsor Brush, her crossbred dachshund Tinker, the labradors Harvey and Sherry, 1975

William Narraway: 'I asked to paint the Queen as if approaching guests'. The original portrait (1976) was destroyed by fire

Pietro Annigoni: Painted in 1954, the artist's first portrait of the Queen depicts her in the cloak and insignia of the Order of the Garter. 'I tried to paint Her Majesty looking into the future'

planned even to mounting a dummy horse saddled and bridled within the Palace for the King's inspection. With his passion for regimental correctness, he was concerned with the design of her bearskin tricorne hat, and murmured to Aage Thaarup, the milliner, that it was not at all what he expected. But his amiable nod expressed his satisfaction.

In June, however, a bombshell fell. As the King wrote to Queen Mary, 'I have a condition on the left lung . . . the photographs showed a shadow. . . .' For Philip and Elizabeth their assured vision of the roving life between London and Malta faltered in a directive of indefinite leave. Aboard *Magpie* Philip glumly watched his white uniforms packed away. 'Saturday 21 July. Left Malta at 7 a.m., feeling very sad' runs the entry in a journal kept by a member of his staff.

Meanwhile, a long discussed proposal for the couple to visit Canada had swollen from a ten-day trip to three cities to a coast-to-coast tour, embracing towns, villages, hospitals, regiments, pulp-mills and parks. 'I will do whatever they want' was the Princess's only comment, as each provincial government extended its schedule. The maps and plans of the journey could no longer be spread over desks and tables, and when Lester Pearson, the Canadian Minister for External Affairs, flew to London, he found himself at Clarence House with the enthusiastic Edinburghs 'crawling over a huge map unrolled on the floor'.

To their elders the programme seemed choked and complex beyond physical capacity. They were to leave on the liner *Empress of France* on 25 September. When suddenly the King's health showed an unexpected decline and his surgeons advised the need of a lung resection. The Edinburghs' sailing was at first postponed and then cancelled at a sympathetic and earnest request from Ottawa. The King, however, progressed satisfactorily. 'Very thin but very plucky', Queen Mary described him. The tour was, after all, decided upon and after a backstage tussle with the Cabinet on the risks of flying the Atlantic, an experience then unknown to royals, the Edinburghs flew out by BOAC airliner on 8 October. It is doubtful whether the Princess realised that her father had cancer. Under the circumstances, it was mere routine that she should carry a sealed envelope containing, as she knew, a draft Accession Declaration, no more unusual than the black outfit always packed for contingencies with her wardrobe. The tour indeed was now also to include a side-trip to visit President Truman in the United States, so confident were the doctors of the King's progress.

It was not to be another over-emotional visit as in Paris three years earlier. After a score of sustained tours at home, the Princess was confidently ready for anything, even if Philip's response was less certain. The extraordinary press coverage was to include 125 accredited correspondents on the royal train, and no fewer than 4,500 additional passes had been sought to cover one phase or another. In Ottawa a reception for 400 correspondents appeared to be attended by 600 extra relatives, 'My wife, Ma'am, my husband, my daughter. . . !' At one reception Philip growled, 'This is a waste of time!' finding himself shaking hands with recognisable faces enjoying a second time round. So numerous were the mayors, reeves and municipal councillors that the Canadian press itself urged that too many brass-hats were seeking attention. Whereupon Philip cleared his throat for another speech to point out that since his wife could not meet all the Canadian people, 'it was right and proper to meet their elected representatives'.

Quebec was astonished that the Princess spoke French perfectly. Ottawa spectators wept when a golden-haired little girl who had just presented a bouquet stood with her head leaning against the Princess's side, like a poignant symbol, during the singing of 'O Canada'. One correspondent cabled an account of a day that included thirteen functions, two speeches, an official luncheon and a State dinner. Through it all, of course, the Princess was reliably 'smiling, gracious and untired'. Behind the scenes, there came a reassuring letter from the King patterned very like another he had written at that time. 'Everything has gone according to plan and I have been most beautifully looked after. I have been sitting up in a chair and have had my meals up as well. So I am getting stronger and can walk to the bathroom.' Elizabeth's high spirits at this good news lightened her whole personality. That night she gaily joined in the square-dancing at Government House, a dance so impromptu that Bobo had to dash to a department store for a suitably Canuck skirt and blouse, and Philip hodowned with the price tag still visible on his jeans. Enjoying themselves thoroughly, they allowed no time to change and drove to the station still in their square-dancing rig, to the delight of the crowds.

The Princess liked to see the local papers night and morning, although the frenetic build-up usually bothered her. Aware of the thousands who waited for the merest glimpse, she ordered her car to circle stadium areas twice and to slow down to 4 m.p.h. wherever people had gathered. Philip complained that the deafening motorcycle escort hid her from the public and Philip had it reduced. When he took up the idea of a bubble top to enable people to see her in bad weather, Toronto aircraft operatives produced it within a day. The *Toronto Star* had waspishly enquired, 'How Can She Leave the Children?' Now it flooded the streets with special editions.

The trip developed, in fact, into a national jamboree, and the tour train's whistle-stop progress across the prairies was matched by the skylarking aboard when Philip's valet, John Dean, produced a shopping bag full of practical jokes, and his purchases were commandeered. Rubber snakes leapt from tins of nuts, bread rolls squeaked, ferocious imitation spiders appeared. 'We heard screams of laughter as the Duke chased his wife along the corridor wearing particularly horrible joke teeth,' wrote Dean. 'A mock bell-push gave an electric shock. But by then the Princess examined every unfamiliar gadget with suspicion.' At every level-crossing, or at the cue of the train whistle, they hurried to the observation platform where their obvious happiness equalled the mood of the jubilant throngs. In the Middle West, people waited in a blizzard, and a Calgary welcoming committee wrapped the visitors in electric blankets to enable them to sit warmly outdoors at night and watch a rodeo.

Back in the east, the Princess acknowledged the flop of a little joke on Niagara Falls, 'It looks rather damp.' Local patriots looked so mortified that she hurriedly had to add the requisite 'But it's marvellous! Magnificent!' Their two-day visit to Washington, with its intensive security, gave a first impression that in the land of the free there were more police than people. Privately the Princess noticed with glee that her visit shared editorial honours in *Life* magazine with a gangster's funeral. In the limited time they took in the sights, going as far as Mount Vernon, and admirably suffered the now over-familiar ordeal of being a sight themselves. The British Embassy reception had allotted two hours to shake hands with 1,600 guests, and the press descriptions supported the statistical evidence, right to the Princess's concluding hand-shake with an aged Embassy messenger, and final courtesy in thanking the bandleader (practically unheard) for his music. A Washington columnist gratifyingly summed up opinion. 'Royalty would not suit this country's scheme of things, but how glad we are for the British that they have a Princess so capable.'

In Canada again, in the swing of the homeward tour from New Brunswick to Newfoundland, only personal highlights remain in retrospect, the broadly smiling young mayor content to hand over a typescript and say, 'The speech, Ma'am,' the mayor who insisted on singing a ballad of welcome. Nature herself fittingly brought the tour to a crescendo as the visitors left St John's in a tender which was soon swept end to end by heavy seas. Remarkably, Prince Philip succumbed, though Elizabeth was unaffected, an immunity she retained throughout the gales encountered by their liner *Empress of Scotland* on the voyage home.

Throughout the tour the Princess had continued to receive her airmail copy of *The Times* and *Hansard's Parliamentary Reports* and conscientiously somehow found time to read them through. She was nevertheless unprepared for the trays of personal press clippings awaiting her in London, bulking more in column space than any other event of her career. Said Mr Churchill in grand hyperbole at the welcome-home Guildhall banquet, 'None has surpassed in, um, brilliance, and, um, in living force, the mission you have just discharged. The whole nation is grateful to you and . . . to Providence . . . for having endowed you, um, with the gifts and personality. . . .'

The widespread satisfaction delighted the King, yet again observing the fruit of his own training. As his biographer, Sir John Wheeler-Bennett has said, 'In Princess Elizabeth he saw emerge certain of his own traits . . . his own combination of humour and dignity, his penetrating mind, his pragmatic common sense, his eagle eye for detail and his deep devotion to public service. All these things pleased him. . . .'

However, the King at last acknowledged that he would be unable to face the long proposed tour to New Zealand and Australia, and arrangements were now complete for Elizabeth and Philip to undertake it instead while he could cruise on a quiet private visit to South Africa in the sunshine. Studying the agreed Australian itinerary, Elizabeth may well have echoed her father's cry in 1947, 'It's astonishing what they expect of us!' Seeking to compromise with her insistence that every wish on the part of her hosts should be met, Martin Charteris presented a document of subdivided columns with every day and hour meticulously accounted. On 7 February the royal travellers were to board the liner *Gothic* at Mombasa for a week of official engagements in Ceylon (Sri Lanka), inaugurating the tour that was never to be. But first the Princess had agreed to spend a holiday week in Kenya.

Her parents had at last persuaded her to see the wonderland they had described so often, and with her father's Christmas gift of a movie camera she planned to make a film to show him the scenery and wild life he remembered so well from the visit early in his marriage. A day of intense happiness occurred at Sandringham when he chanced to put his walking-stick to his shoulder and remarked, 'I believe I could shoot now', and on New Year's Day 1952, indeed, the King enjoyed a shoot around Heath Farm with Philip, the royal secretary Michael Adeane and others, and made the laconic entry in his game book '101 pheasants, 11 rabbits. Fine and cold. Birds flew well.'

Elizabeth and her mother, reassured, played truant a few days later to go racing at Hurst Park. Then every passing day became precious, seeming to give a last opportunity in five months to enjoy the sturdy three-year-old Charles and the seventeen-month-old 'totters' of little Anne. The evening of 30 January saw a happy family theatre party with Elizabeth, Philip, Margaret and the King and Queen at Drury Lane as a *bon voyage* celebration. The musical show, *South Pacific*, had been the King's choice; and the royal group were moved by their own prolonged ovation. Next day the Edinburghs were due to leave London airport at noon for an overnight flight to Nairobi, and the King and Queen dared the January chill to come and see them off. The final photograph of the tired and haggard King George VI has been seen perhaps too often, and we are too seldom shown the happy picture of Princess Elizabeth framed in the doorway of the airliner, gaily smiling and waving in unclouded farewell.

The next day it caused local pleasure that the Princess should be visiting her first African hospital within twenty-four minutes after leaving the plane. The maternity hospital was new and, four hours earlier, had housed not a single patient. A selection of expectant and recuperating mothers

133

and babies, borrowed from other institutions, helped, however, to produce the requisite effect and fill every bed. In such sharp contrast to the London chill, a theatrical first impression of Nairobi was unavoidable: the African women in their flamboyant headbands lining the streets, the exotic blooms, the vast colourful Afro-European crowd at a garden party where, as a reporter cabled, 'fellows in leopard skins were eating cream buns next to women dressed for Ascot'. The next day the Princess fulfilled her ambition to visit the game reserve of the Nairobi National Park. With her 16 mm film camera, she was particularly charmed by the small and shy dik-diks, a predilection endearing to the game-warden, more accustomed to people interested only in lions. However, the Princess had never previously seen an African lion, and in the Nairobi reserve she was able to film one with its kill ten yards from her bush wagon. 'This has broken my luck,' she said.

The following morning, the royal party – with Pamela Mountbatten and Bobo, Martin Charteris and Mike Parker – packed into cars for the ninety miles drive up country to Sagana Lodge, Nyeri. This had been a wedding present from the people of Kenya, a cedarwood bungalow pleasantly reminiscent of the little house in the grounds of Royal Lodge. The travellers were coated in red dust long before the lodge was reached, laughing at each other's discomfiture, yet from the windows of the Lodge one could gaze rewardingly at the snow-capped peak of Mount Kenya, and the garden ran steeply down by zigzag paths to the tumbling Sagana river.

The stay was full of African alarums and excursions: a herd of elephants came near and the Princess dashed to take pictures, a wild elephant was loose in the night in the compound and the staff were alerted in case marauding baboons should break in and try to eat the new lampshades. This had already happened not far away, at the resthouse of Treetops, where the Princess was to spend the nights of 5–6 February, and she prudently decided to forego a wish to raise her personal banner there in case a baboon should steal it.

Destined to be written into history, the fame of Treetops, Mr Sherbrooke Walker's hotel-in-a-tree, was already worldwide, though in those days it consisted of little more than a dining-room, three bedrooms and an observation balcony built into the branches of a giant wild fig-tree, thirty feet above the ground. On 5 February, the Princess spent the morning watching the Duke play polo some miles away, and they arrived at the forest path approaching Treetops shortly before three o'clock. As soon as Elizabeth stepped from her car, she heard the trumpeting of angry elephants in the forest ahead and the sounds grew more awe-inspiring as the royal party made their way in single file along the 600-yard approach trail through the dense bush.

Watching for her from the observation platform, the hunter, Jim Corbett, has told how a herd of forty-seven elephants chanced to mass in the glade below him only a few minutes before the Princess came into view. Among them, three jealous bulls began screaming with rage, and presently were crowded within ten yards of the foot of the access ladder to Treetops when Princess Elizabeth appeared with her guide. A white pillowcase was fluttering as a danger signal; but a hurried consultation between her escorts decided that the Princess should go on, and, unhurried and undeterred, she made her way towards the elephants – and the ladder – over the open ground. Hastening to greet her, Jim Corbett was to reflect that he had seen some cool acts of courage, but few to compare with this. A minute or two more and the Princess was on the balcony and soon busily filming the elephants, which milled about below her for over an hour.

When tea-time came the Princess remained so absorbed that she asked if she could have a cup where she sat. In the clearing below her, two-thirds of it lake, the rest the hard-trodden ground of salt-lick, she had seen a cow elephant suckle its young, while a family of twelve baboons came from the forest and one bold female climbed to the balcony to be rewarded with a sweet potato while Elizabeth promptly filmed her in close-up. Two male waterbuck raced from the forest in a desperate battle, ending their combat in a mêlée of splashing in the lake, where one mortally impaled the other with its horns and then defiantly trotted off. Five warthogs and a dainty doe bushbuck came to browse, and the Princess alternately used her movie camera and scribbled elaborate notes for her intended commentary, often exclaiming how much her father would have enjoyed the scene.

As the shadows lengthened and the frogs became vocal, more animals than had ever been seen before at Treetops – as Corbett noted – emerged on the open ground. In the sunset, as the group talked in low voices, the Princess affectionately told Corbett of her father's shooting prowess. She knew precisely where he had been shooting at Sandringham that day and where he intended to shoot the next day, and Colonel Corbett was to record that 'the young Princess who spoke of her father that night with such affection and pride never had the least suspicion that she would not see him again'.

At dinner a contretemps occurred when the spirit-lamp for the coffee was accidentally swept from the table, setting light to the straw matting on the floor, and frantic efforts were made to stamp out the blaze before the African steward calmly extinguished it with a wet cloth and the peril dissolved in laughter. Afterwards, from the balcony, the Princess could see nine rhino on the salt-lick, half lit by a flood-lamp that simulated the moon, and remained with her husband and her friends looking into the night.

Part Three

Her Majesty Queen Elizabeth II

'We do now hereby with one voice and Consent of Tongue and Heart publish and proclaim that the High and Mighty Princess Elizabeth Alexandra Mary is now, by the death of our late Sovereign of Happy Memory, become Queen Elizabeth the Second, by the Grace of God Queen of this Realm and of all Her other Realms and Territories, Head of the Commonwealth, Defender of the Faith, to whom her lieges do acknowledge all Faith and constant Obedience, with hearty and humble Affection. . . .'

*The proclamation of
Queen Elizabeth II,
8 February 1952*

10

Queen Regnant

On the morning of Wednesday 6 February Elizabeth was up at the first dawn light, waiting with a light-meter until the first rays of the sun should improve her picture of two quarrelsome rhino in the clearing below. She was fresh, 'with eyes sparkling', after only a few hours sleep. Kenya time is three hours ahead of Greenwich and no-one can know whether she was now Princess or Queen. (Between 9 and 10 a.m., when the royal lady left Treetops, the servants at Sandringham House had not attempted to disturb the King in his sleep.) 'It's been my most thrilling experience yet,' she said, as she bade goodbye to her hosts. 'Ma'am, if you have the same courage in facing whatever the future sends you', replied Mr Walker 'as you have in facing an elephant at ten yards, we are going to be very fortunate.' His guest smiled, the Duke laughed, and the car sped away.

The royal couple spent the rest of the morning fishing for trout in the ice-cold Sagana stream, and after an early lunch retired for a short siesta. At about 1.30 p.m. local time, Major Charteris had just finished lunch at the Outspan Hotel just across the valley and was on the point of leaving for a visit of his own to Treetops, when he was summoned to the telephone booth. Here he was confronted by a local reporter, who, white as chalk, said abruptly, 'The King is dead. It seems he died in his sleep.'

The news had come in a Reuter newsagency flash to Nairobi, but no official confirming message had come, for the Governor of Kenya and his staff were all on the train for Mombasa. While Major Charteris tried to contact the deserted Government House, nothing was said, and the tragic tidings were still unconfirmed, when the Queen strolled out to find Bobo and to say that she and the Duke would be riding earlier than usual next morning. At a radio set, Mike Parker failed to intercept any announcement, though the tone of the programmes suggested that his information was true. Nearly an hour had passed before he went round to the wide window of the lodge and beckoned urgently to Prince Philip, who came out and was told what had happened. 'He looked as if you'd dropped half the world on him,' Parker remembers. Then Philip went back into the Lodge and he broke it to his unsuspecting young wife that her father was dead and that she was Queen.

Major Charteris has said that she bore the shock bravely, 'like a Queen'. In a little while, she sat down to write messages to her mother and her sister, and to Queen Mary and the Duke of Gloucester. She called Bobo and asked whether mourning had been packed in her wardrobe. (Always carried against a Court contingency, it was with her luggage on the *Gothic*.) Then the Queen sat down again to write a series of telegrams to her various expectant hosts in the Dominions, regretting that her visit must be not cancelled but indefinitely postponed. While she thus stifled the first shock of grief in these tasks at her desk, it fell to Major Charteris as her private secretary to ask by what name she wished to be known as Queen.

'Oh, my own name – what else?' she answered.

The question then was whether it would be correct to sign her telegrams 'Elizabeth R' (Regina) before the calling of the Accession Council. Charteris had translated a cipher telegram which arrived requesting her permission to call the first part of the Council, for her Proclamation, and the new Sovereign agreed that her queenly signature would be constitutionally correct. Pale but composed during this discussion, she presently could not trust herself to speak, and her husband led her away from the house and along the bank of the stream where they had fished so happily that morning . . . that abyss of time.

Fortunately, the new Queen had not long to delay before beginning the journey back to London. At five o'clock all was ready for departure from the lodge. A Dakota aircraft was waiting at Nanyuki airfield, forty miles away, for the Mombasa flight planned to leave the following morning. But first the Queen summoned each member of the staff who had attended her, the cook and houseboy, the Askari officers and police and drivers, to give each of them a signed photograph and a gift. Her African chauffeur flung himself down to kiss her feet. All along the dusty roads to Nanyuki, Africans stood with bowed heads, offering their silent tribute of sympathy. Did the Queen remember as she travelled, did she know, the strange circumstance that also in the month of February in Kenya, in the year before she was born, her father had similarly ended a holiday in haste and sped along the African roads on learning of the death of a friend?

At the airfield, precisely on the Equator, the waiting contingent of local newspaper cameramen were asked not to take photographs, and the cameras were respectfully lowered. The Queen was still wearing a flowered frock with white hat and gloves and with royal habit she managed to briefly smile and wave as she entered the waiting Dakota. Then the Dakota took off into the darkened sky and those left behind knew that they had taken part in a moment of history.

There was very little conversation in the cabin of the aircraft on the 500-mile flight to Entebbe. The sky was spangled with brilliant stars and bush fires gleamed in patches of crimson in the darkness below. The pilot received a warning forecast of thunderstorms; and presently a radio message from Mr Winston Churchill, her Prime Minister, was delivered to the Queen at her seat. 'The Cabinet in all things awaits Your Majesty's command.' At Entebbe airport, the Queen was met by Sir Andrew Cohen, Governor of Uganda, and his wife, who were in deep mourning (as it chanced not primarily for the late King, but for a family bereavement). Then an anticipated thunderstorm broke with tropical violence, and the plane to London was delayed for an interminable wait of three hours.

It was nearly midnight local time before the Queen and her husband walked across the wet tarmac for the take-off, and they retired at once to their sleeping berths in the rear cabin. The early hours of 7 February saw a touchdown for refuelling at El Adem, and after breakfast the time dragged as they crossed the Mediterranean and sighted the Alps. Presently the Queen appeared in the black coat and dress that had been brought from the *Gothic*. It was the same aircraft from which she had waved farewell to her father only a week before, and now she concerned herself with the shock to her mother and sister. In the late February afternoon, as the aircraft landed at London airport, she could see the black-clad group of statesmen, drawn up awaiting her, and the Duke of Gloucester and Lord and Lady Louis Mountbatten first came aboard. 'Shall I go down alone?' said the Queen, realising that this indeed she must do, and Prince Philip and the others drew back out of sight until she had descended the stairway. Beside the plane, Mr Churchill, Mr Eden, Mr Attlee, and Lord Woolton were next to acknowledge her, in that order, as Privy Counsellors. As Lord Woolton recalled, 'This symbolic scene . . . the new young Queen coming, unattended, down the gangway from her plane – was one that will never be forgotten. . . . It was a period of deep emotion for everyone – and most certainly for the Queen, and yet, having shaken hands with each member of her Council, instead of going to her waiting car, she went along and spoke to the air crew – royal courtesy took precedence over private grief.'

The Queen wore no veil and her face was still unveiled to the people as she reached Clarence House at five o'clock. There Queen Mary was waiting to pay homage. 'Her old Granny and subject', Queen Mary had said, 'must be the first to kiss her hand.' The Duke of Norfolk was also waiting to see her, his hereditary duty as Earl Marshal being concerned with the funeral. Which day should be chosen? Was it to be a naval occasion? Within twenty minutes he had cleared from the Queen's mind the massive problems which had beset her in the plane. Details fell into place in his grasp as readily as in her own.

The following morning Queen Elizabeth held her first Privy Council at St James's Palace, walking quite alone and unattended from the old Throne Room into the Entrée Room where Privy Counsellors, dressed in mourning, were awaiting her. All made her a deep obeisance. The young Queen was twenty-five years and ten months old and nearly all those present were at least twice as old, other than her husband. She was 'very serious, but completely composed'. Walking to the table she took up the copy of her Declaration, which had been mounted on a board, and read it 'in a clear and controlled voice', as Lord Woolton noted:

'Your Royal Highnesses, My Lords, Ladies and Gentlemen,

'On the sudden death of my dear father I am called to fulfil the duties and responsibilities of Sovereignty. . . .

'My heart is too full for me to say more to you today than that I shall always work, as my father did throughout his reign, to uphold the constitutional Government and to advance the happiness and prosperity of my peoples, spread as they are the world over.

142

'I know that in my resolve to follow his shining example of service and devotion, I shall be inspired by the loyalty and affection of those whose Queen I have been called to be, and by the counsel of their elected Parliaments. I pray that God will help me to discharge worthily this heavy task that has been laid upon me so early in my life.'

Her grandfather, as a man in his mid-forties, had found his speech to the assembled Counsellors the most trying ordeal of his life. Lord Wootton considered that the young Queen showed 'magnificent self-control'. Mr Churchill was later to speak of 'too much care on that young brow'. Dr Garbett, the Archbishop of York, thought that she spoke clearly and directly 'and showed such great self-possession, such modesty and simple dignity that I am certain all who were present went away with the knowledge that the Queen has not only charm but the other and greater qualities necessary'. When she had withdrawn, all the Privy Counsellors left the Palace, in Lord Woolton's words, 'in a spirit of optimism and confidence for the new reign'.

Shortly afterwards, in her own room at Clarence House, the Queen watched her Proclamation by television as no other monarch had ever done and heard the change in the royal title that had been agreed at the Commonwealth Conference three months earlier, proclaiming her head of the Commonwealth. After lunch, leaving for Sandringham by car, she could note, almost anonymously, the remarkable token of respect for the late King shown by her people. Nearly every man was wearing a black tie, as if for his own brother. When the Duke of Norfolk, duty-bound as Earl Marshal, issued an order 'that all persons do put themselves into mourning', he unwittingly produced a howl of wrath and execration for a 'peremptory order . . . both intrusive and silly', showing 'an unawareness of ordinary feeling'. Such was the outspoken and immediate temper of the new reign.

At Sandringham the body of the late King remained on his divan bed, in case the Queen should wish to see him, and she thanked her mother but declined. Such was her clear understanding of the memories she wished to cherish and of the limits of her emotional control. . . .

The funeral of King George VI was held at St George's Chapel, Windsor, in the wan sunlight of 15 February 1952. In three days nearly a third of a million people had filed past the catafalque in Westminster Hall, and each evening posies of little flowers, forbidden by the police but surreptitiously carried in, strewed the grey carpet. The Queen paid a visit for a short time to stand unnoticed at a side door, the mourning tableau of State so like the sombre scene she remembered for her grandfather in her childhood that past and present merged. At Windsor the cry 'God Save the Queen!' followed the committal, and the Queen made her last reverent curtsey. The epilogue was to be spoken three years later, in pouring London rain, when she unveiled the memorial to King George VI in the Mall. 'Much was asked of my father in personal sacrifice and endeavour. He shirked no task, however difficult, and to the end he never faltered in his duty. . . .'

Walking down the steps of St George's Chapel, she was already an accustomed Queen. On the very day of her Accession there had been documents to sign. Within the week there were appointments to approve, a new judge in Hong Kong, appointments to the court of the Bank of England, audiences with Prime Ministers and High Commissioners. At Clarence House, during that first dreadful week, a succession of European mourners called at Clarence House and stayed to luncheon. 'Both Elizabeth and Philip tried to be casual,' wrote King Peter of Yugoslavia. 'Everything was bottled up, suppressed. Yet every texture of their lives has been shattered, every hope banished. They told me they felt anaesthetised, living in a vacuum. They cannot yet see how anything can work out, and neither can I.'

Queen and husband turned to their familiar desks as to an opiate. The Prime Minister made his first report on 12 February, a letter on proceedings in the House reached Her Majesty daily, and she began a series of audiences with her Ministers. With every minute closely charted she missed no opportunity to give love and companionship to her bereaved mother and to Margaret. She called on the stricken Queen Mary every other day, and in late afternoon she sought out the nursery as her source of strength. Husband and wife indeed both drew the first grains of comfort from their usual hour with the children. And before long the Queen could not help but be stimulated by the brisk confidence in the new reign that ran through the nation, responsive to the dawn of a new Elizabethan age.

In mid-March, when Queen for less than six weeks, she

held her first investiture at Buckingham Palace, with the Duke of Edinburgh at her side. She had rehearsed with her father's naval sword, and that day fifty-one new knights received the accolade. Seven posthumous awards were also to be made to the next-of-kin of dead heroes, and the Queen decided to deal with these decorations first and received the parents and widows in an ante-room. So it came about that the widow of Flight-Lieut Alan Quinton received the first award from the Queen, a George Cross for an airman who had given an air cadet the only parachute in a crashing aircraft. Later that day, promptly linking her reign with that of Queen Victoria, the Queen also invested Private William Speakman with the Victoria Cross won for the highest courage in Korea. In April, the Queen ceremonially distributed the Maundy money at Westminster Abbey, and so performed her first public function outside the Palace walls. Her mother, henceforth to be known as Queen Elizabeth the Queen Mother, saw that her daughter had adopted her own maxim of 'Begin Gradually'. On her twenty-sixth birthday at Windsor, the Queen yielded her colonelcy of the Grenadier Guards precisely ten years after she had received it from her father, and only then, after two months, did she enjoy the first breathing space since the return from Kenya. In the privacy of Badminton, with the Duke and Duchess of Beaufort, she was able to watch the three-day Olympic Horse Trials, and so find that complete relaxed absorption and self-forgetfulness which horses had always offered her.

With her husband and sister, she found this so recuperative, indeed, that she whisked her mother away the following week on the pretext of looking at some horses at Beckhampton. The Queen subsequently found with dismay that her racing and sporting proclivities were to gain an undue share of attention: far less publicity was apt to attach to her enjoyment and knowledge of the paintings at Windsor Castle and Buckingham Palace. As E. S. Turner has summarised, 'All had their own idea of what the Court ought to be. Some wanted it to encourage art and letters, opera and music. . . . Some wanted the Queen to lay fewer foundation-stones and visit more colonies. . . . Others, again, wished [the Court] to discountenance blood sports or to show more respect for the Sabbath. Still others wanted to see the royal children sent to ordinary schools. A few thought it would be a gracious gesture to receive the Duchess of Windsor.'

The Queen was gradually to acquire the art of compounding

these differences. Meanwhile she had her father's advisers to guide her into the intricacies of statecraft, greying secretaries and officials such as Sir Alan Lascelles and Sir Ulick Alexander, whom the press impatiently dubbed the Old Guard, although the young Queen relied deeply upon their experience. Faced with a difficulty she would often ask, 'How would my father have handled this?' and so settle the matter.

Hopefully, both the Queen and Prince Philip could not help but clutch at the vestiges of their former Malta–London plan of life, grasping vainly at the thought that their appalling transition might not be so forlorn a change after all. With needful optimism they began to imagine themselves still living with some privacy at Clarence House while the Palace could function as the State headquarters of monarchy, with the widowed Queen Mother perhaps still residing in the private wing as she would prefer. As the paramount link between the Queen and her government, Alan Lascelles presented the prospect to Churchill in as favourable a light as possible. But the old man, approaching his eighties, taking an invincibly romantic view of the young Queen in her Palace, was emphatic that anything less would not do. In her youthful inexperience, the Queen supposed at first that she might win him round. But he proved adamant and by April the hopeful pretence had to be abandoned.

Some months earlier, the artist Edward Halliday had mentioned to Prince Philip his interest in painting some conversation pieces that might capture the atmosphere of a house and family at home. He had been encouraged to make sketches of the Princess's sitting-room as it would often be found at the family hour, with the children's books and toys scattered on the floor, and at half-past nine on the morning of 10 April the Queen and her husband gave him a forlorn and final sitting for his theme. The children were brought in, little Princess Anne played with her toys on the floor and three-year-old Prince Charles snuggled beside his mother with a picture book on the settee. The two corgis completed the family circle, and the table lamp was tilted to what the Queen called 'our angle'.

It was very literally the last hour at Clarence House. When Halliday had finished his sketches, the Queen and her husband left to attend the Maundy ceremony at Westminster Abbey and that evening they went to Windsor Castle, where they were to spend Easter. Ranking as a twenty-sixth birthday gift from Philip to his wife, the finished painting seemed bathed in a golden light, a synthesis of all their happiness at Clarence House. Years later, Prince Charles often admired it at Windsor and appropriated it for his own rooms not knowing its inner story – his favourite picture, as he says – a sequel his parents regard as tenderly appropriate.

With their possessions transferred, the Queen and her family moved into Buckingham Palace on 5 May. Through their last days at 'Clarence' they felt like being driven from Eden. Yet the old Palace seemed more homely and welcoming than they had expected. With the Queen Mother still in residence in her own suite, taking her time as most dowager queens have done, the royal couple moved into the Belgian Suite downstairs, as if repeating the makeshift of their early married life. The Queen preferred not to use her father's study and ultimately settled – in fact over a year later – into the pleasant bow-windowed sitting-room that had been her mother's. 'They lived for months in a welter of moving and furnishing decisions,' said an intimate of those days. 'There were always domestic issues to discuss until they reached, as they said, a firm perspective.' Such as, one wondered? The Queen Mother was devoted to a white marble fire-surround, a wedding anniversary gift from her husband, and the moving of similar household gods led into a multitude of problems, few fully solved until her move to Clarence House a month before the Coronation.

Meanwhile, with the conclusion of Court mourning, the first Coronation Council was held at the Palace under Prince Philip's chairmanship. The Queen lived in a busy whirl of secretaries, visitors, diplomats, politicians, architects, designers and portraitists. At one time, she went into brief formal residence at Holyroodhouse and then travelled to Devon for a 'visit of recognition' to the farms and manors owned by the Duchy of Cornwall, where every tiny village turned out to cheer and wave. In five months, Alan Lascelles reminded her, she carried out 140 engagements. Indeed, an inspired article in *The Lancet* suggested that her health and vitality should be protected from her hereditary sense of duty. The caution proved to be vividly justified when, two weeks later, shortly before an investiture, she was seized with a sharp attack of abdominal cramp. Princess Margaret was asked to be ready to act as deputy, but the Queen recovered sufficiently to undertake her programme before taking to her bed for the rest of the day. The passing indisposition sharpened the demand of a Parliamentary spokesman who pleaded, 'We should lighten her load by denying ourselves the pleasure of her frequent appearances at public functions.' So was the criticism against Queen Victoria completely reversed for her ebullient great-great-granddaughter.

Prince Philip, too, went down with jaundice and one of his intimates found him in bed, looking very disgusted and dejected, 'in his most depressing room, hung with paintings of Spanish grandees. . . .' The indignation of the doctors, however, produced no perceptible relaxation.

It has been said that Queen Elizabeth 'took to queenship as a duck to water'. It amused her to see the first Windsor milk-bottles with the initials E.R. and she said, laughing, she had not felt like a queen till then. She considered that royal profiles on postage stamps had in the past sometimes made the chin or forehead slope unnaturally and took her time in critically deliberating with the Duke of Edinburgh on her portraits from which a semi-profile was finally selected. Not unflattered by her postage stamps, the Queen later motored out to High Wycombe to examine the first sheets as they came off the press.

In the same spirit, when desiring Norman Hartnell to submit designs for her Coronation gown, she knew precisely what she wanted and instructed that it was to conform in line to her wedding dress and should be in white satin. Ultimately Mr Hartnell submitted nine designs, with samples of the intended floral emblems. All these, the Tudor Rose, the Thistle, the Shamrock and the Leek were the subject of infinite research and patient toil, but all the authority of Garter King of Arms did not foresee the Queen's 'wise and sovereign observation', as Hartnell royally put it, that she was unwilling to wear a gown bearing emblems of Great Britain without the emblems of the Dominions. So the lotus of Ceylon and India, the protea of South Africa, the wattle of Australia, the specific fern of New Zealand, the wheat and jute of Pakistan, and so on, were all worked into a floral garland for the triumphant, ninth final design.

From Marlborough House, Queen Mary contributed suggestions of Victorian precedents. In her eighty-sixth year, she confessed to growing more frail, feeling weary and unwell and directed the Duke of Norfolk that if she should no longer be of this world for the Coronation the ceremony should on no account be postponed. In a happy gesture which she knew would please her grandmama, the Queen elected to wear Queen Victoria's Parliamentary mantle of royal purple and ermine when opening her first Parliament, and Queen Victoria's diadem graced her brow. On the homeward journey, relaxed and exhilarated after duty accomplished, she was smiling gaily at some incident in the crowd when a press photographer captured one of the finest photographs of his career. The resulting picture of the young and happy Queen was widely reproduced and framed and hung in offices, clubs, schools, shops, hotels and restaurants throughout the world, making a small fortune for the cameraman Charles Dawson. (The Queen enquired his name.)

On the Palace balcony Prince Charles, then nearly four, was brought out for the first time to see the crowds with his two-year-old sister. And then characteristically, after a day of royal splendour, the Queen changed her clothes and took both the children off to the birthday party of two-year-old Viscount Lascelles in Bayswater, a homely celebration which had been deferred and timed to enable the Queen to be there.

One of the final formal events of Accession Year was a State dinner given for the seven Commonwealth Premiers and other delegates to the Commonwealth conference. If it could be said that no reigning Queen had opened Parliament for seventy years, no Sovereign so young had ever presided over a family so international and representative. For the Divine right of Kings Elizabeth was substituting a right to serve. Her very duties as Head of the Commonwealth were primarily unwritten, an embroidery canvas to be filled to the Queen's devising.

One may make these grandiloquent observations but the obverse side was noted by Norman Hartnell one December day when he motored up to Sandringham with seven of his ladies and assistants to present a collection of dresses for a distant Australian summer. In one of the Sandringham bedrooms the Queen and her mother and sister sat crowded side by side on a sofa at the foot of an enormous bedstead to watch the display, and the mannequins entered through a capacious white bathroom. Months before the Coronation the details of wardrobe planning were already being considered for the Commonwealth tour nearly a year ahead.

As the complex preparations for her Coronation lumbered under way, cumbrous and massive as the gold State Coach itself, the young Queen found that she had to iron out a major mistake. So short-sighted in retrospect, the Coronation Commission took a majority decision that no part of the ceremony should be televised. The new medium, it was felt, would detract from the religious solemnity of the occasion and the irretrievable watchfulness of the cameras would increase the strain upon the central figure. The result was of course uproar, 'a volume of public protest that surprised both the Court and Downing Street'.

Nor was public opinion to be mollified by Churchill's compromise proposal to the Commons that the processions would be televised west of the Abbey screen. Among the diehards, the Queen's Secretary, Alan Lascelles, later explained to Harold Nicolson that he regarded the monarch as the subject of a myth: dangerous, then, to allow arc-lights to illuminate the myth. But just as her father had welcomed the filming and broadcasting of his Coronation, so the Queen urged that the direct link of television with her peoples could give millions a sense of participation. In the end, it was left to the Queen herself to settle the problem in a face-to-face discussion with the Archbishop of Canterbury, Dr Fisher, over lunch; and television, as we know, phenomenally enhanced the impact of the ceremony upon the whole world.

The suggestion then arose that to spare the Queen undue fatigue after the long hours of ceremony the long processional route through the streets should be curtailed. The Queen rejected this and asked that the route should be extended by way of the Thames Embankment, making space for thousands of children to see her ride by. Again, the order of the presentation of the Bible in the ritual was changed and, at the Queen's behest, the Moderator of the Church of Scotland was introduced into the ceremony to present the Bible jointly with the Archbishop of the Church of England. An ancient royal emblem, the armills or bracelets, had been discarded from the Coronation ritual for centuries. Now the member nations of the Commonwealth presented a pair of armills of pure gold and the Queen saw to it that they came to be included in the text as 'symbols and pledges of that bond which unites you with your peoples'.

Queen Mary, who had seen three Coronations including her own, lived to offer her own perceptive advice. 'Your father needed to make up his own mind and choose his own officers to carry the standards, to hold the canopy, to bear the regalia,' she cautioned her granddaughter. Her early warning caused Philip and Elizabeth 'to talk Coronations' day and night, examining each separate aspect of the pageantry and symbolism, but Queen Mary died ten weeks before the ceremony and did not live to see the many felicities arising from her advice. Thus the Queen selected Viscount Montgomery of Alamein to carry the Royal Standard, a choice imaginative and correct; and instead of a landed duke Earl Alexander of Tunis was appointed to carry the Orb, the poetic symbol of Christian rule.

At the Court of Claims, that historic tribunal revived with each Coronation to enquire into the various claimants advancing their hereditary right to take part, the Lord of the Manor of Worksop claimed the right to present the Glove which traditionally protects the right hand of the monarch in carrying the Sceptre. The Manor turned out however to be held by a limited company and the Committee of Privileges decided the right could apply only to an individual. The omission of the Glove would shorten the ceremony a little, but this too was a respite the Queen declined and indeed amended by a thoughtful touch. Lord Woolton's ill health no longer permitted him to carry the heavy upright Sword of State, and the Queen appointed him to present the lightweight Glove instead.

Again, the precedents of Queen Victoria's crowning stipulated that the maids of honour should be unmarried, aged about twenty, preferably of similar height and build and of no less rank than the daughter of an earl. 'We need quins and one extra,' said Princess Margaret, volunteering to find the suitable maids from among her own acquaintance. The youngest, Lady Jane Willoughby, was a schoolgirl who found it 'very nice to get countless days off school to come up for rehearsals'; the eldest, Lady Rosemary Spencer-Churchill, delayed her wedding three weeks to maintain unmarried status.

A minor crisis arose from the acute shortage of royal carriages and of coachmen to drive them. The Queen had naturally hoped that the street processions would be, as they say, 'completely horsed', but in an unlucky phase of post-war economy more than half the suitable vehicles in the Royal Mews had been sold. As it turned out, Sir Alexander Korda, the film producer, had purchased a number and was happy to loan several two-pair broughams and open landaus for a glittering farewell appearance. Then members of the Coaching Club also offered to serve the Queen in borrowed royal livery, but royal coachmen are traditionally clean-shaven, and some of the Club's finest beards and moustaches were gallantly sacrificed.

Like a vast mosaic the meshwork of pageantry was pieced together, until the Queen rehearsed wearing the heavy 8 lb St Edward's crown, and, in the Palace Ballroom and Picture Gallery, measurements of the Abbey nave and theatre were marked out with wands and tapes to enable her to rehearse her movements step by step. In her first Christmas broadcast from Sandringham the Queen had spoken 'nervously but with unfeigned sincerity' of her Coronation need of support from her people. 'Pray for me on that day . . . pray that God may give me wisdom and strength to carry out the solemn promises that I shall be making, and that I may faithfully serve Him and you all the days of my life.' In the Abbey, late in May, she preferred to play no part in rehearsals, the event was too sacred for that, but she closely watched the Duchess of Norfolk as her stand-in, and helped with rehearsing the difficult passage of the descent from the Throne.

Bobo, now styled the Queen's dresser, inspected the richly furnished and carpeted robing-room in the new-built Abbey Annex and made the dismaying discovery that no-one had thought to provide the Queen and her ladies with mirrors. The Queen regarded it as a great joke but, cutting it fine, full-length looking glasses were not fitted until three days before the Coronation itself.

Earlier, a stranger and more serious omission, which came to the Archbishop of Canterbury's attention, was that no written material existed to help prepare the Queen for the personal dedication which alone endowed the Coronation with true meaning, and he had to compile a little devotional book himself. 'It took the form', as he said, 'of a simple meditation and prayers for each day, covering a whole month leading up to the Coronation. Each day had a theme, with the little meditation and one or two prayers.'

On Coronation Day, 2 June, the day broke with the thrilling news that Mount Everest had been climbed to its peak for the first time in history, and by the British team of Hillary and Tensing. Millions regarded it as a rich and auspicious portent, as if God had handed out tablets from the mountain itself.

Many thousands, in those youthful years of television, were to spend the day glued to their pioneer sets. The people were massed twelve to twenty deep down the length of the Mall and presently along all the processional route through London to watch the Queen and her consort ride by in their baroque Gold Coach.

Those who watched the Queen in the Abbey tell of her air of being mystically alone in the midst of the multitude, her rapt attention dwelling upon every moment of the ritual. 'The sense of spiritual exaltation that radiated from her was almost tangible,' noted one of her Heralds, Dermot Morrah. 'Calm and confident and even charming,' wrote Henry Channon. At the moment of sacrament before the Anointing, it was noticed that Prince Charles, not yet five, had been brought into the Royal Gallery and seated between his aunt and his grandmother, each whispering to answer his questions, each a hostage to his good behaviour.

As the Queen took her seat in the ancient Coronation chair she cast one fleeting glance towards him. The Crown was slowly settled upon her head, and her hands presently rose to steady it. Symbolism may shine in every movement at such times. As the first to pay homage, her husband uttered the old-style phrases, 'I, Philip, Duke of Edinburgh, do become your liege man of life and limb, and of earthly worship, and faith and truth I will bear unto you, to live and die. . . .' Then, in the afternoon, wearing her Crown, carrying her Orb and Sceptre, the Queen went forth from the warmth and music of the Abbey to ride in unremitting acknowledgment through the streets where the London rain lashed down upon the immense cheering throngs.

11

Round the world and more

It was to cause Princess Margaret sad regret that in the very month of the Coronation the first clouds of 'the Townsend affair' swept across the horizons of public curiosity. In the eventual summing-up, the Queen's sister had no cause for self-reproach. 'What will happen to her?' the gossipy Chips Channon pondered in his diary as early as 1949. 'There is already a Marie Antoinette aroma about her.'

In hindsight, a chain of events hung with curious inevitability upon the decision of George VI to form a group of young war heroes as personal Equerries of Honour. The then thrice-decorated Wing-Commander Peter Townsend was one of the first to be appointed and one of the few to stay the course.

His transfer to the Palace as an equerry was to be for three months. In 1952 he was still there as Deputy Master of the Household, good-looking, good-humoured, treated as one of the family and nearly indispensable. On Sunday afternoons the Queen and Prince Philip and Margaret occasionally strolled through Windsor Great Park to have tea with Peter and his wife Rosemary at Adelaide Cottage, the Townsend's grace-and-favour home, very much like any family group visiting friends. It was a shock when Peter instituted divorce proceedings, though obvious in retrospect that his marriage had been falling apart for years. In the King's reign, divorce would have entailed resignation even for the innocent. But the world was changing and after being awarded a decree nisi, Townsend remained at his post, and was to accompany the Queen Mother to Clarence House as comptroller. Nor was it long before a member of the royal staff wrote of wondering 'whether a romance were developing between Princess Margaret and Peter. We watched what seemed to be a ripening friendship. . . .'

154

On his very first day at the Palace, as he tells in his autobiography, Peter Townsend had been introduced to 'two adorable-looking girls, all smiles'. Elizabeth, he felt, 'played her role dutifully, punctiliously, charmingly ... with a touching, spontaneous sincerity'. Margaret early gave him the impression that, behind the sophistication and self-assurance, one could find 'a rare softness and sincerity'. Then, one afternoon in Coronation year, he had found himself alone with Margaret in the red drawing-room at Windsor. 'We talked for hours – about ourselves. She listened, without uttering a word, as I told her, very quietly, of my feelings. Then she simply said, "That is how I feel, too." It was, to us both, an immensely gladdening disclosure, but one which sorely troubled us.' In reality the Princess lost no time in telling her sister, and the Queen indeed sensed what was coming as soon as Margaret entered her room.

The sisters had long since discovered that they could read one another's thoughts. 'It's no trick, it's telepathy,' Margaret once said. 'We really can do it.' Margaret evidently confided that if any man could make her happy it would be Peter, and the Queen's response was of affection, anxiety and doubt, realising only too well the difficulty implied by divorce.

The Queen's first response was to invite both Margaret and Peter to dinner together with herself and Prince Philip. 'Both were in high spirits and the evening passed off most agreeably,' Townsend was to write many years later. 'There stands out one unforgettable impression: the Queen's movingly simple and sympathetic acceptance of the disturbing fact of her sister's love for me.' The main element was the need of time to consider and perhaps find a solution to the obvious dilemma. 'The Queen Mother was never anything but considerate,' Townsend added, 'never once hurt either of us, behaving always with a regard for us both.' The Queen first privately consulted Winston Churchill as her Prime Minister, who bluntly gave his view that it would be disastrous, during Coronation year of all years, to consent to the marriage of her sister with a divorced man. The Royal Family was confronted yet again with the riddle that had beset the Duke of Windsor, with the sexes reversed, namely the Church of England's Canon 107, which still forbade divorce and would bind the Queen within her Coronation oath as Defender of the Faith.

That hoary statute, the Royal Marriages Act of 1772, could exempt Margaret from the Queen's veto when she was twenty-five, and a civil marriage was marginally possible. Tenderly the Queen must have indicated to Margaret how long she and Philip had necessarily waited, facing endless delays and obstacles, until presently everything had turned out for the best. One or two close family friends also gave analytical counsel of great value. Sixteen years older than Margaret, Peter may have unconsciously offered a father image in her youthful bereavement; and in the trauma of divorce a lonely man may over-eagerly react to the natural wish to rebuild his desolate world.

Peter Townsend tells that both Margaret and he were prepared for a sentence of exile, harsh as it was. Separation was agreed as a temporary expedient, so that they might both indeed be sure of their hearts. Townsend accepted his posting as air attaché in Brussels, while Margaret had been due to tour Rhodesia with the Queen Mother, part holiday, part duty. But what then? At this juncture, one of Margaret's friends, the enterprising Judy Montagu, a champion of good causes, approached the Queen with the prospect that Margaret might care to join with several other friends – Colin Tennant, Lord Plunket, Lord Porchester, Mrs Gerald Legge and others – in staging an Edgar Wallace play for an invalid children's organisation. The Queen saw that this could offer at least a sense of diversion through the winter and demurred at the prospect that Margaret might play the lead. But to help with the production side could cause no criticism, and indeed provided Margaret with an alluring extra interest while the Queen and her husband were absent on their six-month Coronation tour of the Commonwealth.

The two sisters had never previously faced so long a separation. The leave-taking on 23 November was an evening of drizzling rain, and Margaret rode to the airport with her sister and brother-in-law to find thousands of people waiting along every mile of the route to glimpse the Queen and wave goodbye. So compelling still was the Coronation fervour; and the magic of it, as so often, filled the Princess with awe and made the unpromising day 'end with a glow'.

The cruise of the liner *Gothic* stemmed from the late King's Commonwealth plans and postponement. It had twice been planned for him as a six-month Commonwealth tour, and his elder daughter was attempting it in his stead in 1952 when she was recalled by his death. 'I will be back,' she had promised on that day of destiny, on leaving Entebbe. But Philip foresaw that to repeat the eastward bound African journey would awaken too many painful memories. By air and sea the tour was revived in reverse, and the briefest possible recital of the commencing itinerary still conveys its speed and scope. '24 November: Arrive Bermuda. 25: Jamaica. 29: Cristobal (Panama Canal). 30: Depart Balboa. 17 December: Arrive Fiji. 20: Tonga. 23: Arrive Auckland. 30 January: Depart New Zealand (Bluff). 3 February: Arrive Sydney (Australia). 1 April: Depart Fremantle. 5: Arrive Cocos Islands. 10–21 Visit Ceylon. . . .'

The Queen's longer journeys are often described as though they were cineramas of sightseeing, set to a soundtrack of hurrahs and jubilant anthems, though Philip was in fact concerned at the strain on his wife's physical and emotional resources, the clocked and disciplined days, the total subjection to the vibration, jolting, roar and drone of thousands of miles, and the maelstrom of different beds into which they would almost certainly fall, dazed and exhausted. Yet the Queen slept while flying the Atlantic. At a touchdown for refuelling in Newfoundland a crowd was singing, 'For She's a Jolly Good Fellow', though it was the middle of the night, and they both hurriedly dressed and went out to greet them.

Seven hours later, summery, smiling, Elizabeth was visiting 'the first of my Parliaments overseas', an ambiguous phrase, for Bermuda boasts the oldest Commonwealth Parliament outside Westminster. After a day of shrilling children, of triumphal arches of flowers and seashells, the travellers were lured to sleep by croaking bullfrogs and next morning rose before 6 a.m. to head south to Jamaica and discover the wonderful colour and gaiety of the Caribbean, one first impression uppermost in mind as subsequent events showed, 'Margaret must come here! Margaret must see this!'

On the 120-mile drive across the island the impromptu slogan 'Welcome young Missus Our Queen', awaited them, chalked on walls and fences and sung with every calypso chant. The journey was punctuated by stops of the royal cavalcade at every village for the Queen to receive flowers – and fruit – until her car resembled a greengrocer's truck. In a following car, the Governor-General's wife, Lady Foot, took note of the royal method. They inadvertently passed an old lady who stood at the roadside clutching a bunch of flowers

157

that had long since wilted in the sun. 'The Queen turned round and gestured. We knew of course what she meant us to do. We stopped and spoke to her and took her little bunch.' . . . 'Alice, Alice, did you thank the old lady?' the Queen asked Alice Egerton, her lady-in-waiting. 'Did you get her address?' and the following day the old soul received a letter of thanks – in perspective – 'a leaf taken from Mother's book. . . .'

At Kingston, the *Gothic* was awaiting them, the same rented re-fitted Shaw Savill liner that had stood by for them nearly two years earlier at Mombasa, its royal suite a curious combination of flowered chintz and Victorian furnishing salvaged from the sixty-year-old yacht *Victoria and Albert*. Here the Queen was joined by 'her globe-trotting court', as they were described: Michael Adeane, who had succeeded Tommy Lascelles as private secretary, Martin Charteris as asst private secretary, Commander Colville to handle press matters and others. While the *Gothic* made her way through the Panama Canal, the Queen underwent an appalling excursion ashore.

As royal records tell, in separate cars, the royal couple lost sight of each other in that desperately excited human sea. 'The spectators quite lost their heads, the lack of police control was complete. Ordinary cars began cutting in from side streets and the Queen's procession came to a halt', and staff and police organised a sort of rugger scrum to enable Philip to reach his wife. Colon town was filled with frenzied thousands, dancing with wild abandonment and pressing forward, heedless of safety. It was a dire object lesson of the future precautions to be taken elsewhere.

Yet within a day or so the Queen was enjoying 'a super spell' of lazy freedom. 'Running across the Pacific with the gentle trade wind behind us, in the words of the ship's Captain Aitchison, blue sea, blue sky, and the temperature in the mid-seventies.' In perspective again, there was also a sub-plot. The Queen had casually invited Pamela Mountbatten how she would like to go round the world with her in rota with Alice Egerton as lady-in-waiting, and she responded eagerly. Pammy just then had been triumphantly dieting. 'You can always choose the menus,' said the Queen playfully, which, Captain Aitchison tells us, 'Lady Pamela did with great ease'. The invitation also 'paired Pammy nicely' with the acting Master of the Household on board, Viscount Althorp – 'Johnnie' to the others – who was responsible for the table placings and would one day find himself neatly placed as the eighth Earl Spencer, father of today's Princess of Wales.

'He was invaluable to me. He was of that rare type to whom people instinctively go for aid when in doubt or trouble,' wrote Captain Aitchison. 'Whenever I wanted information or wanted something delicate done, I went to him, and he was always ready to help.' In spite of his helpfulness and his good looks, however, Johnnie Althorp was still a bachelor, and it was considered fortunate by all concerned that his thirtieth birthday celebrations occurred in New Zealand during a full weekend assigned for 'leisure'. Three months later it happened that Pamela celebrated her twenty-fifth birthday in Ceylon in the midst of the Rara Perahera, that sumptuous parade of 125 decorated elephants and a thousand whirling dancers voted the greatest spectacle of the whole tour. But by then the Queen no longer entertained any hope of a match between Pammy and Johnnie.

A royal tour permits scant room for romance. In Australia, for instance, the royal party travelled 2,500 miles by road, 900 miles by train, 10,000 miles by plane in thirty-five different flights, and in fifty-eight days had no more than six days and seven half-days free. If one could select a single incident from the two months of emotion, it might be of the Queen in Sydney, enduring for ten hours the tumult of a million people who were 'letting it rip'. But returning to Government House she did not fail to turn smilingly to her chauffeur, 'Thank you very much, driver. This has been a trying day for you!'

The scope and variety of the Queen's first progress through Australia has indeed probably never been eclipsed. Her journeys took in Cairns and the Great Barrier Reef in the north to Tasmania in the south, with Melbourne, Ballarat, Adelaide, Perth and Fremantle strung along a route embracing steel-works, sheep shows, cattle stations and a flying doctor base. Within two months she made more acquaintance with her territories than a sequence of Governor-Generals had achieved in ten years, with a slimming effect so obvious that Bobo had to take in most of her frocks. Aboard the *Gothic*, Captain Aitchison discovered that the Queen enjoyed 'pottering around in the little pantry attached to her suite, and enjoyed getting things for herself. Smith, her steward, could never get used to the fact that she so rarely rang for him.'

The junior officers thought it would be nice to give the Queen a gift from *Gothic* on her birthday and, on being sounded, both Adeane and Lord Althorp suggested a clock. 'Her Majesty always needs to know the time.' On the anniversary, east of Aden, the Queen 'did indeed seem very pleased with it'. As she was soon due to leave the ship to fly to Entebbe, the Queen in turn wished to hand out a few surprise presents and Royal Victorian Medals. Captain Aitchison was asked to kneel on the royal deck and was knighted then and there, so surprised that he wrote home to his wife with the news and kicked himself for ever after for forgetting to address the letter to 'Lady Aitchison'.

At every port everyone eagerly looked forward to extra mail from home. The regular letters from Princess Margaret grew perceptibly happier with every landfall. The leading lady in her Edgar Wallace play *The Frog* was kept busy by the Westminster City Council, and so the Princess was having great fun as understudy in a satisfactory number of rehearsals. A postscript announced that £10,000 was already in the kitty for the Invalid Children's Association, and the leading lady – Raine Legge, the later Countess of Dartmouth (and Countess Spencer) – was nearly word-perfect. Within the correspondence one can catch the latent coincidences. At Aden or earlier Lord Althorp decided to mention that many of his letters were from a young lady whom he was hoping to marry. Indeed, he was enabled to fly home before the concluding African leg of the tour, and the Queen and Prince Philip expressed their gleeful hope of being home in time for the wedding.

The Queen Mother also wrote with fuller detail confirming a radio message that young Charles and Anne were safely aboard *Britannia* on the maiden voyage to Malta, where the royal parents were to be reunited with their children.

Fifteen years earlier on that famous occasion when George VI had visited Dartmouth, he had to be warned that the royal yacht was hardly seaworthy, and later that year the proud *Victoria and Albert* went to the breaker's yard after forty years' service. Plans for a new dual-purpose ship were approved, only to be cancelled by the outbreak of war. It was not until 1950 that the King approved a smaller royal yacht – to be alternatively used as a hospital ship – and ordered the vessel from John Brown's yard on Clydeside. Elizabeth and Philip followed her progress with lively interest. 'The late King felt most strongly, as I do, that a yacht is a necessity and not a luxury to the ruler of a seafaring nation,' said the Queen at the launching of *Britannia* in Coronation year. Prince Philip took part in the speed trials, and no sequel to her father's project could have been more seemly in the Queen's eyes than that her children should be the first passengers on the maiden voyage. Her heart must have leapt at the thought of her children aboard when she first glimpsed her new ship from the balcony of King Idris of Libya, although four patient hours of diplomatic ceremonial had to be faced ashore before she could clasp Charles and Anne in her arms.

Mr Churchill insisted on going to meet the royal yacht at the mouth of the Thames, and at first did not recognise his revered Queen in the sun-tanned young figure in slacks who greeted him as he came aboard.

The sublime pageantry when the *Britannia* sailed into the Pool of London remains etched in history. Her Majesty's other chief Ministers were waiting at the pier, 200 jet aircraft roared overhead, and the Queen completed her journey by the royal barge to Westminster Pier, where a Sovereign's Escort awaited her for the jubilant ride home through the welcoming cheers.

The Queen and the Duke of Edinburgh had circumnavigated the globe in 173 days. Elizabeth was the first monarch in history to travel round the world and the first Sovereign for two centuries to approach her capital by the shining highway of the Thames. On board *Britannia* at Tobruk the Queen had been engrossed with the children for an hour before she remembered she had not inspected the ship and set out on her tour of exploration. Now she discovered her six personal rooms at the Palace newly decorated, her husband's modern white maple study and his fitted Scottish bedroom marvellously transplanted from Clarence House, her own bed in new perfection, draped and canopied. To the smallest piece of furniture, everything was arranged as she had directed before leaving, all those months before, now new and fresh as the uninterrupted era of monarchy opened before her.

And after a weekend of exchanging news with her mother and sister, the Queen characteristically plunged into business. There were always her 'boxes', of course. But first a Palace sherry party for the Cabinet and Opposition leaders, in itself an innovation. The following day, two hours presiding over a Duchy of Cornwall meeting, concerned with the affairs of her small son, and next the welcome home luncheon in the City. 'I set out to learn more of the peoples and countries over which I have been called to reign, and to try to bring them the personal reality of the monarchy,' she told the assembled company. 'The structure and framework of the monarchy could easily stand out as an archaic and meaningless survival. We have received visible and audible proof that it is living in the hearts of the people.'

She had paused at 'visible and audible' but the hoped-for chuckles from her Guildhall audience never came. Wit was not then expected of Majesty. And what had the Queen expected? Prince Philip sought to analyse her viewpoint. 'To the people we visited we are like Shakespeare's poet's pen, which "turns them to shapes and gives to airy nothing a habitation and a name". We bring into immediate focus all the mystery of all the Coronations of history, and people react in the same way, whatever their colour, whatever their religion.' The Queen felt, as she still does today, that every impassioned welcome was less for herself than for her queenhood, her embodiment of an abiding link with history.

Other links there are, at first strange and invisible, yet forming silently in circumstances tangible with passing time. The couple had hardly been home for two weeks when, with a large contingent of royals, they attended Johnnie Althorp's wedding in Westminister Abbey. His eighteen-year-old bride was Frances Roche, daughter of the Queen Mother's girlhood friend, Lady Fermoy. The Scots Greys formed a guard of honour with arched swords. Twenty-one years later, the bridegroom came into his ancestral title as Earl Spencer. His marriage was blessed with three daughters and a son, his third daughter destined to universal recognition as the present Princess of Wales.

On 20 November 1954, the Queen and Prince Philip celebrated the seventh anniversary of their wedding. But, by the customary jostle of events, Philip had to hurry away that Saturday evening to attend, of all absurdities, the centenary dinner of the Battle of Balaclava.

Taking stock for her biographical pen, his well-meaning cousin, Alexandra, surveyed the Malta years, the birth of two children, boy and girl, the false optimism that had alleviated the anxiety of the King's illness; and then the millrace of the Accession, the Coronation and the Commonwealth tour.

Soon after the Spencer wedding, Prince Philip hurried to visit his sisters in Germany, returning with the pleasant news that Sophie was expecting a third baby, and shortly before Christmas he was present at the christening at Salem of her infant daughter, Princess Frederica Elizabeth Victoria Luise.

The Queen and her husband similarly looked forward to private family hopes which were not immediately fulfilled. The absence of plans for further royal overseas travel, apart from a three-day State Visit to Norway, provided a lull intended for personal contingencies which, in the outcome, betrayed the Queen's deep disappointment. Having agreed as early as 1952 to open the 1954 Empire Games in Vancouver, with the inevitable extensions tacked on, Philip however found himself travelling solo – in the royal sense – that summer through the Northwest Territories into the Arctic Circle. In his room in a two-storey hotel in Yellowknife, he could hear the roaring business being done in the 'beverage room' downstairs and wished that the Queen could have shared the experience. Five years were to pass, however, before she embarked on a similar trip, and meanwhile the fates continued to guard the happy surprise they would have in store.

12

Smooth sailing

In the West Indies, the Queen's thoughts had danced to the theme, 'Margaret must see this! Margaret must come here!' Early in 1955 the Princess's letters home from the Caribbean were lyrical. She was finding her feet as both admirer and ambassador, and the newspapers of three continents shone with calypso headlines for a month. A Palace secretary underscored a phrase on her 'shining-eyed enjoyment', a new assurance, a sense of being herself, as if the sea-change had brought wings'. Among her photographs the Princess made sure of including the unexpected banner, 'Jamaica Burial Society Welcomes Princess Margaret'.

The wider vistas however produced no change in Margaret's dilemma of her prospective marriage. It was accounted fortunate by some that Peter Townsend had never visited the West Indies to leave his imprint there. Princess Margaret was now in her twenty-fifth year; the Queen all but in her thirtieth, content as yet to turn over every aspect of Margaret's wishes in her mind, vigilant for every amelioration of circumstance if she should prefer to retire into private life.

Another detachment loomed in the retirement in his eighty-first year of Sir Winston Churchill, whose admiration for his Queen remained unbounded. Elizabeth was touched by his veneration, aware that he kept a framed picture of her over his bed, and amused by his tricks in extending his weekly audiences, a glass in his hand. He had twice refused the offer of the Garter from her father, but accepted it from her now. 'She has written a five-page letter to me in her own hand,' he told his physician in astonishment. When he was persuaded to retire, it was with the shining idea of entertaining her to dinner at 10 Downing Street, a precedent her father had established.

He also already wore the Order of Merit, the second distinction within her bestowal. 'Would you like a dukedom – or anything like that?' she enquired, when he tendered his resignation.

His resignation was, in fact, muted by a newspaper strike and it thus fell to the Queen to exercise her prerogative to choose his successor under unusual conditions of silence. There might otherwise have been controversy on the Queen's selection of a divorced man as Prime Minister and Princess Margaret's choice of a divorced man as husband. The Queen was under no obligation to consult Winston on his successor nor constitutionally required to seek advice. Sir Anthony had acted for three years as 'deputy' Prime Minister, but this office held no actual validity in the Constitution. Firmly to lend observance to her prerogative, the Queen allowed the night to pass and did not send for Eden until the following day.

The following month, for the first time in her reign, Elizabeth II granted a dissolution of Parliament for a general election. The Conservatives were returned with an increased majority of sixty, and the Queen opened her first Parliament, as distinct from a Parliamentary session. However, the strikes that were to bedevil Britain for at least the next twenty-five years were already in evidence and, instead of street pageantry, the Queen drove to Westminster in a closed car, which struck some observers as a deliberate demonstration of the dreary republican alternative.

At the weekend of 1 October, Sir Anthony and Lady Eden were guests at Balmoral, a critical occasion not lost on Peter Townsend. 'Eden could not fail to sympathise with Princess Margaret, all the more so while his own second marriage had incurred no penalty,' Townsend stresses in his autobiography. He [Eden] had to warn that the Princess that my second marriage – to her – would bring her the most grievous penalties: she would have to renounce her royal rights, functions and income. The Princess now had confirmation, for the first time, of the consequences of a marriage to me.'

But to this authentic note the then Archbishop of Canterbury, Dr Fisher, has added, 'The Princess was seeking and waiting all the time to know what God's will was'. She regarded her dilemma as a deep moral one. 'She got plenty of advice, asked for, and a good deal unasked for,' the Archbishop added. Certainly any sneer of financial considerations in the event of marrying a penniless air attaché was false, for Queen Mary is known to have left the Princess a fair fortune, and the Queen's own private revenues were sufficient to shelter her sister from any adversity.

The outcome still remained unresolved, the options open, when Peter Townsend returned to London on 12 October. The press speculations exceeded anything that had gone before, and Townsend was fortunate in that the Queen's close friend, Lord Abergavenny of the Nevill family, gave him private sanctuary at his home in Lowndes Square. Returning from Scotland on 13 October, Princess Margaret kept pace with her programme of the day, including a portrait sitting with the painter, Denis Fildes. The meeting with Peter was arranged for that evening and, keeping in touch with Clarence House from Balmoral, the Queen heard that 'Mr Fildes says the Princess has never looked more beautiful'.

'In her sitting-room at Clarence House we at last found ourselves once more in our own exclusive world,' wrote Peter Townsend long afterwards. 'We realised that nothing had changed. Time had not changed our accustomed, sweet familiarity.' Yet to what degree were they in reality strangers to one another after seventeen months?

At the weekend, the couple were the guests – separately, it was stressed – at the home of the Queen's Elphinstone cousin, Mrs John Wills, in Berkshire. Aloof or otherwise, the Queen returned from Scotland on Monday the 17th, while through the week the sentinel reporters continued to chart Margaret's various meetings with Townsend under the roofs of their mutual friends. The Princess, however, was as skilled in dissembly as her mother, and on 18 October, Townsend was reduced to noting that the Prime Minister's audience with the Queen 'lasted ninety minutes instead of the usual thirty'. On the 19th a dinner with the Archbishop at Lambeth Palace, with the Queen and Prince Philip, Princess Margaret, the Queen Mother and others passed with little comment. On the razor's edge of the following day, there were flurries both at Downing Street, where the Cabinet was believed to have discussed a Bill of Renunciation (of royal rights) to be placed before Princess Margaret, and in a committee-room of the House of Commons, Hugh Gaitskell – who in fact was Peter's cousin – informed his Opposition Shadow Cabinet that the Princess intended to marry Townsend.

Strangely, on 21 October, it fell to the Queen to unveil the fine memorial statue of her father in the Mall. It was a day of heavy rain, and the Queen's words, speaking from notes made weeks in advance, fell irrevocable as the rain itself. 'Much was asked of my father in personal sacrifice and endeavour. He shirked no task however difficult, and to the end he never faltered in his duty.'

Swimming in the seas of journalism, Randolph Churchill asserted that the Princess called on the Archbishop a few days later and said, in words worthy of Elizabeth I, 'Archbishop, you may put your books away; I have made up my mind.' This was an instance of poetic license. According to the Archbishop 'The Princess came and I received her in the quiet of my own study. But she never said, "Put away those books". There were no books to put away. Her decision was purely on the grounds of conscience.'

Phoning that Sunday from Lowndes Square, Townsend discovered, as he has said, that 'the Princess was in great distress', and Townsend grasped his fate. Indeed, it was he who drafted the words 'I have decided not to marry Group Captain Townsend. It may have been possible to contract a civil marriage. But mindful of the Church's teaching . . . conscious of my duty to the Commonwealth. . . .'

'That's exactly how I feel,' said the Princess when she first saw the memo, the very same words she had used to Peter when their love episode began. It remained only for the message to be perfected, discussed, revised, in a flurry of dispatch riders between the Princess spending that final weekend with the Nevill family, and Windsor Castle. The Queen, it is said, suggested changing a word or two. More mature and cautious advice would have preferred no statement to be issued at all. A simple fade-out could have elapsed, without explanation, with the Group Captain's further withdrawal to Brussels.

Even the firm reality of the Princess's decision vanishes into Townsend's phrases. Reading the statement that evening, Harold Nicolson wrote with truth, 'This is a great act of self-sacrifice – I feel rather moved,' and *The Times* accurately added, 'She is loyal to the Queen, her sister.' Princess Margaret's determination not to detract by a dust-grain from her sister's dignity, indeed, not to flaw by an iota the lustre of the Crown, were the ultimate unshakable bastions of her resolution.

And I am tempted to add a personal curlicue. From Princess Margaret's side, Peter hurried to his mother, staying with her sister, his godmother, in Sussex, to tell them that there would be no marriage. Their house was next to the home of my closest friend, the gardens touching, and in those gardens today, the passions effaced, one remembers little more than a passing storm, a storm in a king-size teacup.

'My husband and I. . . .' The words had crept incautiously into speeches part written by Martin Charteris, part by Prince Philip, vetted by Michael Adeane, with additions by the Queen herself, a conjugal phrase so quickly exploited by satirists that she soon used it warily until venturing her Silver Wedding quip, 'Everybody really will concede that on this day of all days I should begin with the words 'My husband and . . . .' But the rest was lost in laughter.

The ever-improving collaboration had been built up step by step, and as if the *Gothic* world-circler had not sufficiently disclosed the husband-and-wife teamwork it was demonstrated afresh on the next dual overseas tour, the 1956 compass of Nigeria. Philip's first flip through an old reference book at Balmoral had been unpromising, the then largest British colony 'affording possibilities of good health during temporary residence'. They had made a joke of that, light relief against the real work of genning-up. The Queen suggested a Nigerian equerry to provide running information. Philip urged, 'Why not two?' The first Africans to enter the Royal Household, their guest-lists added up to the largest multi-racial garden-party Lagos had ever seen, Philip watchful throughout in steering the Queen from white residents to talk to Nigerians. Or as London newspapers put it, she 'constantly broke through the difficulties of race and custom'.

It was Philip who learned in advance that flowers withered in the Government House air-conditioning, and jogged somebody's arm, 'Let's not catch a chill!' Philip too who provided the cue, 'cool and calm', when the Queen inaugurated the new Federal Courts and attended the House of Representatives in full evening dress and tiara in a temperature above ninety. In London and Lagos the back-stage diplomacy of the Duke of Edinburgh's office helped also with the choice of leisure highspots to set before the Queen. Lagos offered her the impact of a stamping, whirling dance team thousands strong. Kaduna, capital of the northern peoples, staged a Durbar of 8,000 mounted warriors, an Agincourt scene of unexpected medieval richness.

On the working aspect again, Philip notably eased the Queen through the hours at the Oji river leper settlement, visiting every class and compound, the children, the blind, the permanent sufferers and the curable, seen by and seeing 1,000 patients. Both asked many questions, a technique less in concealing emotion from each other, than facing advanced stages of the disease unflinching. But the visit was well publicised and achieved its purpose in lessening the exaggerated African fear of the contagion of the illness. Over the years, moreover, the Queen and her husband have driven the lesson home with a sequence of adopted leper children. One after the other, the Queen and the Duke of Edinburgh make their separate adoptions, paying for all their medical and other needs until the boy or girl can be sent home 'discharged without trace of leprosy'.

During the homeward flight, the royal aircraft touched down at Kano on the southern fringe of the Sahara, enabling the Queen to see the great mud-walled city on which until a century earlier no white man had ever set eyes. In ceremonial robes of green and gold, the Emir of Kano rode out to meet her, through an avenue of Moslem horsemen decked in heirloom armour handed down from the time of the Crusades. Masked Tuaregs watched from the crowd. A camel-boy who gazed open-mouthed at the unveiled Queen wore a rough toga that recalled ancient Rome. Stamped into impressionable memory, the adventure fired the Queen's lifelong fondness for travel. And home again she could not but appreciate how Philip, from the planning stage onward, had devised a marvellous escapade combined with the flavour of a useful State mission. Trade statistics with the Republic of Nigeria were to double within the next few years. It was the same with her State Visit to Sweden later that year, so pleasurably spiced with the equestrian events of the Olympic Games. Without Philip's tactful hint on timing to his aunt, Queen Louise, it could have been different.

Another journey was a husbandly impromptu. Prince Philip had snatched a brief taste of naval life by attending the Mediterranean Fleet exercises and proposed that the Queen should fly out for a look at Corsica and Sardinia. Though the sun infuriatingly refused to appear the incognito Queen had the fun of going ashore with Princess Alexandra of Kent to eat spaghetti in tiny restuarants and stroll amid the fishing-nets on the quays. But the rain fell and the wind blew, and it was probably just as well that Princess Margaret had not joined this forlorn adventure.

It irked the Queen in those days to read nonsense about Philip walking one step behind her, for she had long since signed a parchment Warrant giving him 'Place, Pre-Eminence and Precedence next' to her. His name is thus written into the highest position in the land, after her own. He rides with her in the State carriage to the Opening of Parliament and accompanies her into the House of Lords ceremonially holding her hand, slightly to the side of the processional line. In the early years of her reign he was seated on a chair of State in the alcove to the left of the Throne, *outside the canopy* and demoted one step down.

In 1967, when Prince Charles and Princess Anne first accompanied their parents to the Opening, an Act of 1539 controlled the placing, to the left and right of the Queen, also outside the canopy, and a dilemma had to be decided. Since ancient law omitted thought of a husband, Prince Philip received his rightful place, in the Queen's eyes, beneath the canopy on the Consort's throne. The Consort's throne was brought from Lord Cholmondeley's home at Houghton, where it was traditionally stored and placed in position beside the Queen's throne, the officially recognised Throne of Great Britain. But in church law Elizabeth and Philip are man and wife, in partnership. In public or private, their very lifestyle lies in sharing.

The Duke of Edinburgh candidly dislikes comparison with Queen Victoria's Albert. Writing in private, the Prince Consort described himself as 'manager of the Queen's private affairs, sole confidential adviser in politics and only assistant in her communications with her government'. Prince Philip assumes much less but undertakes more, and shrugs away the equivocal tight-rope. 'What is unique about this regiment?' he enquired at a Welsh Guards dinner. 'I will tell you. It is the only one in which the Colonel is legally married to the Colonel-in-Chief.' The two brasshats indeed long since divided duties through nearly every possible activity. The Duke goes out to dinners while the Queen prefers to stay home with the television or in meeting her friends. No-one has ever numbered Philip's after-dinner speeches, except to give evidence to a Civil List committee that he attends eighty-three speechifying luncheons and eighty-three similar dinners an average year, and no estimate has been taken of the hours spent in preparation.

When the time allows, the Queen enjoys reading the rough text of her husband's speeches, not in any sense to give approval but from wifely interest in what he is going to say, and occasionally persuades him to improve on a point she thinks will go down well. In return, as mood and opportunity offer, it is evident that he retails some of the previous evening's after-dinner conversation, keeping a finger on the pulse of the nation. A Bishop's wife at Balmoral noticed them sitting together on a garden bench, out of earshot, 'chatting so animatedly to each other you wouldn't think they had already been together all afternoon'.

In taking the pulse-beat, a clinical advance was made with the abolition of the débutante Courts, the debs in line to curtsey to the Queen on her dais, and among their elders the hum of polite chitchat engrossing none. Instead of the Courts, the oval-table luncheons were instituted, which over twenty-five years, 1956 onward, have indeed proved successful. Eight guests are adroitly blended, leading personalities in every walk of life, business men and authors, churchmen and scientists, industrialists, theatricals . . . and the alchemy works. The Master of the Household usually greets the guests and introduces them to one another; two gentlemen of the Household effectively get things going over sherry. Occasionally another member of the family is present – Princess Margaret, Prince Andrew, perhaps the Kents. Before the Queen appears, two corgis scamper in, probably the only dogs in the world trained to run ahead as deputy heralds; and in the laughter at that, guests hardly notice being formed into a line for introductions.

Relaxed, surprisingly enjoyable, the occasion drifts towards three o'clock, clearly one of the happiest joint ideas of wife and husband. Similar dinner parties for twenty, formed of married couples, have seemed less effective, and a trial conversazione for actors, authors, musicans, people in the arts, did not work at all. Eminents accepted invitations but failed to turn up. Philip, for once, must have felt like George III, who dreamed up an Order of Knights of Minerva for authors, which ran into such a muddle of rivalry and petty spite that the idea died on its feet. Frosty garden-parties, on the other hand, gave way to the larger, and still successful, Commonwealth gatherings in the Palace gardens with guest-lists 7,000 strong. All these experiments and changes at court in the middle years of our twentieth century were the outcome of Queen and husband consulting together.

Dermot Morrah, for thirty years a leader-writer of *The*

Times, once curiously put his foot in his mouth by announcing, 'The Duke of Edinburgh has practically no official powers or functions. . . . None of the mystical aura of monarchy surrounds him. He has no share in the Queen's daily intercourse with her Ministers of State. Officially he is scarcely known to the Constitution. In the main work of the monarchy, because of the nature of the people's feeling, he can do little or nothing.' Prince Philip in fact once supplemented this pronouncement by telling a lecture audience, 'I am always wary of sticking my nose into things which do not directly concern me', which seemed to leave very little.

The comment was, of course, mere persiflage and fun, as he intended. *The Observer*, however, once observed with candour that a decision on any standpoint of the monarchy is no longer resolved by any one person. 'It emerges from the interplay of opinions – of the Queen and her officials, Prince Philip, the Prime Minister and others.' Pointedly, too, *The Observer* asserted that the Queen often defers to her husband's judgment 'and always likes to know that he has agreed to a course of action before the officials make a move'. *Le Roi – c'est moi* was in fact acknowledged to have become *La Reine – c'est trois* – the Queen, Prince Philip and the private secretary, if not others besides. No critical challenge of this assumption has ever come from the Palace. By Bagehot's celebrated definition, the Queen has the right to consult, to encourage and to warn her Ministers. As a husband, Philip has a right to encourage and to warn his wife. As a Consort, by virtue of being also a Privy Councillor, Prince Philip has in fact a constitutional right to advise the Queen, not excluding the important power to counsel her in her royal prerogative of choosing a new Prime Minister.

In any discussion of Prince Philip's status, this issue is perhaps the most commonly overlooked. The Privy Council, the most ancient form of the Queen's government, is the central executive of the Constitution; and it is during the formal ritual of holding a Council that the Queen agrees to the supreme acts done in her name, from giving assent to Acts of Parliament to a declaration of war. Much of the business of government is given by Orders in Council to which the Queen assents by saying the one word 'Approved'. But in the wings beforehand, vital acts of approval are usually preceded by a process of exchanging viewpoints and discussion.

It nevertheless remains a quirk in history that Prince Philip was away for four months and often out of touch in frozen Antarctica at a time when the Queen had to make a controversial constitutional decision while deprived of his company and moral support. This is what comes of the royal need of planning ahead for events while unaware of future contingencies. In 1954, Philip had undertaken to open the 1956 Olympic Games in Melbourne and husband and wife were dismayed months later when the international planning committee fixed the opening date for 22 November, only two days after their wedding anniversary. Philip at first entertained the idea of making a dramatic thirty-hour flight by jet, leaving Windsor on the 20th and thus demonstrating British aircraft speed and supremacy. But the politicians were already concerned at the personal hazards the Queen's husband might face in flying jets at that stage of development, and this time all the Prince's energetic persuasions failed to survive Cabinet discussion.

For a far graver reason, there was even some hazard that the entire voyage should be cancelled in view of the Middle East situation. At the outset a major change of plan was necessary when President Nasser of Egypt seized and closed the sea route of the Suez Canal. It was forcibly argued at the time that the *Britannia's* tour could give the world no better reminder of the cohesion and strength of the Commonwealth. But at the head of government affairs in London Anthony Eden was a desperately sick man, and early in the New Year he had to tell the Queen of his doctors' advice that he could no longer serve her without detriment to her service.

Two foremost figures seemed to have almost equal claims as Britain's next Prime Minister, Mr Harold Macmillan, Chancellor of the Exchequer, and Mr R. A. Butler, Lord Privy Seal and Leader of the House of Commons. Both were close on balance of merits, each had a considerable body of opponents and neither commanded the unanimous support of the Conservative Party. It was for the Queen alone to decide. Her private secretary, Sir Michael Adeane, had no experience of any similar dilemma. The Queen sought the advice of Sir Winston Churchill and the Marquess of Salisbury, Lord President of the Council, among others, and on 10 January these senior statesmen dutifully attended at the Palace. In his memoirs Sir Anthony Eden gives no indication that the Queen sought his advice, although she no doubt sought the advantage of his opinions while he was at Sandringham. The deliberations continued through the morning. As on the occasion when Sir Winston Churchill retired from office the Queen allowed precisely eighteen-and-a-half hours to pass before she showed her mind and sent for the new Prime Minister. Mr Harold Macmillan was occupied only twenty minutes in being received and offered the post of Prime Minister and First Lord of the Treasury. By that time the heat of the Suez crisis had dissolved, and a United Nations salvage fleet had begun the interminable task of clearing the Canal.

The Queen had long since been aware of Philip's thrilled enthusiasm for the Commonwealth Trans-Antarctic Expedition, which he had heard about from Sir Vivian Fuchs, who was timed to start overland from the Weddel Sea shortly after the end of the Games, while Sir Edmund Hillary was to begin a trek from the Ross Sea. 'I had visions of visiting both ends of the expedition,' Philip later wrote, 'but they soon faded . . . . At one time I had hoped to take *Britannia* into the Ross Sea, but I didn't think the risk of being iced up for nine months was worth it.' He had clearly been convinced by his wife's arguments.

There is a story that Queen Juliana of the Netherlands once asked her sister-monarch, 'What do you do when your husband wants something and you don't want him to have it?' Elizabeth supposedly replied, 'Oh, I just tell him he shall have it and then make sure he doesn't get it. . . .' But Juliana cannot recollect the conversation, and colleagues say that the Queen 'is far more likely to keep quiet and then think of other alternatives'. Sensitive to Philip's every mood, the Queen's contribution to the Melbourne journey rapidly became evident. 'In discussing these ideas and looking at charts and maps,' wrote Prince Philip, 'it soon became obvious that there were a good many island communities and outposts in the Indian Ocean, the South Pacific, Antarctic and Atlantic which cannot be visited by air and which are too remote and too small to get into the more usual tours. Although it meant being away from home for three months, including Christmas and the New Year, I decided to try to arrange the journey. . . .' He flew out on 15 October, joined the *Britannia* at Mombasa, and visited the Seychelles, Ceylon, Malaya, Papua and New Guinea, Darwin and Alice Springs and reached Canberra on 20 November – twelve hours ahead of London time. A telephone call to his wife was made just as she was awakening to their anniversary day. Neither had dreamed that their tenth year of matrimony would find them talking to one another from opposite sides of the world.

Something of their private exchanges echoed also in a broadcast which Philip taped and forwarded, 'The Lord watch between me and thee when we are absent from one another.' He knew his wife would get the message. The Queen's thoughts, too, were reflected in her own Christmas broadcast. 'It is sad for us to be separated . . . we look forward to the moment when we shall again be together', and with this she coupled a special wish for 'every man and woman whose destiny it is to walk through life alone'.

Unhappily, it made their comparatively brief separation less bearable in that the media, no longer with cause to pursue Princess Margaret, now invented a completely mythical rift between the Queen and her husband. The Queen had grown used to the wild fabrications from the continent, and in occasionally glancing through French or German magazines notorious for their royal rumours, she was amused by their powers of invention. Reports of her impending divorce, supposed miscarriages and coming abdication, jostled with alleged snubs of Princess Grace of Monaco, the Queen Mother's impending remarriage and wearisome analysis of her many billions' fortune. But the nonsensical 'rift' was taken more seriously. Wise heads nodded 'at no smoke without fire', though any smoke was in fact blowing from the wrong fire and in the wrong direction.

Philip's letters home, one gathers, told of the revolting smell of Deception Island 'a maternity home for 250,000 Adelie, Chinstrap and Gentoo penguins'; the lively sight of one of his team 'defending himself against the dive-bomb attacks of two enraged gulls with a rib-bone of whale'; and, among the whaling fleets, 'the yacht chased the catcher as the catcher chased the whale. Turning and jinking the whale never allowed the gunner to get in a decent shot' – men's talk, as the Queen cheerfully summed up.

But the supposed marital disharmony grieved both the Queen and Philip because, in fact, it concerned their close friend, Mike Parker, the Australian from Philip's naval days who had joined him as secretary. Lieut Commander Michael Parker had been separated from his wife for a year and now found the disruption of his marriage irreparable. His future was dark with divorce proceedings, and the *Britannia* was approaching Gambia on her homeward run when Philip had to send the Queen the unhappy news of Mike's resignation. For ten years he had been at the hub of the royal circle, with Martin Charteris, Patrick Plunket, the Rupert Nevills and others. Now the Queen could still hope to meet him as a friend, but change was in the air, with regret at losing Mike's good company mingled with the sadness of a family bereavement.

'You must write it all down, cousin Louie,' the Queen had often said to Princess Marie Louise, a granddaughter of Queen Victoria. 'Do please write it down, it's historic and therefore so thrilling', and now the old lady had gone, while her published memoirs were still fresh in the bookshops. Queen Mary's brother, the Earl of Athlone, onetime occupant of Clarence House, had also died and, in this dolorous atmosphere, the fifth year of her reign ended with the distaste and annoyance of rumour.

A week or so after her accession anniversary, Elizabeth flew to join Philip in Portugal. It had lent fuel to the flames that the *Britannia* had berthed at Gibraltar on 6 February and to the uninitiated Philip could readily have flown home to help his wife with a day laden with memories. The public could not know that Philip was taking part in Fleet exercises, and in the sensitive aftermath of the Suez crisis it was deemed undiplomatic to stress these activities. However, the couple were to have a weekend to themselves before commencing a three-day State Visit to Portugal. The Queen met Philip's plane and, as she went aboard, hundreds of frenzied pressmen noted with dismay that the Venetian blinds were drawn at the aircraft windows.

As Queen Alexandra of Yugoslavia has written with sentiment, 'Philip and Elizabeth had planned their reunion with ardent anticipation. . . . After nearly ten years of marriage a couple need to contrive an occasional romantic new meeting with one another, and the fatherly President Lopez of Portugal proved an understanding fellow-conspirator.'

The Presidential car and the police cordons in fact enabled them to outdistance all pursuers, and in a lonely bay beyond the romantic Setubal peninsular, the private serenity of the royal yacht awaited them.

13

A Queen for the space age

In the ground-floor secretarial rooms at Buckingham Palace the large wall maps showing the Queen's movements, past and future, visits accomplished or scheduled, became more densely speckled with coloured pins, the map of Great Britain pin-clustered not only around the great cities but through the Western Isles and studded towards Land's End. On the map of Europe the purple studs of forthcoming State Visits were placed upon Paris, Copenhagen and the Hague. On a map of North America the pins denoting the opening of the future St Lawrence Seaway spread west and south as accepted invitations lengthened into a fresh grand-scale tour in Canada and the United States. The maps showing the movements of other working members of the Royal Family were lined afresh with Marina the Duchess of Kent's visit to Ghana, the Queen Mother's renewed visits to Rhodesia and Nyasaland, Kenya and Uganda, New Zealand and Australia, and the then Duke of Gloucester's visits to Ethiopia, Norway, Germany and Nigeria.

Prince Philip returned from Antarctica driven by new ideas, his own travel projects extending indefinitely, beyond the 'near hops' of Germany and Belgium to India and Pakistan, Singapore, Hong Kong, the Solomons. As cousin Alexandra said, he 'set every member of the Royal Family travelling with a deepened sense of mission, strengthening the links of Commonwealth where it had once been a major event if royals visited a small provincial town'. On the reception side, the list of State Visitors extended from that kindly uncle, the King of Sweden to Feisal of Iraq, Haile Selassie of Ethiopia, de Gaulle of France, emperors, kings and presidents honoured with colourful ceremonial, fruitful in creating and strengthening the top-level friendships that further the amity of nations.

In her thirties, young yet maturing, Elizabeth II perceived the value of friendship between heads of nations with almost Victorian intensity, but also saw her Commonwealth role in fostering a worldwide brotherhood of nations as clearly the most far-seeing modern extension of the monarchy. In his audiences, her new Prime Minister, Harold Macmillan, found himself invited to sit comfortably beside her, which helped easy conversation, he felt. One of her prearranged overseas visits – to Ghana – was preceded by a bomb plot and a violent explosion occurred close to the very dais where she would be seated beside President Nkrumah a few days later. There was equally the very real risk of her being the unintended victim of an assassin's bullet aimed at her host. 'But how silly I should look', the Queen pointed out, 'if I were scared to visit Ghana and then Mr Khrushchev went a few weeks later.'

Mr Macmillan saw that on this issue of personal risk she might resist advice even to flouting the will of Parliament. 'The Queen has been absolutely determined all through,' he confided to his diary. 'She is impatient of the attitude towards her to treat her as a *woman*. . . . She has indeed "the heart and stomach of a man". She has great faith in the work she can do, in the Commonwealth especially. She doesn't enjoy "society". She likes her horses. But she loves her duty and means to be a Queen and not a puppet.'

Mr Macmillan was to serve the Queen as her Prime Minister for over six years, one of the longest administrations of her reign to date. He had cautioned her at one of their earliest meetings that his government might not last six weeks. 'She smilingly reminded me of this,' he wrote six years later, on his retirement.

When he fell ill and the necessity arose of choosing a successor, she visited him in hospital, and the worried matron moved his bed down a floor, rather than risk the Queen being stuck in a notoriously temperamental lift. Macmillan had some memoranda ready in an envelope on the advice available from his colleagues. She shook her head and told him, 'I do not need any other advice than yours', and then sat and talked of more domestic topics, of her hopes of visiting Western Germany, about personalities, of Prince Charles's schooling, and of Mr Macmillan's own long Parliamentary record, reminding him that he had been Premier for only three months short of seven years.

'I believe this is a record for the twentieth century,' she

wrote to him afterwards. 'If it has been exceeded at other times their conditions cannot have been comparable with the arduous circumstances of modern political life.' In fact one has to seek back ten years before she was born, to discover the long nine years of Mr Asquith's Liberal regime. The error was excusable. The Queen read like lightning and could remember all her current reading. In his memoirs Mr Macmillan had described the extraordinary task this involves. 'The Queen has a duty to be fully informed of all the affairs not only of the United Kingdom but also of all the countries of the Commonwealth, as well as foreign countries. This duty is always conscientiously performed. All Cabinet papers, all departmental papers, all foreign telegrams are sent to her and carefully studied by her. All the Cabinet's decisions are available to her immediately. All great appointments under the Crown must never be a matter for formal approval.' During three working months between a visit to Denmark and a joint visit to Canada and the United States, she was estimated in addition to have carried out 200 official engagements. The American magazine *Look* called her 'the most overworked young woman this side of the Iron Curtain'.

She regarded it as sufficient relaxation to slip off her shoes and put her feet up for thirty minutes. In a memo on Denmark, I noted, 'The Queen breakfasted at 8 in order to arrive at the Carlsberg Brewery at 9.30. She was shot up and down in goods lifts, she admired the huge Jutland draught horses in the dispatch yard and noticed that the white delivery trucks were of British make. Forced to shout above the noise of the machinery, she was amused to find her cipher formed in thousands of gold-topped beer-bottles. For a few minutes at mid-morning she found herself in the sedate tranquil home of Niels Bohr, the atom scientist, talking of flowers and gardening, and of her children. "I miss them when I'm away for long. But they understand why I have to go." Then she went on to visit a crèche, a school and municipal recreation centre, to attend a reception for 3,000 people of the Commonwealth communities and to watch a gala ballet performance. Somewhere during this time, an hour was spent in her streamlined study aboard *Britannia*, a secretary at her side, dealing with current business.'

Nor can we omit the accomplished success of the State Visit to France, the first to be watched almost continuously by the television cameras, a triumph of French elegance in the entertainment that President Coty offered his guests and a delight to the Queen in the obvious affection with which she was received. State Visits run to a basic pattern: the processional drive, the laying of a wreath, the State Banquet, the gala performance, the visit to some highlight of industrial or social conditions and the reception. The old illustrations of Queen Victoria and Prince Albert ascending the staircase of honour at the Hotel de Ville in 1855 curiously resemble the scene when Queen Elizabeth and Prince Philip mounted the steps of the Opera House. Queen Elizabeth appeared on the floodlight balcony of the Opera and a crowd 'estimated at half a million people, massed in every radiating street, gave a great sigh of admiration and pleasure'.

Millions of TV viewers, too, shared with Elizabeth the sumptuous enchantment of the cruise by night past the floodlit banks of the Seine, where every quay was a panoramic stage, each turn of the river revealing a fresh tableau, a vividly illumined flower-market starting from the darkness with its strolling mannequins; cavaliers and grenadiers parading; folk dancers leaping through a medieval crowd; men and women in eighteenth-century costume crossing and re-crossing a bridge with their bobbing lanterns. Choirs sang, and the stained-glass windows of Notre Dame – floodlit from within – glowed like jewels. Coloured cascades from fire floats shot high into the air and fireworks crackled dazzlingly in the night sky to complete the spectacle.

In October 1957, Russia launched the first satellite, Sputnik I, and inaugurated an unfathomable new era in the human story. While the news was still being discussed, Elizabeth II sat nervously before two unwieldly television cameras set up in the State dining-room at Buckingham Palace facing her first TV rehearsals. The Queen had worried the previous year with the certainty that the twenty-five-year-old tradition of the Christmas broadcast established by her grandfather was out-moded, 'old hat as the ark', in her phrase. There was no going back.

Prince Philip had pointed the way ahead by making an Antarctica film for schools. The title 'My Trip Round the World' had been burnished into 'Round the World in Forty Minutes'. The BBC made a demonstration film to show the Queen the various techniques she might use, to chat im-promptu, read from a script or memorise a talk with the safety-net of a teleprompter. The Queen chose the latter but was so disastrously nervous that two takes had to be scrapped.

'Take off your shoes. Be comfy,' Philip advised. Back in the summer the Queen had agreed to a TV broadcast to the Canadian people as a preliminary to opening the Canadian Parliament in Ottawa. In the United States she was then to address the United Nations Assembly in a filmed and televised broadcast to the world. Facing the cameras in Ottawa the producer noticed the 'congealed terror' in her eyes. Seated next to him, Prince Philip advised, 'Tell her to remember the wailing and gnashing of teeth – it has a special meaning.' The producer obeyed, the Queen flashed a smile of instant amusement and next moment, visibly eased, was on the air.

The Opening of Parliament, wearing her Coronation gown in a temperature under the film arc-lights of 93 °F was no trouble after that, and no newspaper could complain that the Speech from the Throne was in platitudes. The Queen added her own phrasing and recalled the words of the first Elizabeth to her last Parliament, *Though God hath raised me high, yet I count the glory of my Crown that I have reigned with your love.* 'Now here in the New World I say to you that it is my wish that in the years before me, I may so reign in Canada and be so remembered. . . .' Cousin Alexandra, keeping her pencil poised at that time to catch the contrasts of royal travel, noted that at the State Banquet that evening Prince Philip had a quizzical eye for the pantry-peekers, the correspondents elected by ballot to watch the Queen and himself eating turtle soup and duckling. One of the woman peekers wore slacks to climb a ladder and peer over a fifteen-foot curtain.

The American visit began in Jamestown, celebrating the 350th anniversary of the British settlement from which grew the fabric of the United States, and the Queen made obliging jokes about George III and slept that night in Williamsburg. Next day, President and Mrs Eisenhower awaited them at Washington airport. 'My, you look pretty,' said Mamie, with American verve. With the American gusto for statistics, the royals were estimated to have enjoyed seeing some of her own Blake watercolours on loan in art gallery, her visit to a ball game, and an impromptu exploration of a supermarket. Now there remained the Broadway welcome and the United Nations.

'Welcome, Liz and Phil,' said every shop-window in New York with a mass-produced poster, but their hosts prescribed that they should ride in separate cars, and they found that the bubble tops insulated them from the excitement to a remarkable degree, the car roofs soon darkened with paper. At the UN the Queen acknowledged the standing ovation with 'a sweet composure and calm', before and after – so said one witness – reading her basic speech that the Commonwealth nations could be pledged to add their tried element of strength and accumulated experience. That same day they lunched with 1,500 people and had dinner at the Waldorf with 4,000. At an American-style press conference, she had of course been asked how she survived her 'terrific schedule of appearances'. 'That's not difficult,' the Queen replied. 'I survive by enjoying every minute of the day.'

At home, however, the Queen watched two tele-recordings of herself without enjoyment and underscored her Christmas script with self-critical admonitions in large red letters. 'It is inevitable that I should seem a rather remote figure to many of you – a successor to the Kings and Queens of history. . . . But now at least I welcome you to the peace of my own home.' It harmed no-one to see the Queen smile with relief at her husband beyond camera range as she finished. And a family note mentions that it delighted Prince Charles to see himself and his seven-year-old sister on a monitor screen before the engineers left Sandringham.

From every journey, from even a day of duty away from home, the Queen returned to her children with loving delight. This above all was her private world, the playtime in nursery or sitting-room, the conversation with their nanny 'in a kind of code', the daily talks with their governess, Catherine Peebles, 'Mispy' to the children. The fun at bath-time slipped into the phase of games in the sitting-room, wherever there was space for Charles or Anne to curl into a ball for a romp of head over heels. (The Queen had early altered the hour of her weekly audience with the Prime Minister to avoid encroachment on 'the children's time'.)

Looking back at those delectable years, perhaps the Queen best remembers the domestic crisis when Nanny Helen Lightbody handed in her notice. In the equivocal relationship of nanny and parents, there had been few perceptible skirmishes through all the eight or nine years since the Windlesham era. Seconded from the Duchess of Gloucester's household, when her two boys, the Princes William and Richard, were beginning their schooling, Nanny Lightbody had survived the transfers to Clarence House and then to the Palace, the overtired tantrums of Coronation night, the months for the children without their parents and their voyage to Malta on *Britannia*. Bad as she considered travel for children, she met the changes of scene to Sandringham, Windsor or Balmoral, placidly and unfussed.

The first trouble came from clear skies while cruising with the family aboard the royal yacht around the northern tip of Scotland. In wet weather, the children snuggled to their grandmother, Prince Philip's mother, who could tell Bible stories more vividly than anyone and had more to tell of children in Greece who were hungry in wartime. When their parents were ashore, Grandmother assumed authority. 'You may be sure I know how to handle children,' she said once, crisply settling a difficulty with Nana. Whether Nanny Lightbody resented this divided rule is more difficult and delicate to tell, but the atmosphere was not without strain.

Then Prince Charles was launched into primary school at Hill House, near Knightsbridge, and Miss Peebles, the governess, proposed that three little girls should join Princess Anne for classes, and the institution of four or five for nursery lunch did not altogether meet with favour. Perhaps the breaking point was when Princess Sophie, Philip's sister, came to London to keep the Queen company during Philip's Antarctic absence, bringing her little two-year-old daughter, Princess Frederica. The under-nurse, Mabel Anderson, readily managed the fair-haired little creature. But Miss Lightbody pleaded that she wanted to have charge of babies again, and since the Queen and her husband did not foresee that they would be having any more children, she took her departure 'by amicable agreement'.

Miss Mabel had the possible advantage of being nearly the same age as the Queen. While Elizabeth and Margaret were in the dungeon air-raid shelter at Windsor, sitting close to the hatbox containing St Edward's Crown, Mabel was sheltering with her mother and younger sister under a staircase during the air-raids on Liverpool. Her father, a policeman, had been killed in the blitz – my records still shelter the horror of the certificate of death on duty, 'Dead body found 5 May' – and, with a link of coincidence, Mabel had taken her only specialised training while living in Elgin with her widowed mother, a mile down the road from Gordonstoun. Miss Peebles, too, followed the royal Scottish tradition, Glasgow-born and early assuming her vocation in Australia before taking charge of Princess Alexandra and Prince Michael of Kent. 'Very good at exercising a gentle discipline. She teaches children self-control and a sense of humour,' wrote her former employer, Viscountess Clive, in recommendation.

An essential difference between Anne and Charles, 'Mispy' quickly discovered, was that the girl could amuse herself while Charles liked to be amused. When he was smaller she had felt that he had 'only a vague relationship to the external world', a report her royal employers took in good part. Indeed, the vagueness lessened when Charles first copied a meaningful phrase from his Beacon Primer, 'Here is baby sister. She likes to play horse', a prophetic first encounter with the media.

The Queen chose Hill House day school for Charles after a friend had reported it as the only local primary where the pavement outside was washed weekly and the basement railings kept dusted. Inviting the headmaster, Colonel Henry Townsend, to tea, the Queen discovered that his wife had been theatre sister to Sir John Weir, the obstetrician who had been present at Charles's birth, and she needed to know no more.

Arriving for his first day at school, a press photographer recognised Charles at once – to the Queen's annoyance – as the only boy wearing an overcoat with a velvet collar. But when her car was travelling through one of the quieter Chelsea streets one afternoon, she had the pleasure of seeing him in a two-by-two file of schoolboys, all in identical russet shorts and cinnamon sweaters, on his way to a nearby soccer field. Unrecognised herself, 'I wanted to tap on the window and thought better of it', the cameo remains in memory. Prince Charles's first school report told of 'good well-formed writing, aptitude for history, promise in French, good in geography', and when he appeared in the end-of-term school show at Chelsea Town Hall as one of ten little Indians, his mother was in the audience. Hill House made a point of 'educating the boy to be part of a world community' and in Prince Charles's year at least forty boys of every shade of colour were pupils from the neighbourhood's foreign embassies.

Again, the Queen and Prince Philip, with Princess Anne and Mispy, formed a family group at the summer school sports, when Charles showed his new sporting prowess and was overtaken in the fifty-yard sprint only by looking an admiring second too long at his mother. Some of the members of his class still remember being presented to her, one of the few occasions when Charles could pull his rank, and, like any mother, the Queen readily showed his school report to her friends. There were adequate pointers to the future, in the professional assurance that he was 'tremendously observant, never cheeky to the staff. . . a boy with some creative capacity with a receptive and sensitive mind as well as individual determination'.

Despite fading hopes in some respects, 1958 had been planned as a leisurely year and, on the flimsiest excuses, the Queen contrived to visit a number of prep schools to help her to decide the vexed question of where Charles should next go as a boarder. The elder side of the family championed Ludgrove, the proved route to Eton followed by the Queen's uncles, David Lyon and the Duke of Gloucester. Prince Philip preferred his own school, Cheam, leading on to Gordonstoun and, inevitably, before long the Queen accepted her husband's view. Both travelled down from Balmoral to see him safely received. Charles shuddered with apprehension; another of the Queen's cameo memories. Watching his arrival, one of the welcoming teachers thought that he looked scruffy and very miserable, the only boy who needed a haircut.

His mother was as concerned about him as any woman sending her small son away to school for the first time and privately called to see him after two or three weeks to make sure he was settling in. And he was, except that, as his detective let fall, he 'wasn't being given a chance'. A day rarely passed without one of the national newspapers publishing a story about Charles and the school, his teachers and his friends. 'Can't it be stopped?' the Queen asked. 'Can't we talk to the newspapers?' As a result, her press secretary, the sailorly Commander Colville, called a press conference to point out to the offenders and others that unless the news stories ceased she would have to take her son away from school to be privately educated. The assembled editors saw the point, the news surveillance simmered down and the schoolboys gradually accepted Charles as one of themselves. His worst remaining ordeal during his five Cheam years was in the first year when, with other boys, he was invited into the headmaster, Peter Beck's, study to watch the closing ceremonies of the Commonwealth Games in Cardiff.

The Queen was expected to perform the closing ceremony,

hugging with glee a secret she planned to disclose, but she fell victim to an attack of sinusitis and the Duke of Edinburgh introduced her recorded message instead. 'By a cruel stroke of fate,' came her voice, 'I have been prevented from visiting Wales today, a memorable year for the Principality. I have therefore decided to mark it further by an act which will, I hope, give as much pleasure to all Welshmen as it does to me. I intended to create my son Charles Prince of Wales today.'

The Cheam boys watching the television turned to Charles clapping and cheering, and Peter Beck saw him wince with embarrassment. 'When he is grown up, I will present him to you at Caernarvon,' the Queen went on. Watching the scene at Cardiff as her taped message ended, she could see the crowds rise in a roar of cheering. Her quiet room at the Palace echoed with spontaneity of the great crowd singing 'God Bless the Prince of Wales'. But for the blushing Prince it was probably the moment when he felt the cold touch of his future and the 'awful fate' that lay in store. He was not yet ten years old.

As the New Year of 1959 opened, the Queen approached the seventh anniversary of her Accession with the not unreasonable satisfaction that some of her deepest ideals for the work of the monarchy within the Commonwealth were paying off. The Duke of Edinburgh early abandoned the customary Sandringham break to fly off on a three-month working tour through India, Pakistan and the Far East. The Queen Mother embarked on a visit to Kenya and Uganda. The then Duchess of Kent and Princess Alexandra undertook a tour in Latin America, paving the way for Philip's goodwill visit in 1962. The Duke and Duchess of Gloucester prepared to visit Nigeria, while Princess Margaret took up a full schedule in the Caribbean. 'Between us, we are going to many parts of the world,' the Queen ended in her Christmas TV broadcast. 'We have no plans for space travel at the moment!'

But the year promised travel plans, in a sense, off the world map, into the frozen wastes of the Arctic Circle, the journey to the Northwest Territories which her husband had foreshadowed to John Diefenbaker, 'The Queen's wanted to see them ever since I was there.' Months in advance, it had been foreseen that the end of his Far East visits clashed with his needful presence in Bermuda to celebrate 350 years of British settlement, and he would not be home for his wife's thirty-third birthday. They talked by long-distance phone: Charles was out of isolation with chickenpox, a nuisance that Anne had caught it, but mother and son had gone riding together that morning, Cheam was making him really good company.

Nine days later the Queen met her husband at London airport. On the point of completing her 'family portrait' book about Philip, Cousin Alexandra privately noticed an unusually long weekend at Windsor and noted in her book that within three days he was vigorously playing polo, having 'travelled farther than any prince in the records of man'. This was the month that saw Philip in jaunty mood at the Chelsea flower show, examining an automatic sprinkler that next instant drenched the nearby press photographers. The general opinion was that 'he was innocent but shouldn't do it again'. And the Queen that month, during a provincial visit, was asked if she would like to greet an old lady of 105 who was waiting in her car. 'They shouldn't have done it: it might have killed the old lady.' She was speaking from acute experience. Old ladies keel over in crowds and end the day in 'intensive care'. A bank manager visiting Buckingham Palace died of a heart attack.

If Prince Philip's idea of a fun trip with his wife into the Yukon tended to fade, the packaged programme tightened inexorably. The central essential had been to share the opening of the St Lawrence Seaway with President Eisenhower. But even the eager Canadian press was critical of the demands of the Queen. Was it necessary that she should spend three hours inspecting a Quebec nickel-mine, and be called upon to admire frozen-food plants, sawmills and a Salvation Army hostel? 'You must remember, I'm not going out for a holiday, but to work,' the Queen reminded Esmond Butler, her Canadian press equerry. The influential editor of *Maclean's Magazine* suggested that the schedules should be scrapped. 'Let the mayors and dowagers repine. Royalty will have an easier time.' But the Queen did not wish for ease, and it was only on the eve of departure that there was a hint, an intimation, that in her own private life her dearest personal wish might after all be fulfilled.

The royal couple kept their hopes to themselves and it was only afterwards that they noticed the curious and reassuring elements in the journey. They were due to fly into St John's, Newfoundland, but the coast had been blanketed all week in a sea fog which the meterologists predicted would continue, and an hour from arrival it seemed that their aircraft would have to be diverted. Instead the fog-banks suddenly rolled aside and the plane unexpectedly landed in sunlight. The Queen and Prince Philip had no sooner left the airport, in fact, than the mists closed down while the sun still shone on the road ahead. In mid-town the people broke through the thin police cordon, shouting and cheering. Most crowds have a distinctive sound, sometimes clapping, often a sound like breaking surf, sometimes the drum-beat of 'Liz! Phil! Liz! Phil!' but surrounding the car the people of St John's were calling 'Bless you! God bless you', again and again.

A correspondent cabled that Prince Philip 'seemed subdued, in contrast to the Queen's obvious high spirits'. The Queen was more truthfully elated at her private hopes while her husband was gravely concerned as he considered the strain on her of the arduous six weeks ahead. On the first full day the Queen opened a new terminal building at Gander airport, flew into the backwoods to the tiny settlement of Deer Lake and lurched and bumped thirty miles over a rough dirt road to visit a papermill. Twenty-four hours later she stood in the open pit of a Labrador iron ore mine, coated in the blowing red dust, deafened by the bulldozers. Forty-eight hours more and, regardless of sinus troubles, the white powder of an aluminium smelter assailed her. But the Queen was replying in her own way to complaints that she did not meet the people. The miners of Sheffeville rubbed their grimy hands on their stained working togs before shaking hands and, in their prefab homes, the Queen talked sympathetically with their wives – 'I find it difficult keeping my floors clean, too.' She met nuns and smeltermen, geologists, engineers and lumber-jacks; she talked with fishermen, fur dealers, and Indian trappers.

The opening of the St Lawrence Seaway with President and Mrs Eisenhower aboard *Britannia* was duly accomplished with a five-hour cruise through the first three locks, in a bedlam of gun salutes, pealing bells and sirens. In the Beau-harnois lock the royal yacht was so close to the concrete that the heads of the two nations in mock alarm tried to fend the ship away with their hands. 'As close as that!' the Queen spread her fingers to Mr Diefenbaker.

At about this time the Queen confided to her Canadian

Prime Minister her happiness that she might be going to have a baby. Greatly concerned, Mr Diefenbaker at once offered to cancel or curtail the tour, though the Queen would not hear of it and indeed reminded him somewhat sharply that the decision was for herself alone. No doubt the royal couple now felt that there was no turning back. The royal yacht leisurely cruised through Lake Huron and Lake Michigan to Chicago, where another fantastic welcome, all fireworks and fanfares, was similarly followed by a placid cruise into Lake Superior. The mid-July programme in Vancouver and Victoria was, however, prolonged and demanding, and when the Queen arrived in Whitehorse those concerned with the tour were shocked at her pallor and obvious exhaustion.

Tapping their typewriters, the accompanying press party used up their resentful adjectives, 'brutal', 'onerous', 'punishing'. As I wrote at the time, 'they watched the Queen grimly struggling through the ceremonies in the dusty streets as if at a pitch of exhaustion, continuing by will-power alone. . . .' The programme made no concession to the heat, but when the Queen went to bed at 7 p.m., complaining of feeling unwell, the news buzzed more noisily than the mosquitoes in the Press Room at the RCAF barracks. That evening the Queen at last explained her symptoms to the tour doctor, Surgeon Captain Steele-Perkins, but otherwise preferred to wait until she returned home. Next day the Queen's arrangements for the day were cancelled and explained in good faith, 'The Queen is suffering from a stomach upset and from fatigue. She will not be going to Dawson City and will stay indoors today. Prince Philip is going to church alone and will go to Dawson City. . . .'

Mr Diefenbaker again suggested that the tour should be broken off, and the Queen refused as before. But the next bulletin announced, 'The Queen is better but is not fully recovered', and on 21 July the Queen appeared in Edmonton as arranged to undertake a programme of handshaking, tree-planting and the like. To Philip's regret, though on his strongest recommendation, the tour of the northland was however abandoned. (The Queen crossed the Arctic Circle two years later with Prince Philip, the Prince of Wales and Princess Anne during the tour of the Northwest Territories, July 1970.)

Now the progress was eastward and homeward on a whistle-stop run through the prairie provinces. The larger townships boasted bands; every hamlet had its cluster of shrill Brownies –

'They're a real tonic,' said the Queen – and the evening drink aboard the royal train was promptly dubbed a gin-and-Brownie. And when the train stopped for the night in some lonely siding, when the last stray visitors had gone away, the Queen and her husband were seen sitting quietly together on the observation platform, free at last to exchange their own serene and hopeful thoughts and to hear the chirping of the crickets under the great bowl of the prairie sky.

14

The second family

It will long be remembered that the birth of Prince Andrew, on the afternoon of 19 February 1960, heralded a phase of strangely alternating events of pleasure and sorrow. Immediately on the Queen's return to England, indeed, her cousin, the young Duke of Kent, told her of his hopes of marrying a young lady, Katharine Worsley, at that moment on holiday in Canada, while explaining diffidently that he was talking of hopes still in the future. Elizabeth, amused, disclosed her own delicious secret. Her indisposition at Whitehorse turned out to have nothing to do with her pregnancy but her own doctors now confirmed her happy anticipations.

No child had been in prospect for a Queen of England since the advent of Queen Victoria's last baby, Princess Beatrice, in 1857, when royal hopes were never discussed. Elizabeth ensured that the Commonwealth governments were informed and then slipped away to Balmoral, while Commander Colville took the unprecedented step of calling a full news conference in the Palace ballroom. The Queen found this venue amusing and enquired, 'And how did your ball go?'

Never averse to a good story about himself, the Commander recounted the journalists' questions: whether the Queen wanted a boy or a girl, whether twins were in prospect, whether the Commonwealth governments already knew. He had answered that the Commonwealth governments had been informed through their Governors-General, and up spoke a dismayed Indian, 'But we have no Governor-General! We're a republic!'

'The Queen will undertake no further public engagements,' ran the communiqué. 'Her Majesty deeply regrets the disappointment which her inability to carry out her projected tour in West Africa may bring to many of her people in Ghana, Sierra Leone and the Gambia. Her Majesty also much regrets that she and the Duke of Edinburgh will be unable to visit Shetland and Orkney next week. The Queen . . . is in good health.'

There were the usual 'cot trimmings' of news. The old ladies of a drapers' retirement home happily knitted and stitched a fifty-six-piece white layette. The Queen was said to have acquired a fondness for honey, and sticky packages inundated the Palace mail-room. The people of West Virginia dispatched a US government booklet on infant care. The government of Kenya sent a gift-rug of nine lambskins, and the Diplomatic Corps subscribed for an antique silver cup of the year 1693 for the baby. Then, privately, these news items were accompanied by another event causing great happiness at Balmoral. For over two years the Queen had known of Princess Margaret's deepening friendship with the gifted young photographer, Antony Armstrong-Jones, and as usual had no difficulty in reading her sister's mind.

Much was implicit in Margaret's repeated playing of the recordings of *West Side Story* with its modern-style Romeo and Juliet theme; implicit, too, in her constant chatter of Tony, with his extraordinary hideaway down the river at Rotherhithe, his *Vogue* photographs, and Margaret's undisguised pleasure in the photographs he had taken for her twenty-ninth birthday.

The Queen Mother indulged the couple, and the Queen, casually but deliberately, dropped in for tea at Clarence House one day when Tony was there. They had in fact met earlier when he had come to the Palace, on the Duke of Kent's recommendation, to photograph Charles and Anne.

In that lovely lazy anticipatory summer at Balmoral, Margaret 'quite shamelessly wangled' Tony as a house-guest nearby at Birkhall. 'They both carried cameras everywhere and spent hours taking photographs of the scenery – and of each other,' another guest noted. Cousin Pammy Mountbatten also introduced an interesting newcomer into the circle one weekend, a young artist-designer named David Hicks.

The Queen befriended both young men, both intending bridegrooms, 'as though each came of a long-lost branch of the family'. One story was that Pammy and David discovered that they had been born within a month of each other and instantly considered themselves two of a kind. By that criterion,

Margaret and Tony were only separated by five months. Tony was born in March 1930, Margaret making her début with more celebrity in August. David Hicks was the only son of a London stockbroker, Tony the only son of a London barrister. Both came of the same Chelsea–Belgravia strata and had trodden the same London pavements, Tony to his first studio in Shaftesbury Avenue, David to the nearby Central School of Art. David Hicks, moreover, shared a house with his widowed mother in the next street to where Tony had been born. Whatever Queen Mary might have said about marrying into the arts, there was good sense in Philip's viewpoint that in matters of the heart people had to find their own way.

Margaret and Tony agreed to follow the then unbroken system of royal alliance by waiting six months before a formal engagement in the late autumn. 'The chief topics here are brides and babies,' wrote a Balmoral visitor.

At Sandringham, too, a concourse of Mountbatten kinfolk gathered immediately after Christmas, with sufficient Hesse, Hohenlohe and Hanover youngsters to have amply satisfied Queen Victoria. There were mysterious midnight peals from the security alarm on the landing, bringing the families together in their dressing-gowns, and coot-shooting expeditions by day to the frozen wastes of Hickling Broad. After Twelfth Night the entire flock of relatives departed for Broadlands and the festivities of Pammy's wedding on 13 January. As bridesmaid at Romsey Abbey Lady Pamela had chosen Princess Anne and two of her aunt Princess Sophie's daughters, the brunette Clarissa of Hesse and the blonde little Frederica of Hanover, with one or two Knatchbull cousins. The weather was cold and snowy, and as a mother-to-be the Queen felt it best to remain at home in Norfolk but could not resist ringing Broadlands during the wedding reception to hear all the details. The snow had caused a power failure, she learned, but everything was being marvellously staged by candlelight.

In the course of a string of family confabs while thus happily awaiting her baby the Queen also cleared her mind of the pressing emotive problem which her Prime Minister, Harold Macmillan, described in Cabinet as 'The Queen's Affair'. Seven years of growing experience had elapsed since Churchill had persuaded her to follow her father and grandfather in taking the dynastic family name of Windsor, legalising it by declaring to her Privy Council 'Her Will and Pleasure that She and her Children shall be styled and known as the House and Family of Windsor'. Was her husband's surname, then, to be erased and banished from future record? The issue was first brought back to Cabinet notice in 1959 and, after ministerial agreement, the Queen had 'something to say' at a Sandringham family dinner party, something she confessed to having 'had in mind for a long time', something close to her heart.

Without changing the name of the Royal House, she had 'always wanted to associate the name of her husband with her own and his descendants'. And so while continuing to be known as the House and Family of Windsor, her wish for her children and descendants was for them to bear the name Mountbatten-Windsor. This was thought at first only to apply to grandchildren and their descendants, but Princess Anne as a bride gave her surname as Mountbatten-Windsor. Prince Charles, too, could not but follow this precedent at his own wedding, or so legal experts expected.

'My decisions have had to include The Queen's Affair,' wrote Mr Macmillan. 'The Cabinet agreed to the plan which the Lord Chancellor managed to work out with Her Majesty . . . the name of Mountbatten-Windsor – like Spencer Churchill,' he added. An odd example to cite, twenty-one years to the month before Lady Diana Spencer became engaged to the Prince of Wales.

Two days after the birth of Prince Andrew, the Queen faced the other side of life's coin in being told of the sudden death of the Countess Mountbatten, Philip's Aunt Edwina, in Burma. Two days more, and she had to be told of the death of Queen Victoria's last surviving grandson, the Marquess of Carisbrooke, at his home in Kensington Palace. The Queen decreed a week of family mourning, but decided equally that prearranged events should not be affected. Princess Margaret and Tony Armstrong-Jones had come to her hand in hand while little Andrew lay beside her in the Belgian Suite, and Mr Macmillan found himself officially expressing his condolences to the Queen on Lady Mountbatten, while privately informing Hugh Gaitskell, as Leader of the Opposition, of Princess Margaret's impending betrothal. Above all, indeed, the Queen recognised that the thirteenth year of her marriage was one of 'domestic joy and felicity'.

As with Diana Spencer twenty-one years later, Tony

Armstrong-Jones was at once offered the security of a guest-room at the Palace, a dignified remove from the intense glare of public curiosity abruptly turned on him. Margaret was anxious that not a whisper of her betrothal should leak out even a day too soon, and, to the Queen's undoubted glee, when Andrew was just a week old, the engagement announcement burst on the world as a complete surprise.

When Cecil Beaton first photographed the baby at a month old, he correctly sensed that there would be no official press release of any christening pictures. The Queen and her husband agreed that their relations with Andrew should be 'of pure pleasure'. The little boy was already different, with the 'dark look' of another Mountbatten side of the family, taking more after Earl Mountbatten's daughters, Patricia and Pamela, or Prince Philip's eldest sister, Margarita, than the Saxon fairness of Philip and Anne. Immersed in contented maternity, the Queen did not reappear in public until 5 April, when President and Madame de Gaulle began a State Visit, thus leaving the warmth of public favour and approbation entirely to Margaret, in the glow of her wedding preparations.

The better the Queen knew Tony the more she felt the couple were perfectly matched, so similarly mercurial, so nearly of the same age and even height, so very alike in their artistic tastes and interests. If it seemed untimely that Tony's father had been tracked down on honeymoon in Bermuda with the third Mrs Armstrong-Jones, this was better than the wounding assumption that he would share in Margaret's Civil List allowance, which automatically increased on her marriage, and a sheaf of hurtful inaccuracies about his family. He was resolved indeed to meet a full share of household expenses from his professional income, difficult though it was to be sure whether his photographic career could continue. Indeed, he was persuaded to close his studio and accept a public relations post with the Design Centre. The Queen and Prince Philip considered there might be many bridges to cross and could only suggest taking each in turn. Among many such bristling problems, the Queen's sister found herself advancing into an unknown future with few signposts or prescriptions.

Meanwhile, on the day the de Gaulles flew home, the new baby was christened Andrew Albert Christian Edward. President de Gaulle had lightly suggested that the baby should have a French name. 'But, of course, we named our first son

Charles and we shall name our second André,' the Queen responded. Both were among the President's own Christian names and, if he recognised that the Queen was being ingeniously diplomatic, he could not help but feel flattered. The name Andrew was primarily that of Philip's father – Andrea within the family. Christian was a compliment to Philip's sister Sophie who had given her elder Hesse daughter the equivalent Christine. The name equally echoed Christabel, the little-known last name of Princess Alexandra, who was a godmother. The other sponsors were the Duke of Gloucester and Lord Elphinstone (uncles of the Queen) and the Earl of Euston and Mrs Harold Phillips, who were among close personal friends. The ceremony took place in the Music Room at Buckingham Palace and the baby was 'beatific, wide awake and friendly'.

Privately, the inner circle of the Royal Household considered it a godsend that maternity had remitted the incessant flow of State activities, if not the constant presence of State business. In the quiet months before and after Andrew's advent the Queen found time to be her womanly self, to go shopping, see more of her friends and indulge in purely feminine chatter, even to spending an hour or two choosing wallpaper patterns for Windsor. She and Philip often went to the theatre, enjoying such pleasurable anonymity one evening that they were ushered into the wrong seats.

At Windsor Castle, too, they launched upon the fulfilment of an old dream in supervising the remodelling and furnishing of a set of guest suites in the King Edward III Tower, having decided that a shabby and old-fashioned wing should be renovated in a fresh and contemporary manner. 'Self-service lunch with HM and an hour of discussion after', noted her architect, Sir Hugh Casson. 'We pack up, pleased the main decisions are made.' The Cassons were encouraged to commission fabrics and furniture from modern designers, and the Queen methodically set in motion a thank-offering quest for the work of a dozen or more young artists whose paintings would be representative of the moment and could form a contemporary royal art collection within the guest-wing.

'They have reopened the unoccupied rooms,' wrote Queen Ena of Spain. 'Elizabeth has brought the sun in and chased out the clustering shadows.' Another unaccustomed visitor dwelt on the effect of 'striped fuchsia wallpaper, sounds strange but looks fabulous, the wide sitting-room carpeted in a deep blue-green and bright with lamps and flowers'. Independently of Casson and Hicks, the Queen had discovered tastes of her own in modern decor. She paid an impromptu visit to look over a much-vaunted modern hotel near London airport, and hurried to the new Berkeley Hotel in Knightsbridge to tour it from penthouse suites to swimming pool with a discriminating eye. The British artists whose works she purchased included Ivon Hitchens, Mary Fedden, James Taylor and Robin Darwin; and with her new guest suites satisfactorily completed, she turned to other enterprises of a watchful chatelaine.

On presenting Marlborough House, Queen Mary's former home in the Mall, for use as a Commonwealth centre in London, she called in occasionally to see for herself how alterations were progressing. The Queen had always felt there was something vaguely wrong about the painted ceiling in the entrance hall depicting the nine muses. It turned out that they had been wrongly rearranged when brought long ago from the Queen's House at Greenwich. Cleaned and set into their original positions, they are now one of the glories of the historic Wren mansion. On the staircase, similarly, battle-scenes and landscapes of the great Duke of Marlborough's day emerged in fresh repair from behind smoke-screens of varnish, and other exacting overhauls were set in train at Holyrood-house and Hampton Court.

As a connoisseur, and by her mid-thirties she was truly that in many fields of art, the Queen early set herself the lively ambition of passing on to her successors a royal heritage in better state and more perfect condition than she had found it.

All the major works of art had disappeared into safe hiding during the war, and five months after the end of hostilities a major exhibition of the King's pictures was staged at Burlington House. The works had never before been hung in order from period to period, from the newly luminous Holbeins and the great Italian pictures to the portraits by Zoffany and Reynolds. Through the winter the King had given a series of memorable parties at Burlington House at which Elizabeth met many senior painters and sculptors of the day, and from their admiration of the royal collection the Princess learned the necessity of sharing the enjoyment of art, expressed today in her readiness to show her treasures to the public in ever-increasing degree. Year by year fresh priorities are agreed – for the cleaning of pictures, for example, and new assignments made.

Both for the Queen and Philip it was as if the coming of their 'second family' inaugurated a renaissance in attachment to these ideals. The old bomb-damaged private chapel at the Palace had, for instance, remained derelict for twenty years and when the prospect of rebuilding arose the royal couple suggested a small modern chapel affording extra space for an art gallery, where the public might enjoy selections from the royal art collections – pictures, furniture, china, silver, old master drawings and even rarities from George V's stamp collection.

The Queen's Gallery became an exhilarating family interest. Prince Philip proposed the illuminated panelled ceiling, Princess Margaret – and indeed Lord Snowdon – recommended a pastel canvas wallcovering as the most sympathetic background for the paintings, and the Queen chose the pearly-grey rayon canvas itself and in fact footed the bill for the additional cost of the gallery – structural alterations, fixtures and fittings – from her private resources.

Through twenty years the changing exhibitions have naturally tended to reflect the Queen's personal tastes and interests, Gainsboroughs, landscapes, animal studies, child portraits, Dutch pictures, soldiering through artists' eyes, her Sèvres porcelain, her ultimate responsibility as custodian of the world's largest array of Leonardo drawings, and not least her choice of modern artists displayed in her Silver Jubilee exhibition, ranging from Graham Sutherland and Paul Nash to the abstracts of Alan Davie. The Queen has learned to live with the shadow gaps on her walls caused when pictures are loaned to other exhibitions. There are 900 loans in Britain alone in a sample year. But her interests extends to the very fabric of monarchy, a first-viewing of the cornice lighting illuminating the Holbein ceiling at the Chapel Royal, an incognito call to see the restoration of the lake and grounds at Claremont, her patient insistence and support over fifteen years which triumphantly saw the miracle of the painstakingly restored Mantegna processional pictures at Hampton Court, and equally her thoughtful planning with Philip of the simple perfection of the garden in eighteenth-century style at Kew Palace.

The cruelty of rumour has exacted a forfeit from royalty since the widowhood of Queen Victoria, and indeed since the Gillray sketches of Georgian days. It was sadly said that Elizabeth II looked 'dour' during Princess Margaret's wedding, when indeed she could hardly conceal all but maternal emotion at seeing her sister happily wed at last.

It was a perfect day, and early in the morning from a Palace window the Queen had trained her binoculars on the remarkable arch of roses sixty feet high at the top of the Mall, and watched the growing crowds as she had done on her own morning as a bride. The more remarkable public manifestations of the day however were reserved for television where they were later seen by the Queen, as by most of us.

Towards the close of the afternoon a royal Rolls emerged from the Palace forecourt with a single escort car and one suddenly realised that this was the bride and groom, shorn now of royal panoply, Mr Armstrong-Jones and his wife in fact on their way to embark at Tower Pier for their honeymoon. As I wrote at the time, it was a touching *coup de théâtre*, and the crowds ran across the Mall to welcome them like ripples upon a shore. There were no troop cordons now. Not for the first time, the Princess was among the London crowds. Along the Strand and in the City, where the office homegoers joined those who were waiting, the limousine was engulfed by well-wishers, twenty deep, on either side. There were too few police; the people near the car were enclosed themselves by happy, more distant throngs, and the car moved at a snail's pace through the miles of smiling faces.

The Queen had felt 'rather like a guardian angel' in the background, an angel rewarded, too, with the first letters home from the Caribbean. 'It was so very wonderful for us both', Margaret wrote from one of the islands, 'just to lie on those deserted beaches, without a soul in sight. Neither of us ever wanted to be rescued in the evening and we would gladly have lived in a little grass hut.' When they eventually returned home, indeed, it was to live in one of the smaller, and all the more desirable, houses within her gift. The story is that one day, in gleeful mood, she mentioned an available house in the village cluster of Kensington Palace. It turned out in fact to be the same Georgian 'dolls' house', a charmer overlooking a green at the back of the old palace, where Margaret had once admiringly said she would like to live, a wish her sister had noted and remembered ever since.

Undoubtedly Elizabeth entered the tenth year of her reign contented in seeing Margaret so romantically settled, illusory as this may have seemed in the long term. At Sandringham, too, at Christmas, the young Duke of Kent sought out the Queen to ask her formal permission for him to marry Katharine Worsley, who was nearly three years younger than Margaret. Elizabeth saw clearly that Eddie Kent's sister, Princess Alexandra – six years younger than Margaret – and Angus Ogilvy would be next. Now nearly thirty-five herself, the Queen had a pleasant sense of affectionate seniority among an emergent new band of active royal partisans. Cousin Eddie was soon to represent her at independence celebrations in Sierra Leone and Uganda, with visits to Kenya and Tanganyika. Princess Alexandra's roster ranged from the independence of Nigeria to an impending official tour to Japan, Burma, Thailand, Aden and Tripoli.

The Queen could see her own engagements extending five years ahead and, contingently, far beyond. With the thought of another baby, of perhaps rounding off that optimistic prospect of the 'second family', so far limited to one, there had to be diplomatic space in the calendar. The project of a visit to India and Pakistan had matured within six months but the Queen did not foresee that her Accession anniversary, so burdened with memories at home, would pass in the crisp air and barren landscape of the Khyber Pass or that she would cut a cake for little Andrew's first birthday surrounded by sari-clad women in the sultry atmosphere of Madras. In any event, who could have imagined that, so soon after the bitter birth-pangs of India in 1947, thousands of Union Jacks would flower in Delhi and that the travellers would find India's millions demonstrating their affection and friendship for the embodiment of the Raj?

In retrospect, the whole experience was an extravaganza. On her first night in the former vice-regal lodge the Queen learned that Mr Khrushchev had slept in the same room before her, probably in the same bed, and her team's wistful hopes that she might outvie the ovation given to him only shortly before were to be more than fulfilled. Everywhere were crowds, smiling, cheering, nevertheless individuals demonstrating their regard in tens of thousands. She attended the Republic Day parades standing at the side of President Prasad, that devout and homely old man who talked of a term in His Majesty's gaols as 'gone in a minute'. The parading camels were draped in Union Jacks and knelt to her. As one of her vignettes the Queen remarked subsequently of the contrasting wild excitement of the people at one point 'and the deadpan faces of their bullocks standing behind them'.

Here was the India of burning contrasts which Uncle Dickie Mountbatten had described so often, 'nothing like it anywhere else in the world'. In industrial Ahmedabad, 'the real India' confronted her, the rickety balconies crammed with people, others packed in front of the crumbling buildings so close that they could have touched her, crying such English words as they knew, 'Hullo!' and 'Happiness!' She attended a tiger hunt in Jaipur which provoked dissent in England. Yet an influential Indian editorial set the balance, 'No-one seriously thinks that if the British monarch watches her husband take a shot at a tiger they bring down the Commonwealth. No-one grudges them their fun.'

Unashamedly a tourist, the Queen constantly used her movie camera, on the tiger, on the painted elephants, on the crocodiles which Philip pursued with speedboat and gun on the lakes of Udaipur. She photographed the Taj Mahal in watery sunshine but returned with her husband for the fitful moonlight. The tour swooped from Delhi south-west to Karachi, intermixing a little Urdu in her greetings in Pakistan. North then to Peshawar and the bleak heights of the Malakand Pass, where Churchill had first seen action as a war correspondent, and the royal couple charmed the old man with a telegram, 'We both send you greetings from Malakand.' In the little kingdom of Swat, they motored through pines to the edge of the glaciers, through scenes of magnificent film material. In the rarity of perfect weather, there was a flight along the Himalayas to Nepal, their plane circling Everest at 28,000 feet and Elizabeth, unashamedly a tourist, filled reels of colour with the incomparable scene.

So it went on, the crescendo welcome of Calcutta, the voyage on a decorated barge upstream past the burning crematoria of the Ganges, a parade of 327 elephants. It was all of a piece that on St David's Day, back in Delhi, a young Welsh girl presented the Queen with daffodils flown from Wales, and that the Queen's farewell broadcast that same day was forthwith translated into fifteen different dialects, 'The happiness and friendship which we found was a triumphant vindication of the vision of the statesmen who changed the old empire into a free association of equals. . . .' The words summed up much of the Queen's overseas philosophy.

Four dreamlike days of the homeward route were spent in a State visit to Iran. From their jet, the couple transferred to golden coaches with the Shah and Queen Farah and drove from the airport to the strains of 'Bonnie Dundee'. Michael Adeane had done his work with a reminder that it was exactly 400 years since Elizabeth I sent letters of friendship to the Shah Abbas the Great. From Teheran the Queen and the Duke of Edinburgh visited Isfahan, with its blue domes and minarets, and no-one dreamed that it was only a score of years to the year of the American hostages.

'Halfway to seventy. . . .' The press could not be expected to omit that phrase, though the Queen preferred to forget it when she celebrated her thirty-fifth birthday at Badminton. In her early twenties she had written that 'the time has whizzed by'. Now a commentator noted, 'She keeps an antique hour-glass on her desk to signal discreetly the passage of time during an audience. Now, as she steps briskly into maturity, the sand-glass of her own life needs adjustment.' Martin Charteris, as assistant secretary, correctly assessed the result when he passed the newspaper to its victim. She merely laughed and said, 'Oh dear!'

But with this signpost passed, the Queen and her husband flew to Sardinia, where the carpets draped in salutation from the windows of Cagliari were reminiscent of the bedspreads hung from the balconies for their reunion in Lisbon four years before. A spaghetti lunch served at a tiny hotel on the isle of Vulcano was inevitably remindful of Malta. Then there followed a State Visit to Italy. In Rome, the story went the rounds of a South African tourist, pausing at the Palazzo Barberini to enquire what was going on, who was ushered into a Common-wealth reception and found himself shaking hands with the Queen. On their final day the royal couple were received by the Pope, and the Queen was conscious of change. As Princess Elizabeth her audience had been with the scholarly Pius XII. In the same room she was greeted by the genial and fatherly Pope John. That day, too, brought an apt and lasting memory. If the Queen had begun to think herself beyond travel emotion, she came near to tears when the band of the Palatine Guard began to play 'God Save the Queen', and the crowd of thousands in St Peter's Square, nuns, priests, visitors, took up the anthem.

Next, another weekend in Florence with Queen Helen of Rumania, and then Venice, where Elizabeth had looked forward to the Torcello taverna where Philip had skylarked in his teens, but his wife now found it transformed into a restaurant of elegance. She had hoped to sail in a gondola and this too was brought about in a secret trip by water back to the *Britannia*. The Venice evening ended with sumptuous fireworks followed by a vivid thunderstorm. 'And did you arrange this, too?' the Queen kidded the mayor. Again, in Milan, the Queen paid a morning visit to the Scala, expecting to see the empty auditorium of the opera-house. But instead the curtain rose on a stage set and lit for the second act of *Lucia* with singers and orchestra to surprise her with twelve minutes of complete perfection.

Not that travel impressions may dim private memories. In the flow of personal events the Duke of Kent's charming June wedding to Katharine Worsley in York Minister must have vividly brought back to the Queen her remembrance of him as a baby in the year her father came to the throne. His wedding was but a week after the withdrawal of South Africa from the Commonwealth, the unhappy outcome to a Security Council anti-apartheid vote. Some of the continental wedding guests had not gone home when President Kennedy visited and he and Jackie of course dined at Buckingham Palace. As a Princess at Windsor, the Queen had introduced one of her Guards officers, the Marquis of Hartington, to Kathleen Kennedy, and the two had married. Hartington had been killed in Normandy, Kathleen had later died in an air crash . . . and now her younger brother sat beside the Queen as President of the United States.

In the autumn Princess Margaret was expecting a baby and the public came of their own accord to the conclusion that the Queen would wish to honour her brother-in-law. The editor of *Burke's Peerage* had put on record that a peerage seemed more fitting than a knighthood, and the editor of *Debrett* published his unwise view that the title could not be less than that of marquess, the degree between a duke and an earl. Tony demurred at the prospect but the Queen enquired if he would accept her gift of an earldom, and couched as it was, he accepted with real pleasure. The same style of Countess was thus conferred upon his wife as upon his mother, the Countess of Rosse. In the last analysis, any lingering disinclination was overcome because his wife wished it so and his title as Earl of

Snowdon was announced on 1 October. The subsidiary title, requisite to a first-born son, of Viscount Linley of Nymans came into use with the birth of Princess Margaret's 6 lb 4 oz son on 3 November. At the christening party the Queen Mother proposed that with a little trick photography Tony might have made it seem that twins had been born. A little humour just then might have disarmed the carping critics of the title.

Though 1963 was intended as a restful year, free of travel except for Queen Juliana's silver wedding celebrations, the fates seemed at first oblivious of the Queen's own hopes of rounding off her second family. Instead, family attention centred at first on the wedding in April of Princess Alexandra and Angus Ogilvy, which itself cast a separate mantle of happiness over everything. The day after her thirty-seventh birthday the Queen gave a State Ball at Windsor Castle for the wedding guests which was surely the largest and merriest party seen within those ancient walls for more than a century. After the family dinner party – with the additional three reigning Queens of the Hellenes, Norway and Sweden – the Queen and her husband were hilariously dancing Scottish reels long after midnight.

In deciding how to keep her huge but weary house-party occupied the following day, the Queen judged that exercise might not be popular and swept them all, kings and queens, princes and princesses, on a sight-seeing tour in two motor-coaches around Windsor and along the Thames valley, with Prince Philip in his element as host and guide.

Prince Charles, too, amused his elders with a new 'grown-up almost cosmopolitan air', after concluding his first year at Gordonstoun. The transition to the Kurt Hahn curriculum of his father's school had been accomplished with none of the lonely trauma that first beset him at Cheam. Forewarned was truly forearmed, and his two Hanover cousins were at Gordonstoun ahead of him, with cousin Alexandra of Yugoslavia's son, Alexander, and presently Charles's Mountbatten cousin, Norton Knatchbull. The quartet pulverised the ice rather than broke it. The Queen had previously visited the school with Philip, admitting to Robert Chew, the headmaster, that the world of school remained a mystery to her but that she had read the prospectus approvingly. Indeed, she appeared to have committed it to heart. Her son's allotted school house, Windmill Lodge, was a stark modern bungalow roofed with green asbestos, embodying little more than locker-rooms and an austere dormitory, and if her heart sank at the curtainless windows and bare light fittings she kept it to herself.

According to Prince Philip, the schooling issue had been put squarely to Charles, 'This is the situation you're in. These are the choices.' Prince Charles has said, 'He left me to decide. I freely subjected myself to what he thought best, because I had perfect confidence in my father's judgment.' But the Queen giggled at the picture of juvenile domesticity on reading that the day began at seven with a wash and cold shower and a morning run, 'the boys then make their beds, clean their shoes and do part of the housework'.

Catching up, Princess Anne had also outlined her targets at the same time, so firm and sure that her mother took her to see Benenden School two months or so after Princess Alexandra's wedding, when they were all staying at Goodwood. To send the heir to the Throne and then his sister to their separate public schools were entirely new approaches of royal democracy.

At Balmoral Castle the local Scottish doctor, George Middleton, was a regular caller to attend staff ailments and his call on the Queen gained no attention, and Commander Colville excelled himself with the brevity of his announcement on 16 September, 'It is announced from Buckingham Palace that the Queen will undertake no further engagements after Her Majesty leaves Balmoral in October.'

The Queen pretended to find it an overstatement, asserting that she expected to get back to work eventually. Princess Margaret was also able to tell her sister that she, too, had 'intimations'. It was indeed a delight to the two sisters to find that they were sharing pregnancy together. At Christmas, the last of the many Christmases at Sandringham before a permanent change to Windsor, the New Year of 1964 was greeted by four expectant mothers in the house-party, for the royal sisters were then joined by Princess Alexandra and the Duchess of Kent. None were more aware of the elements of comedy than the mothers themselves, resigned to laughing at mutual clumsiness and formidably going out for walks together.

Prince Edward was born in the Belgian Suite at Buckingham Palace on the evening of 10 March, and Princess Margaret gave birth to a daughter, Sarah Frances Elizabeth, on May Day. The baby Edward was fully named Edward Antony Richard Louis in the private chapel at Windsor Castle the following day, with Princess Sophie of Hanover as a god-mother and the Duchess of Kent as godmother by proxy, her own baby girl, Lady Helen Windsor, being born four days earlier. Prince Edward was the first royal baby to be christened at Windsor for many years. Princess Alexandra's son, born 29 February, had been the first baby boy to be baptised in the converted Palace chapel since its reconstruction as chapel and art gallery, and Margaret's daughter was the first baby girl to be named there. In her own deep thankfulness the Queen had indeed cause for saying, like Queen Victoria, that everything had worked out very well.

15

The Wider Family

At the approach of her forties, the Queen celebrated Christmas at Windsor Castle for the first time, setting the festival within a new personal context which she has observed ever since. She had once said that if she had been born into ordinary life she would have lived in the country with lots of horses and dogs, and now indeed this pattern was realised with the creation of a private home within the Victoria Tower at the south-east corner of the Castle, with its separate front door and cosy staircase and high sunny windows. 'Almost our grace-and-favour house', she merrily defined it, a haven remote from public bustle, between the gilded range of State Apartments and the new-furnished guest-suites.

The Queen spoke of herself as 'wonderfully fortunate', and in her Christmas TV broadcast – though made in advance at the Palace – she dwelt on the thought that 'when one's house is at its noisiest (with children) it is also the most free from care'. Mixed into that first Windsor Christmas was also the happy realisation that every personal dream had been fulfilled, all save one, and even this was on the point of coming true.

Mystifying as he was to the British public, especially when announced as one of Prince Edward's godfathers, Prince Louis of Hesse was an early Christmas-time guest, with his English wife, Margaret Geddes. With no children of their own, they were among the kindly surrogate parents who had all but adopted Philip in childhood, welcoming him to Wolfsgarten during his mother's illnesses. In many a royal description, Louis (Ludwig in German) and Margaret are 'dearest people', and it deeply troubled the Queen that she had never yet been able to accept their return invitations.

In 1947, the existence of Philip's inconvenient German

connections had been soft-pedalled, as we have seen, and even eleven years later the State Visit of President Heuss of West Germany received a cool welcome from Londoners. Carr Linford colour drawings of Salem, Wolfsgarten and Langenburg, family backgrounds dear to Philip, enlivened the private corner of Windsor. But if the Queen spoke of going on a private visit – and Queen Victoria provided ample precedent – her ministers demurred, debating the effect upon public opinion, while Prince Philip paid his own annual visits regrettably unaccompanied by his wife.

In the end, the children got there first, Prince Philip flew Charles over one Easter to visit his Aunt Sophie and Uncle George at Salem, and after Christmas her two Hanover boys, Guelf and George with their younger sister Freddy (Princess Frederica Elizabeth) were together for a ski-ing holiday. All four were first cousins, of course, and since Freddy was rarely absent, one might catch a hint of far-sighted adult matchmaking. Within a few years Freddy would presumably be a good-looking and self-possessed young lady. The urbane Uncle Philip was becoming an admired figure at the weddings of his elder nephews or nieces; and the Prime Minister of a brief year, Sir Alec Douglas-Home, was shocked and sympathetic on hearing that the Queen was dependent on photographs for her knowledge of the scene.

Yet prospects were improving and, with the coming of socialist Harold Wilson to power, the newly re-elected President Lubke invited the Queen to a State Visit of Germany. It was twenty years and ten days after the end of the war when Elizabeth II first set foot on German soil. And there at once, with President Lubke and Chancellor Erhard, waiting to greet her with Prince Philip at the airport, was Prince Louis, wearing probably the broadest beaming smile of his life.

That evening all Britain watched by television the spectacle at dusk in the gardens of the Schloss Bruhl, near Bonn, when 6,000 German school-children lit candles for the Queen. 'Your country and mine stood on opposite sides,' she said. 'This tragic period in our relations is happily over.' Next morning the ecstatic response was framed in the phrase in a leading newspaper, 'Since yesterday Germany has a Queen. She's called Elizabeth.'

Public and private events were perfectly balanced. The royal couple sailed *en fête* up the Rhine, the most romantic of all the approaches to Wolfsgarten, to find the old Hesse home crowded with relatives, among them the dozen or more of Philip's nephews and nieces who had always been on affectionate terms with 'Aunt Elizabeth'. The Queen said that it felt like a dream to be there that summer evening, to see the rooms where Queen Victoria had visited, to inspect at last, amid laughter, the old measuring board showing Philip's height at the age of ten, and his mark again at fifteen much higher up. The heights of Uncle Dickie as a boy, of the Czar 'Nicky' II and of Philip's mother were there, too: it was from Wolfsgarten that she had ridden out one sunny day to get married. The Queen had but to peep from the windows to see the lake where Philip had rowed for solitary hours as a boy. She drank in the atmosphere avidly; she had indeed thirsted for it for years.

The official programme allowed for a weekend of leisure, and on the Friday evening, in Munich, after a day of ceremonies, the couple attended a three-hour gala performance of *Der Rosenkavalier* at the State Opera House, and afterwards drove direct to their special train parked at the railway station. Asleep soon after midnight, they breakfasted as the train was travelling through the valley towards Lake Constance and Salem where the signal-stop, a little wayside station disused for years, had been made spick and span specially for them. In keeping with the announced privacy of the occasion, the press corps and most of the royal staff had been left in Munich.

It had been Sophie's idea that her guests should travel the short mile through the village to Salem Castle in one of the old open carriages. The Queen thus gained a wonderful first glimpse of the long creamy line of the Schloss from across the green cornfields, the striking mass of innumerable windows beneath the five great gables and, recognising it at once, she cried out, 'There it is!' in great excitement.

Though so large, the effect of the old four-storey pile of monastic buildings is surprisingly domestic. The Queen knew that the school occupied the southern wing but the carriage swung north beneath an ancient archway into a garden shaded by imposing trees. Prince Philip's mother, who had turned eighty, and his widowed sister 'Dolla' were already at the door. Here, too, were Dolla's grown sons, the Princes Max and Philip of Baden, whose resemblance to Philip had often amused the Queen whenever they were at Windsor or Balmoral.

George and Sophie of Hanover had thought up every pleasant

novelty, from the tasting of estate wines to an entrancing tour of the district where the police had sealed off the approach roads so that nothing might mar the precious sense of secluded freedom. Again, Monday saw an official tour of the province of Baden-Wurttenberg under the auspices of its Premier. But now it was the turn of Philip's eldest sister, Princess Margarita, and her son, Prince Kraft, to show off their real-life Ruritania of Hohenlohe-Langenburg.

With its many balconies, the inner courtyard of Langenburg Castle resembles an inn courtyard where Mr Pickwick might feel at home. But the Queen found herself taking tea on a rooftop terrace with an unparalleled view of pinewoods and rushing river in a world of stillness and birdsong and sunshine. As in some fairy-tale, she nibbled Wibele biscuits, the tiny button-size Langenburg macaroons that are supposed to make wishes come true and said, laughing, that she wished above all to come again.

In all this family festival, it is worth noting that the Queen and Prince Philip were on time for their official engagements in Cologne next morning, and it remains notable that the Queen did not attempt to extend her tour to Coburg, with all its memories of Victoria and Albert. The Queen shares the current interest in Victorian and would indeed like to see a definitive twelve-volume biography of her predecessor. Langenburg Castle itself was once the home of Queen Victoria's half-sister, Princess Feodora. But despite the blood-ties of the past, Elizabeth's affectionate interest in Philip's German kinsfolk is distinctly a personal family pleasure of our own day and of her own life.

Like many parents, the Queen was noticing 'how quickly they grow up'. Was it already three years and more since Charles's introduction to Gordonstoun? The time was measured off by maternal surprise, amusement and continuous interest at his developing enthusiasms and achievements, from his taste for the cello, his confident solo singing in *The Pirates of Penzance* to the absorbing enjoyment of watching him playing *Macbeth*, bearded and word-perfect. With his impending transfer for a term or two to Geelong Grammar School and, in particular, to its outback branch, Timbertop, he was entering, for the first time, a phase she had never foreseen and felt she could only imperfectly realise. In her concern she turned to Sir Robert Menzies during his summer stay at Balmoral. 'I should be very sorry for the young Prince if he were at school in the middle of a crowded city in Australia, with people gazing at him, trying to get pictures of him, making him a raree show,' the Australian Premier later set down his viewpoint. Happily Charles's first letter home brightened her whole year. 'I absolutely adore it . . . .'

His equerry-secretary, David Checketts, had settled into a country farm in the Melbourne suburbs, providing Prince Charles with a home from home for occasional weekends, and while there Mrs Checketts presented her husband with another daughter, giving Charles the glee of photographing the baby, giving us some insight into mother-and-son correspondence by sending the results home in a package marked with red ink, 'Exclusive Pictures'.

Eighteen months before Charles passed his A-levels, however, his mother's thoughts turned ahead. The ultimate stage in the education of the heir to the Throne, she felt, became a more public matter, not to be settled by parents alone. Should he go on to university and, if so, where? Should Commonwealth institutions be considered? Should Service training be fitted in? The relative merits of Dartmouth, Sandhurst, Cranwell, might all be considered.

A few weeks after Charles's seventeenth birthday, Prince Philip gave a dinner party for eight in the festive yet practical atmosphere of the evening but one before Christmas Eve. By this expedient, the Prime Minister, Harold Wilson, the Archbishop of Canterbury, Dr Fisher, the Dean of Windsor, Dr Woods and the then Chairman of the Committee of University Vice-Chancellors, Sir Charles Wilson, were all brought together, briefed by Sir Michael Adeane on the problem awaiting them for discussion after dinner. Earl Mountbatten and the Queen herself made up the party. Prince Charles was not present, however, and the Queen remained a listener during the debate.

No full agreement was reached then and there. But presently at Timbertop Charles heard of the considered opinion that a university should come before Service training. Cambridge, Aberystwyth and Dartmouth were each in prospect. Charles added his own personal view. Later on, 'it would be marvellous to have three years when you are not bound by anything, are not married and haven't got a particular job'. Later on, there would be the Services to give one 'experience and responsibility, of life, of discipline, and above all of people and how to deal with people'. Meanwhile, young Andrew's name was put down for Heatherdown school, the gate to Eton. If of his own accord he presently preferred Gordonstoun, as indeed he did, it would be up to him.

With these semi-public issues resolved, the texture of the Queen's private life became if anything more withdrawn from the public at about this time. The Palace press secretariat have recorded that within a year the Queen had been concerned with 500 public engagements, including a tour of the Caribbean, a State Visit to Belgium, 70 public functions in the United Kingdom, 287 audiences and much else besides, in addition to her detailed and unceasing attention to her 'boxes'. The clamour of the tours and the constant press of business had to have a necessary counter-balance of serenity.

'I don't always want to be gazing at my own cypher,' she told a designer, when specimens of a new Crown Derby dinner service were submitted. Clearly there were times when Elizabeth wished to be the woman and not the monarch, herself and not the embodiment of a dynasty. Sympathetic friends knew that the Queen sometimes detached herself from other guests to go walking or riding quite alone. While preparing his biography of Prince Philip, Basil Boothroyd was struck by a Sandringham evening when she 'stole in', as he noticed, with a sticking-plaster on one arm, covering an inoculation for a coming tour of Canada. 'She tucked her shoes under her to kneel on a stool at a mammoth jigsaw. I felt it was no way to treat one's hostess.' 'Don't worry,' Sir Martin Charteris said, 'she's perfectly happy.'

Friends knew, too, that she had become much attracted to modern landscape paintings 'without a soul in sight', and it seemed unusual when she purchased a Lowry at the Royal Academy. But instead of a street scene of scurrying figures her Lowry showed only a fenced courtyard, with the back of an old-fashioned car that had just entered, and not a soul in sight. 'These have been some of my happiest hours,' she told the artist Edward Halliday, after a series of rather non-communicative sittings when she knew he was seeking to paint her in repose.

A significant experiment was seen in the simple life with the deliberate closing of the 'Big House' at Sandringham for much of the year, to be replaced by the seclusion of Wood Farm, formerly the home of a local physician. Philip was in his element in replanning bedrooms and bathrooms and is said to have shinned up the ladders to try tile-fixing for himself. The essential idea was that Wood Farm could be used for weekends, anything from family visits to a day or two's pheasant shooting.

The Queen in fact inaugurated Wood Farm in the autumn of 1967 shortly after Prince Charles had entered Trinity College, Cambridge, not fifty miles away. The dining-room fireplace had been effectively cured of 'smoking bronchitis'. On the walls here and there hung paintings by 'an obscure family artist', otherwise Prince Philip, and 'a vigorous young artist of the new Norfolk school', otherwise Charles. The mantelshelf provided nesting room for samples of Charles's newly made pottery, and the house soon resounded to the stereo tastes of Charles and three or four student friends. At Cambridge the Queen visited Charles in his rooms where, so they say, her son regaled her with sausage-and-mash dished up from his kitchenette. On a later occasion, the College kitchen provided fried chicken. At Balmoral, also, the Queen revived Queen Victoria's favourite retreat of Glasalt Shiel, hemmed in by mountain slopes at the head of Loch Muick. With a domestic wing added, the single sitting-room and dormer-windowed bedrooms were satisfyingly sufficient until recent times for idyllic overnight picnics when the children were younger.

In Windsor Great Park, too, the Queen for a time used one of George IV's smaller lodges as a picnic house, sometimes entertaining polo friends and wives to tea or riding over to it when, like Garbo, she wished to be alone. It was here, I think, that the young King and Queen of Thailand innocently came to call on her unannounced, unhappily bringing with them an aide-de-camp and a young secretary. The Queen had only a page and her former personal footman, Roy Cameron, with her to prepare refreshments. 'It was the only time I saw her nervous,' says Cameron, in his translated reminiscences, as if the whole world had come knocking at this last sanctuary.

In her quest for ultimate non-formality, the Queen will characteristically sit on the floor at any excuse, to talk with young children or play with the dogs, to pore over maps or look at television. Unaccustomed visitors are ushered with great ceremony through the stately halls of Buckingham Palace, and astonished all the more when shown into the Queen's homely living-room. Philip's modern rooms differently bespeak his character with their sparse, uncluttered

213

space; but on this point husband and wife agree to differ. As the Queen herself says, she prefers her 'rooms to look really lived in'. When her domestic staff clean and tidy up her rooms, they then have to restore any untidiness in which they found them.

Indeed, Roy Cameron has described her sitting-room as permanently looking 'as if a bomb had devastated it; toys, magazines and other things lying about in great disorder, her desk heaped with albums, documents, boxes, letters and innumerable photographs of her children . . . . I always endeavoured to restore the untidy order.' Like Queen Alexandra, the Queen always knows where everything should be in this apparent confusion. 'What *have* you done with it? Where *have* you hidden it?' she asks, if a magazine or newspaper is missed in the jumble. The Russian leaders, Khrushchev and Bulganin, on visiting the Palace, were impressed with the 'family atmosphere' but the explicit details that caught their eyes were perhaps the doll on the couch and an unexpected package of birdseed: the Queen is a window-sill bird-watcher.

It was surprising, really, that the Queen presently allowed all the world to watch a barbecue in the Glasalt garden in the TV film *Royal Family*, but with her extra enjoyment of privacy she characteristically considered it appropriate to give the public a fuller understanding of both sides of her life, the official and personal, and when the cameras began their chronicle she ultimately decided that it was unfair to the public for her pleasant hours at Glasalt Shiel to be omitted.

The girl who had once been terrified at the sight of an anchored television camera could not have foreseen that she would spend scores of hours with TV crews at her very elbow. As a teen-ager, however, Elizabeth had happily taken part in a wartime documentary short on the life of the Royal Family, paying great attention to make-up, I remember, although the film was only in black and white. 'How right you were!' said Princess Margaret afterwards. 'We all look like pallid ghosts compared with you!' The Sunday newspaper editor-turned-propagandist, who had helped with this, proposed many years later a film about the Royal Palaces, with helicopters catching new angles of castle towers and turrets and zoom cameras enquiringly exploring State apartments and private fastnesses, and a commentary emphasising history, architecture and art treasures.

A business-like bargain was struck through the Lord Chamberlain, and the Queen's nett share of the proceeds, estimated at £16,000 over two years, paid for a degree of redecoration and new modern lighting in the Palace picture gallery, the cleaning of Van Dycks and the purchase after a Sotheby's auction of a miniature of Queen Henrietta Maria, bride of Charles I. Thereby hangs a tale, for the final bid by the Queen's representative was in fact topped by an unknown American lady who, hearing of the royal interest, pleasantly offered the miniature to the Queen at cost price, a kindly transatlantic gesture.

By this time, moreover, the whole family had been steeped for three years in the making of Uncle Dickie's TV biography, *The Life and Times of Lord Mountbatten*. Script improvements were suggested in a spirit of friendly interest, points of criticism raised with more candour than Mountbatten may have wished, and the family would sometimes troop down to the Palace cinema after dinner to watch the 'rushes' – first print viewings – of Dickie's new-filmed interviews. The soil was ripe, in fact, for a TV movie that would explain the work of the Queen. How could the tasks be explained if cut off like a limb from the Queen's everyday life and interests? The upshot was that Richard Cawston of the BBC was given leave to shoot what he pleased, leaving the Queen to exercise her own editorial rights on the completed picture.

It was a revolutionary idea, a contemporary improvisation on Marie Antoinette's suggested diet of giving them cake, the Palace and every royal setting invaded by the nine-man television crew in sweaters and jeans, the camera craning over the Queen at her desk, holding a Privy Council meeting, giving an audience, receiving her Prime Minister, with Harold Wilson as willing participant. It was all in fact against the rules, quite at variance with the precepts of Walter Bagehot, that astute and quotable Victorian journalist who had laid down that 'the mystery of monarchy is its life. We must not let in daylight upon magic.' Was Bagehot wrong? Was he simply flattering, as well as justifying, Victoria in her recluse-like existence? Our own Elizabeth's great-grandfather had helped the infant motion picture, the baby bioscope, with nothing more than riding his horse round the Sandringham courtyard. Her father surrounded the still camera with caution and discretion: he withdrew photographs of table-settings of a State Banquet, for example, lest they seemed over-lavish during post-war austerity.

By contrast, *Royal Family* featured the ballroom buffet at the Palace reception for British Olympic athletes at which mikes and camera caught up conversation between Princess Anne and a young rider named Mark Phillips; the lunch-time wait for service aboard the royal yacht *Britannia*; the carrots ready on a linen napkin on a silver salver with which the Queen, dismounting at the Palace, rewarded her horse after Trooping the Colour, 'Any more for carrots before they all go?' The Queen was anxious in case some of the everyday family scenes should seem too trivial: Prince Edward and young friends in the nursery schoolroom, the dressing of the Christmas tree, the Ogilvys with their gift trolley. Herself feeding the dogs, herself watching the TV, Charles biking through Cambridge. But counter-balanced, of course, by scenes of the Queen in silver-blue splendour at the diplomatic reception, at the opera with Margaret, in action at an investiture, or with constant change of greeting and expression at a garden-party.

Altogether the Queen was involved through seventy-five days of her time. Guests and staff alike were told of the filming and asked if they would mind taking part. Hence the vivid scenes of the arrival of President Nixon, his reputation then unmarred. Some were transmitted to America forthwith as newsreel, others effectively held in reserve. Other scenes were devised: the Queen discussing her jewels and dress with Bobo, the family lunch-table conversation, Charles and his father at their desks, Philip at his easel . . . the memories still flood through a dozen years later. And there were the chance felicities: young Edward nearly in tears, stung by the snapping cello string, the American ambassador struggling with formal speech as the Queen strives to put him at ease.

The Queen suggested no cuts in the final 105-minute programme. But the secret had been in Richard Cawston's meticulous selection and editing from forty-one hours of film. The unused remainder is deposited in the National Film Archive, an extraordinary gift for posterity. Tinged with the nostalgia that comes to any ordinary home-made family movie with the passage of time, a second programme or even a series could be created with moving effect. Certainly Bagehot was wrong in regarding mystery as necessary. The Queen disillusioned none of us and the mystique remained.

The Queen had entertained doubts about the project at first, but once the die was cast, she had accepted the new drill, as Basil Boothroyd has said, 'with inexhaustible patience and cheerfulness'. Philip, on the other hand, 'vigorously in favour, sparking with intelligent suggestions' then had 'periods of pronounced sulkiness'. The apparent sulks, in fact, coincided with the anxieties of his mother's failing health. Nearing her mid-eighties, Princess Alice had at last been persuaded to move into the Palace, to find shelter and indulgence with her son and daughter-in-law, and the Queen loved to have her mother-in-law living along the corridor.

As Earl Mountbatten said, 'The Queen was the only person who could speak to my sister in her normal voice and make herself completely understood – every word. The Queen adored her and she adored the Queen.' The old lady took an amused and lively interest in the film, remote as it was from her deeper concerns, and in June 1969 she felt well enough to attend the family showing at Windsor. The screening followed closely on her daughter Sophie's fifty-fifth birthday, the Hanover couple were staying at the Castle, and Princess Alice was alert and responsive, her health so completely normal, according to her brother, Earl Mountbatten, that 'people simply couldn't believe it when they met her'. (It was a sunset glow and she died in December.)

But meanwhile the press acclaim of the BBC premiere of *Royal Family* was triumphant, indeed 'a milestone in TV history, a world-beater', as they said. Every synonym of praise, 'record-breaking, fascinating, brilliant, engrossing', was hurled into the stockpot. If the programme had been intended as a warming prelude to the debatable pageantry of the Prince of Wales's Investiture at Caernarvon Castle the following week, now everything was different. The illusion of television had simultaneously made millions feel acquainted with the Queen. The curious processions of mayors and druids, county clerks and Welsh notables moved across the greensward. The fanfares had sounded, the choirs had sung. The Prince of Wales was invested with his ermine mantle, his sword, his new-made crown. But now a nation – and others overseas – watched a mother clasp her son's hands in her own to hear him repeat the substance of his father's Coronation oath of fealty, 'I, Charles, do become your liege man of life and limb . . . and faith and truth I will bear unto you to live and die against all manner of folks.' And it was as a mother that the Queen took her son to the battlements above the King's Gate to present him to the people.

To all manner of folks now, Elizabeth II was an acquaintance or friend, familiar aunt or cousin, a welcome visitor and, to some of her elders, but for lese-majesty, almost an adopted daughter. To her vast audience in faith and truth she could no longer say, as one Christmas, 'To many of you I must seem a remote figure.' That year, after repeats and requests of the family film, the hazard of over-exposure disturbed her more than remoteness, and she decided to forego her usual broadcast, of course with the result that petitions and protests rolled in. All unaware, the sceptre of television had introduced a persuasive and personal new era of family monarchy.

16

Event on event

Time, that masquerader, had again 'whizzed by' and, as with other couples, the Queen and Prince Philip celebrated their Silver Wedding, in November 1972, hardly believing that twenty-five years could have passed so soon. 'It came as a bit of a surprise. Neither of us are much given to looking back and the years have slipped by,' said the Queen at the Guildhall luncheon. 'Now we can see how immensely fortunate we have been. If a marriage succeeds in real life, there is nothing like it. . . . If I am asked what I think about family life, I am for it.'

The television cameras watched her hour upon hour. That morning she had herself set the felicitous scene by inviting 100 other silver wedding couples to share her thanksgiving service in Westminster Abbey. That afternoon, with her husband and Charles and Anne, she walked through the streets of London among her people as no British monarch had done in 300 years. Children ducked under the slim barrier rails to present posies, the royals divided into groups and chatted up the crowds as if at a garden-party. 'The pavements thick with happy people,' I noted that evening, 'though BBC news bulletins all but ignored the event, only a fifteen-minute evening film.'

At the Palace Charles and Anne were responsible for the invitations to the private supper party, 'Prince Charles and Princess Anne request the pleasure of your company . . .' and Charles particularly had fretted over the guest-list, anxious that no friend or kinsman close to his parents for twenty-five years should be overlooked. He had made sure that both his brothers were home from Heatherdown School: they had attended the Abbey service but not the City walkabout. He remembered to ask the new Poet Laureate to write a poem for the occasion, which was delivered by hand to the Palace but has never been published. Two hundred people sat down to dinner. An entertainment followed, commencing with the English Chamber Orchestra playing the Wedding March and a section of the Bach Choir to recall the wedding anthems. The youthful hosts' attempt to keep the celebration a surprise had been successful, and the Queen 'marvelled at everything, often quite astonished, and utterly enjoyed it all'.

The year had opened on a note of romance. On St Valentine's Day, no less, the then Duke and Duchess of Gloucester announced the betrothal of their younger son, Prince Richard, to Danish-born Miss Birgitte van Deurs 'to which union the Queen has gladly given her consent'. The Gloucester brothers, William and Richard, were the Queen's closest cousins, but the intended bride was a complete royal novitiate. They had first met over tea and toast one Sunday afternoon at a students' crowd-in, when Richard was studying architecture at Cambridge and the fair Birgitte was improving her English at a local language school. She had not at first realised Richard's identity: 'We met without intending to meet', in the bridegroom's words.

The newspapers soon presented the affair as the familiar idyll of a student prince and a shop girl, the 'shop' in fact being the showroom of a leading Copenhagen silversmith, and the course of true love had run smoothly through seven years. But was there a hint of royal displeasure? The Queen Mother, the Prince of Wales and Princess Margaret were at the July wedding in the Gloucesters' village church at Barnwell, while the Queen, Prince Philip and Princess Anne remained in Scotland. An enigma, unless overtly to stress to Prince Charles his own narrowness of choice.

Any family difference was in the event tragically effaced not two months later, with the terrible news of Prince William of Gloucester's death in a flying race. Overnight the newly-weds accepted the shattering responsibilities of the family, the Barnwell estate and the tasks of royal rank. Long incapacitated by illness, the old Duke of Gloucester died in 1974, and by these turns of fate the young couple were thereupon Duke and Duchess, the Queen's confidence and esteem fully established.

Shortly before the Silver Wedding, Prince Richard was notably aide to the Queen at Windsor during the State Visit of President Heinemann of West Germany, and some of the

Queen's less-informed anniversary guests took a heightened interest in Princess Richard, the first European recruit to the House of Windsor since Princess Marina forty years earlier. Could it be a sign of the times? Would Prince Charles perhaps find a continental bride? And, after all the speculation, could Mark Phillips, a soldier of no fortune, possibly marry the Queen's daughter?

These were riddles in public and private, and the Queen of course kept her own counsel. She had in fact first met Officer Cadet Phillips at the competitors' cocktail party at Badminton, when he was still only nineteen and emerged splendidly fourth. This was four clear months before her old friend of St Paul's Walden days, Lady Abergavenny, introduced him to Princess Anne after the one-day event at Eridge, and from then on she watched his career with keen interest, gratified when he was the youngest ever reserve with the British Olympics team in Mexico, astonished and apprehensive when her daughter began competing against him, at the army horse trials and elsewhere. At the Rushall Trials Lieutenant Mark Phillips of the 1st Queen's Dragoon Guards came superbly first on Great Ovation while, to the Queen's delight, Anne was fourth on Doublet, a jumper of South American stock which she had given her at Christmas.

Then came that unforgettable Badminton, watched throughout by the Queen, when the twenty-year-old Princess led the twenty-five entrants who had completed their dressage, and next day Mark maintained his lead over the thirty-three fences, while Anne lapsed to fourth on timing. On the third day, one show-jumping error reduced the Princess to fifth and Mark was the immaculate winner. It was to be the year of Anne riding as an individual in the European championships, winning the loner's gold medal, acclaimed in England on a poll vote as Sportswoman of the Year. 'But you don't get all the votes!' twelve-year-old Prince Andrew is supposed to have cheekily reminded his sister when their mother topped a Gallup poll, listing the world's most admired women, for the third year running.

In her Silver Wedding year, the Queen could hardly wait to see Anne and Mark competing again at Badminton, and it was a bitter blow when Anne's horse Doublet suffered a strained tendon only a week before the event and had to be withdrawn. But Her Majesty's sustained interest in Mark was richly rewarded instead by seeing him win the Whitbread Trophy on Great Ovation for the second year running, a double unequalled since the Sheila Wilcox hat-trick in the 1950s. Mark was in the winning British Olympics team at Munich later that year, and it astonished the Queen all the more to find that he and Anne were both aiming at Badminton for a third year.

At earlier trials she was terrified one day to learn the Princess was thrown and trampled on by Mark's horse, Persian Holiday; and next day, Mark was riding the Queen's powerful horse Columbus at the Rushall Trials only to be unseated, half rolled on and knocked out. In the Queen's girlhood it had been national news if she grazed her knee. These two merely made a joke about their bandages. Part of her own interest in horses had been in the racing and breeding of bloodstock, in independently forming her own judgment: her knowledge of blood strains was expert among experts. Now she examined the newest ideas on the Badminton course, incredulous but enthusiastic at the skill and judgment they demanded. But in action that year Anne came merely eighth in the three-day event, while Mark faced a final day of total disaster, twice unseated and indeed neatly ducked in the lake by Columbus.

As it happened, Lieutenant Mark Phillips had already sought the Queen's permission to seek 'a deeper understanding' in his now long-standing friendship with Princess Anne, and at Easter the family gathered for a remarkable celebration. It was fifty years since the Queen Mother's wedding day, and the Queen proposed her mother's health with a toast 'charming, succinct and just right'. The Queen Mother responded in some jeopardy of emotion and then Prince Philip rose to announce the happiness of 'our beloved daughter's betrothal to Mark . . .' This was 'between ourselves', as he said, and it was not until 29 May that the news was made public.

Princess Anne paid Prince Charles the pretty compliment of choosing his twenty-fifth birthday on 14 November as her wedding day. She settled, too, the expectations of a number of languishing hopefuls by deciding to have only one bridesmaid, her nine-year-old cousin Lady Sarah Armstrong-Jones, partnered with young Prince Edward as page. This deprived the press of the bevy of pretty girls who might otherwise have been seen with the group on the Palace balcony or identified from wedding group photographs, among them the attractive young blonde who ran with her father through the Palace courtyard to pelt the honeymoon couple with paper rose petals.

It amused and contented the Queen, however, to watch the various girls whom Charles sought out at the pre-wedding dance. After one of his earlier Australian journeys, as Dermot Morrah recorded, 'the Queen sat out with a friend, laughing quietly as they observed the enthusiasm with which the Prince of Wales sought out all the prettiest partners in the room', at twenty-five his taste running 'rather to the rosebuds of England than to the tiger-lilies'. And at his sister's wedding festivities, he danced more than once with a rosebud of slightly different texture, his cousin, one of his mother's house-guests, Princess Frederica of Hanover, who had turned nineteen less than a month earlier.

Preoccupied with his Services training, first with the RAF at Cranwell, next in the Navy from Dartmouth to the companionable frigate HMS *Minerva* – and with army and parachute training, too – he had last seen his cousin as an over-thin pigtailed schoolgirl. Much earlier than that, before his own launching as a Cheam schoolboy, he had pushed her around in her pram at Balmoral; and on his first teenage ski-ing holidays with her brothers, his Hanover cousins, she was a decidedly junior accompaniment, carrying her own miniature skis, launching herself onto the slopes with enviable courage, already an expert.

Their six-year age difference had always seemed considerable. When Charles was seventeen and rehearsing *Macbeth* as a senior boy at Gordonstoun, 'Freddy' had barely begun as a boarder in the castellated junior school of Salem, Gordonstoun's parent school under Kurt Hahn. As we have seen, Frederica's elder brothers, Welf and George, accompanied Charles through his early terms at Gordonstoun. Though only a year or two older than Charles, Welf was already married and had a baby daughter, having made an impetuous match that ignored courtly and ancient precedents. Princess Freddy graduated from the Salem senior school only a week or two after Princess Anne's engagement, and within three months her brother George married the 21-year-old daughter of a New York businessman. The younger generations were catching up, though fortunately without attracting any whisper of surmise around the renewed friendship of Charles and Freddy as they gossiped of family links and old mutual acquaintance at Salem and Gordonstoun and generally enjoyed one another's company in the wedding atmosphere.

The Queen watched indulgently, her thoughts probably

reflected in one of her husband's television interviews around this time. 'I've never specified whom he should marry,' he said of Charles. 'People tend to marry within their own circles. The advantage, perhaps, is a certain built-in acceptance of the sort of life you are going to lead.' Prince Charles was thinking along those lines, too, with a built-in acceptance that he would not settle to marriage until he had at least successfully finished his training, another three years' programme, 'the traditional thing to do, and very sensible', as he says. 'A period in the Services gives you great experience and responsibility of life, of discipline, and above all of people,' Princess Frederica's future, at the time, was more unsure. She thought of taking an art course, like one of her Hanover cousins. She couldn't see herself settling to a career as yet. She would like to travel, to see the new world: she had friends in America. Charles must have listened sympathetically, with few such personal prospects of freedom.

More than eight years on, we may assume that the Prince was pained if not appalled, immediately upon his engagement to Lady Diana Spencer, to find the brasher newspapers packed with distasteful photo-spreads of 'former' girlfriends and lists of past engagement rumours, the whole nonsensical rollcall of 'loves that could not be disguised in public', close friends and 'future brides'. The BBC flashed pictures of the ladies on the screen one by one as if dealing a pack of cards; and even the discriminating Debrett with their *Book of the Royal Wedding* listed some twenty 'female figures', albeit in a satiric tone.

Art editors scissored mothers and husbands out of photographs to emphasise the portrayal of 'the Prince of Wales at Ascot with Lady Blank' or 'with Mrs Blank, the glamorous divorcee'. Some unscrupulous sections of the press invested him with the libertine mantle of his great-grandfather Edward VII: for Lily Langtry read so-and-so. The dubious effect was of a blithe Lothario, until a respectable royal biographer described him as 'like any other hot-blooded male', regardless of all indications of considerable powers of discipline and discretion.

The Queen commiserated with her son, remembering her own youthful misery under the cloud of rumours about Philip, and indeed Mark Phillips's angered protest after the accidents at Rushall that the crowding reporters made the horses nervous. Yet through ten years of the hue-and-cry for the mythical 'future Queen' – as any possible Princess of Wales was invariably termed – there was no whisper of Princess Frederica

224

save for three lines in a local Scottish newspaper one year mentioning her presence at Balmoral.

A practical difficulty for the media, and a useful protection screen for Frederica, lay in the lack of photographs. If her various visits with her parents had been reported, which they were not, few columnists would have recognised her. Coming to England, clutching a teddy-bear, as a five-year-old bridesmaid to Lady Pamela Mountbatten, the wedding group pictures show her as an enchanting little blonde, so small that her uncle Prince Philip had to pick her up and carry her into Romsey Abbey, safe from the snow and slush. A family group of the Queen's 1965 visit to Germany shows a ten-year-old nearing a gawky bean-pole phase. 'Elizabeth told me how much she enjoyed seeing the children,' wrote Frederica's Hanover grandmama, Princess Victoria Luise. 'When I said goodbye I had a strong sense of remembrance and hope, and told Elizabeth, God bless you.'

From then on, photographs were prudently restricted to school, home and family. For the curious, reference books were limited to the bleak listing of 'Frederica Elisabeth Victoria Luise Alice Olga Theodora Helen, born at Salem, 15 October, 1954'. Each given name was that of a relative, but equally of a queen or empress. In all their widespread conjecture of marital prospects, the press also discounted first cousins. It was a curious blindspot, for Queen Victoria and Prince Albert were first cousins, Albert's father and Victoria's mother being brother and sister. King George V and Queen Mary were each descended from George III, as indeed were Freddy's parents, Sophie and George, and Elizabeth and Philip. Cousinly marriages were the royal norm until very recently.

Early in 1974, the Queen and Prince Philip's visit to New Zealand occasioned a family rendezvous aboard *Britannia* with Charles and Anne and Mark, and possibly with the Hanovers, too, to indulge Frederica's wish for travel. The Palace would describe this as mere surmise, but it would not be the first time the Hanovers' presence aboard had passed unnoticed, as for instance during the summer holiday cruises around Scotland. In the course of the unforeseen British general election which extinguished Mr Heath's government the Queen flew home to summon Harold Wilson for his second term as Premier and then resumed her tour as planned in Australia and Indonesia. In March the kidnapping attempt on Princess Anne in the heart of London emphasised all the more the need for reticence and even secrecy about Princess Frederica. The first *hint* of intentions came, however, when Prince Charles unexpectedly visited Chevening.

In the late 1960s the seventh and last Earl Stanhope had left his country home to the nation, furnished and endowed under a trust offering priority of occupancy to members of the Royal Family. Inspecting the mansion with his mother in the dreary autumn of 1969, Prince Charles had thought it gloomy and uninviting. Shattered tiles littered the courtyard and the place had a deserted and off-putting atmosphere. Five years later, visiting the house in the freshness of spring, the Prince found its repair and reconditioning virtually complete, and it looked incredibly serene and beautiful. Home was the sailor from the sea, and with a young man's fancy lightly turning to thoughts of affection and housing, Charles was enchanted. Twelve minutes by 'chopper' from the Palace across London's south-east suburbs, Chevening was handy to his – and Frederica's – Brabourne-Mountbatten cousins at Mersham, to the Nevills and other friends, as well as convenient to the cross-channel routes for Freddy's parents.

The preliminary furnishing of the inviting second-floor suite of private apartments was entrusted to his Mountbatten cousin-in-law David Hicks. The Queen, too, 'nipped down' to see the restorations, characteristically combining her visit with a side-trip to see her nephew, Princess Margaret's son, at his prep school in Sussex. Perhaps it was a sign of trouble at home that young Lord Linley was frequently at the bottom of his class, and the Queen felt he needed her encouragement.

Princess Anne also praised her brother's choice as she gazed over his 'penthouse view' of lawn and lake and treetops. Four years older than Frederica, she had detected her young cousin's sense of humour when unwrapping the Hanovers' wedding gifts, 'two extremes' as they had promised her, an ice-bucket and a hot plate. Here 'Uncle George' had been an official at the Munich Olympics, sweeping her off with her father at the weekend to visit Aunt Sophie at their old-style village house in the pinewoods, and Anne proclaimed herself an 'Hanover adherent'.

Of the Queen's view of a Hanover marriage, her first motherly concern was for the future happiness of the young people, but one's personal impression is that *at the time* she

226

would have liked nothing better. After the Hessians, the royal House of Hanover was the oldest Protestant dynasty in Europe. Through five reigns and 123 years, the Crown of Hanover had been united with the Crown of Great Britain, and the prospect of a new link with Hanover appealed to Elizabeth II's every instinct of sentiment and tradition. 'Some fourteen daughters of British sovereigns through the ages married German princes,' she had reminded West Berliners in one of her friendly speeches, and a new deal in the marital trend seemed especially fitting for the EEC era in which Britain again entered Europe.

On the cousinhood question, and the old wives' tale of supposed defects in first cousin marriages, the textbooks reported 'no evidence of any genetic consequence, no ill effects in inbred communities . . . it is only the reflection of a sentiment which (wrongly) associates such marriages with incest'. For a time, borrowing on the Palace subscription with the London Library, the Prince of Wales read every book he could find on Hanover and on George III's porphyria, occasionally forgetting to remove a place-marker before returning a volume. And no doubt he put the central question to his much-loved Uncle Dickie, with Lord Mountbatten's invariable persuasive reply, 'If first cousins couldn't marry, I wouldn't be here!'

With his untiring expertise in genealogy, Mountbatten was probably the first to acquaint Charles with the surprising fact that Frederica was British by nationality, a definition subjected to appeal and counter-appeal in legal argument and finally upheld by the House of Lords two years after she was born. In 1705, nine years before the death of Queen Anne without issue, an Act of Parliament had ironed out problems of the Protestant succession by naturalising 'all persons descended from' her second cousin, Princess Sophia, granddaughter of James I, henceforth 'to be deemed natural born subjects of this kingdom'. The musty, resonant phrases might have been forgotten if Frederica's grandfather, Crown Prince Ernst August, had not found himself denied a British passport, an expedient he had often used, and hurried to consult his lawyers. After his death, his eldest son, another Ernst August, continued the struggle in the courts with a tenacity that led to victory. Prince Charles evidently knew nothing of this when, to his great-uncle's glee, he told an interviewer. 'The one advantage about marrying a Princess or somebody from a royal family, is that they do know what happens. The trouble is I often feel I

227

would like to marry somebody English, Or Welsh. Well, British, anyway.'

Visiting German friends in their quaint Bavarian-style house in a Vancouver suburb in 1975, Frederica wrote home rapturously of the beauty and space, the sense of a new-minted life and the easy friendliness of Canadians, and clearly had no intention of following her brothers' enraptured race into matrimony. Not that Charles had precisely proposed as yet or faced refusal. A London journalist, Stuart Kuttner, however, persuaded him just then into an 'engagingly frank conversation'. 'People get the wrong idea about love,' said Charles. 'It's basically a very strong friendship. You have shared interests and ideas in common and also a great deal of affection.'

'Have you any particular girl in mind?' Kuttner persisted.

'Well, that would be letting too much out of the bag, wouldn't it,' Charles replied. 'Obviously, there must be someone, somewhere, for me,' and it sounded as though the someone was a long way off. Various puzzled writers and interviewers noticed that 'secret defence centre' within his outwardly frank yet guarded manner. 'Take marriage,' said Kenneth Harris tentatively, and saw that 'a steely expert wariness gleamed'. Audrey Whiting wondered at 'a sort of inner serenity'. Mountbatten, too, basked to the end of his days in the anticipation that his obscure great-niece might sustain family prestige and become Princess of Wales. 'When Charles finds someone he wants to marry,' he told editor Donald Zec, 'he will never been seen with her in public. Very privately he will try to win her round like any other suitor.' And while the courtship rumours sounded and rebounded entirely in the wrong direction, mother and son, as I read the situation, hugged the rich joke that the media and its inquisitors had completely overlooked a young and beautiful British Princess, a 'Princess of Great Britain', at all events.

Was there a tacit understanding? It seemed as if the firm-minded Frederica promised no more than to give a decision when she was twenty-five. Meanwhile, the prospect of a Canadian university course was very appealing, and in July 1975 she registered with the arts faculty at Simon Fraser University in British Columbia to commence studies that autumn in psychology and a newer feminist course known as women's topics. That same month, the Royal Family gathered in Canada for the Montreal Olympics. Prince George was again an official with the German team; the riding competitions were at Bromont, nearly fifty miles from the city and for ten days the Queen and her family 'had a ball', with Frederica's presence passing unnoticed by the public.

Over the next year or two the opportunities for meeting ranged from Prince Charles's shore leave from the carrier *Hermes* in American waters to a month's course with the RCAF at Blissville, and the side-strings of his visits to Calgary and the West Coast, to both Victoria and San Francisco. The Brabournes with their holiday home in the Bahamas, the trusted Annenbergs at Palm Springs and many others could all have helped the hidden paths of romance. In the summer of 1976 the Hanovers sailed aboard *Britannia* around northern Scotland to the Castle of Mey, and a curious photograph, looking down from a bridge at Scrabster, shows the royal party with the Prince hurriedly dashing out of camera range.* The Queen's gift to Princess Anne of Gatcombe Park made another venue, with winter sports at Klosters and fishing trips in Iceland with Charles's friends the Tryons, equally within the innermost circle.

The monarchy held a trump hand in a British part-Mountbatten Princess concluding her education in Canada and studying, of all subjects, a contemporary course in women's lib. Yet the Simon Fraser authorities appear to have handled her with a special almost furtive secrecy and it was six months before the student body discovered they had 'one of Queen Victoria's relatives' in their midst. Local reporters turned their sights but Freddy refused all interviews. A TV celebrity who tracked her to her small single-storey cream clapboard house found the door firmly closed in his face. Students sharing tutorials with her on 'female roles in contemporary society' adopted a loyally sympathetic reticence. New-built above Vancouver in 1963, a campus in classicist-Mayan concrete within the forestry of Burnaby Mountain, Simon Fraser was highly contemporary itself, and Frederica diligently qualified herself for modern queenship in swotting 'research methods in psychology', 'data analysis' and so forth, under Dr Marilyn Beaumont.

In April 1979, Prince Charles had cause to visit the Lester Pearson College on Victoria Island. Ostensibly his interest was as president of the international (Mountbatten-founded) World Colleges and, with duty done, his speedboat readily

* See back-jacket of *The Queen Mother Herself* by Helen Cathcart, W.H. Allen 1979.

229

outstripped pursuers on what was called 'a private visit to friends' on one of the smaller islands. Princess Frederica was in her twenty-fifth year, her 'SG' studies near conclusion. (She gained her BA, with a major in Psychology and a minor in Women's Studies, but did not appear personally for the conferment of her degree.) Few of her Canadian friends, incidently, called her 'Freddy'. To some she was 'Phil', from her pronounced resemblance to Prince Philip, to others Aly, from Alice, her chosen name.

That July, curiously, she took out a new *German* passport, with all its crowded names, from the Consul General in Vancouver. This was the summer of Lord Mountbatten's hideous death in the Bay of Sligo and the Princess was among the mourners at his funeral in Romsey Abbey. Early on Freddy's birthday on 15 October, the Queen left Balmoral for London leaving the group of young people at the Castle to merrymake as they wished, but no word came of betrothal. At Sandringham the New Year of 1980 saw an unusually large continental gathering and then, as I believe, Princess Frederica's decision on royal marriage came at last, either in person or by letter, and the words fell, 'I want no part of it.'

A strange and fateful phrase . . . yet how does one know? Fourteen months later, on first bringing Lady Diana Spencer before the TV cameras in the gardens of Buckingham Palace, Charles explained his anxiety at the thought of losing her. 'She could have said, "I want no part in it," but she was marvellous . . .' Sounding oddly out of context, he seemed to blush at the words, and they were not used again.

But back in the spring of 1980, the Queen visualised his desolation of heart and deliberately began to deepen his channels of friendship with Diana Spencer. There remained loose threads to draw together in this 'engagement that never was', however, when it became ineradicably clear that henceforth all Frederica's deeper interests lay in Canada and that events were irreparable. Charles responded to the situation with considerable chivalry. Shortly before Easter, during a string of Canadian duties, he flew from Ottawa to Vancouver and an official reception at the Bayshore Inn, on the shores of the Inlet. After the crowded reception, he retired to dine in privacy with Frederica and one or two friends and make his leave-taking. Next day a spectator at the unveiling of an Indian sculpture gave him a single red rose and the camera saw Charles nearly in tears in a poignant moment of unguarded emotion.

That, too, was the week when, after flying to Miami, he played polo with such frantic disregard of fatigue that he ended in hospital with reported heat-stroke, and back in England he abruptly gave the Stanhope Trust three months' notice to terminate his tenancy of Chevening, a decision on which caused him to be criticised as capricious, for only family and friends knew the reason. (A few weeks later, a friend close to the Hanover family telephoned me to say that Princess Frederica had married; although in Vancouver that autumn, at her clearly independent little bachelor house in the suburbs, the Princess assured me that she was not married; and with this enigmatic denouement the curtain falls.)

And so we come to the happier ending, of some hopes fulfilled and others lost, of the Prince and Princess of Wales married and facing their future, the bells of St Paul's and the cheers and good wishes still echoing, and the Queen herself opens a new era at the centre of her family.

Life is seldom as tidy as landmarks and signposts might make it appear and there are always events to marshal, new chains of circumstance to burnish or define. At fifty, the Queen faced the deep sadness of the breakdown of Princess Margaret's marriage: there had never seemed a more romantic and better-matched couple than the Snowdons until the years brought a gradual disillusionment, and in 1978 divorce ironically followed swift behind the previous year's rejoicing of the Queen's Silver Jubilee. In 1980 the Queen Mother enjoyed the plaudits of her eightieth birthday in the love of her two daughters and the knowledge that Princess Margaret's scars were healing. In 1981, in what should have been a phase of joy, Prince and Princess George of Hanover tragically suffered the loss of their eldest son, Welf, aged only thirty-three, the Queen never more compassionate nor more tender in sympathy through all their years of friendship.

In 1982 Elizabeth II completed the first thirty years of her reign, a Queen of faith and high courage and devotion to her duties. God save her and spare her to face as many full and active years again, in the love of her peoples. Only the foolish talk of her retirement, although some argue that her Coronation promises can be passed to younger shoulders.

But for the Queen herself there will always remain her personal vow made those many years ago when she was a Princess of only twenty-one: 'I declare before you all that my whole life, whether it be long or short, shall be devoted to your service . . .'

ABRIDGED BIBLIOGRAPHY

The following are among the books consulted:

The Teaching of History, C. H. K. Marten, 1938

King George V, John Gore, 1941

Heiress Presumptive, Dermot Morrah, 1947

Royal Guides, V. M. Synge, 1948

Clarence House, Christopher Hussey, 1949

Cosmo Gordon Lang, J. G. Lockhart, 1949

A King's Story, H.R.H. The Duke of Windsor, 1951

King George V, Sir Harold Nicholson, 1952

The Young Queen, Godfrey Winn, 1952

Royal Performance, Ian Bevan, 1954

H.R.H. Prince Philip, John Dean, 1954

The King in his Country, Aubrey Buxton, 1955

Village Royal, Phyl Hopkins, 1955

Silver and Gold, Norman Hartnell, 1955

Treetops, Jim Corbett, 1955

The Queen's Majesty, L. A. Nickolls, 1957

Our Gracious Queen, L. A. Nickolls, 1958

The Work of the Queen, Dermot Morrah, 1958

Palace Diary, Brigadier Stanley Clark, 1958

Royal Standard Red Ensign, Sir David Aitchison, 1958

How the Queen Reigns, Dorothy Laird, 1959

The Memoirs of the Rt. Hon. The Earl of Woolton, 1959

Prince Philip, A Family Portrait, H.M. Queen Alexandra of Yugoslavia, 1960

The Mackenzie King Record, J. W. Pickersgill, 1960

The Memoirs of the Rt. Hon. Sir Anthony Eden, 1960

The Queen and her Children, Lady Irene Peacock, 1961

Dame of Sark, Sibyl Hathaway, 1961

Treetops Hotel, Eric Sherbrooke Walker, 1962

Thatched with Gold, Mabell, Countess of Airlie, 1962

The Queen and the Arts, Harold A. Albert, 1963

The Green Baize Door, Ernest King, 1963

'Chips', The Diaries of Sir Henry Channon, 1967

To be a King, Dermot Morrah, 1968

Philip, An Informal Biography, Basil Boothroyd, 1971

Pointing the Way, Harold Macmillan, 1972

The Royal House of Windsor, Elizabeth Longford, 1974

The Queen's Clothes, Anne Edwards, 1977

The Parting Years, Sir Cecil Beaton, 1978

Time and Chance, Peter Townsend, 1978

Mountbatten, Hero of our Time, Richard Hough, 1980

Debrett's Book of the Royal Wedding, Hugo Vickers, 1981

ACKNOWLEDGEMENTS

For photographs of portraits
of The Queen:

With the Queen's kind permission, the Coronation
Portrait by Sir James Gunn: A. C. Cooper

For the portraits by Edmund Brock, Stella Marks
and Wallace King, *Cathcart Archives*; for Alfred
Lawrence, Timothy Whidborne, Douglas Anderson,
William Narraway and Pietro Annigoni, *Camera Press*; and
for Terence Cuneo, *Press Association*.

INDEX

Owen, Mr 36

Parker, Cmdr Michael 118, 120, 127, 134, 140, 175–6
Paul, King of the Hellenes 127
Peebles, Catherine 182, 184
Peter, King of Yugoslavia 91, 144
Philip, Prince, Duke of Edinburgh 12, 37, 64–6, 70, 79, 80–2, 92–5, 116–18, 120–133. As Consort: 139–42, 144, 146–7, 153, 155–8, 161–3, 168–77, 180–81, 184–90, 194–6, 198, 201–205, 207–13, 216–7, 219–20, 225 and *passim*
Phillips, Mrs Harold 196
Phillips, Mark 221–2, 224
Pickford, Mary 93
Pius, Pope 128, 202
Plunket, Lord 62, 78, 156
Porchester, Lord 156
Prasad President of India 200
Psaila, Vincent 126

Ramsay, Capt. Alexander 29
Robertson-Justice, James 118
Rowe, Miss 119, 125
Roosevelt, President 62, 87

Salisbury, Marquess of 95, 173
Sark, Dame of 124
Seymour, Capt. Reginald 12
Simson, Sir Henry 11–2
Sitwell, Osbert 59
Smith, Charles 108
Smith, Horace and Sybil 75
Smuts, Field-Marshal 82, 98, 108
Snowdon, Lord 192–5, 198, 203–4
Sophie, Princess of Hanover 94, 116–8, 126–7, 163, 183, 206, 208–9, 217, 225–6, 229
Southesk, Countess of 80
Spencer, 7th Earl 25
Spencer, 8th Earl (formerly Viscount Althorp) 95, 158–60, 162
Spencer, Countess 156, 160
Spencer, Lady Diana *see* Wales, Princess of,
Spencer-Churchill, Lady Rosemary 151

Stanhope, Earl 226
Steele-Perkins, Capt. 189
Strachey, Lady Mary 82–3, 87
Strathmore, 14th Earl and Countess of 13–4, 17, 19, 22, 28, 39, 57, 62, 79
Strong, Charles 116
Synge, Violet 59, 60, 75, 80

Tanner, Hubert 72, 79
Tennant, Colin 156
Thaarup, Aage 129
Theodora, Princess of Baden 116, 117, 119, 209
Townsend, Col. Henry 184
Townsend, Group Capt. Peter 93, 96, 99, 125, 154, 164–7
Truman, President 129
Tryon, Lord and Lady 229

Vicary-Gibbs, Mrs Jean 87
Viktoria Luise, Duchess of Brunswick etc 225

Wales, Princess of 95, 105, 162, 224, 230–1
Walker, Sherbrooke 134, 139
Welf, Prince of Hanover 204–8, 223, 231
Wellesley, Comm. V. E. M. 85, 86, 87
Wernher, Lady Zia, and family 61, 65, 78, 196
Whateley, L. V. 85
Wheeler-Bennet, Sir John 28, 132
Whiting, Audrey 228
Wigram, Lord 60, 71
Wilhelmina, Queen of Netherlands 72
Willoughby, Lady Jane 151
Wills, Major and Mrs John 166
Wilson, Sir Charles 211
Wilson, Harold 208, 211, 225
Windsor, Duke of (as Prince of Wales and King) 21, 27, 40–2
Windsor, Duchess of (Mrs Simpson) 42, 44
Woods, Dr 210
Woolton, Lord 142, 143, 151

Zec, Donald 228

239